THE COTTAGE,

THE SPIDER BROOCH,

AND THE

SECOND WIFE

How to Overcome
the Challenges of Estate Planning

SANDY CARDY

WITH MICHAEL FITZGERALD

ECW PRESS

Published by ECW PRESS
2120 Queen Street East, Suite 200, Toronto, Ontario, Canada M4E 1E2

NATIONAL LIBRARY OF CANADA CATALOGUING IN PUBLICATION

Cardy, Sandy, 1958–
The cottage, the spider brooch and the second wife : how to overcome the
challenges of estate planning / Sandy Cardy.

ISBN 1-55022-596-0
1. Estate planning – Canada – Popular works. 2. Inheritance and succession –
Canada – Popular works. 1. Title.

KE5974.Z82C36 2003   346.7105'2   C2003-902199-8
KF750.Z9C36 2003

Cover and Text Design: Tania Craan
Cover photo: © George Shelley/CORBIS/Magmaphoto.com
Production and Typesetting: Mary Bowness
Printing: Webcom

This book is set in Trajan and Garamond.

The publication of *The Cottage, the Spider Brooch, and the Second Wife* has been generously
supported by the Canada Council, the Ontario Arts Council, the Government of Canada
through the Book Publishing Industry Development Program. Canadä

DISTRIBUTION
CANADA: Jaguar Book Group, 100 Armstrong Avenue, Georgetown, ON, L7G 5S4

2 3 4 5

PRINTED AND BOUND IN CANADA

ECW PRESS
ecwpress.com

CONTENTS

DISCLAIMER

This book is not intended to be a formal estate planning reference for estate planners, lawyers, or accountants. The purpose of this book is to provide a basic foundation of estate planning information for many Canadians. This book discusses general issues and strategies with respect to the laws surrounding issues such as powers of attorney, wills, trusts, and probate. These laws are governed provincially and the rules therefore vary from province to province.

Any financial projections and illustrations used in relation to the Hilroy family in this book are provided solely for illustrative and discussion purposes. The analysis and solutions contained herein represent the opinion of the authors and should not be interpreted as being applicable to your particular situation. There are many different strategies to consider. This book does not exhaust all alternatives and combinations and is not designed for you to 'do-it-yourself.' This book is not a substitution for the services of a legal or tax expert. Readers are encouraged to consult with a professional before deciding on a course of action.

The analysis in this book represents legislation in effect at the time of publication.

ACKNOWLEDGEMENTS

Michael and I are indebted to the people who provided us with guidance and encouragement on this project over the past two years.

I am very thankful to my agent Don Bastian of Bastian Publishing Services and to Jack David at ECW Press both of whom believed in this book right from the beginning. David Chilton encouraged me to keep moving ahead in the early stages whenever we had the inevitable periods of doubt. The financial professionals who gave their time to give suggestions and make corrections — Bruce Cohen, Miriam Kelly, Joseph Sardella, and Teresa Lee — were invaluable in helping me transform some of the complex tax and legal concepts into meaningful and understandable form.

Stephen Beattie was of tremendous help to us not only in polishing the manuscript, but also critiquing the narrative and aiding us on any editorial questions.

Thanks also to Fina Scroppo, James FitzGerald, and Mark Nolan for editorial suggestions in the early going, and to Joy and Nadine at ECW for their work in the late going. Special thanks to Roland Cardy, David Chilton, Don Bastian, Jon Nussbaum, Stephen Dunn, Judy (Puffer) Higgins, and Mark Smyka for their contribution as 'test readers.' To us, they were critical in telling us if we were on the right path in our efforts to reach those readers who want to know more about estate planning and the communication challenges that can arise in families. Also, Dr. Jon Nussbaum of Penn State University provided many insights on aspects of family communication that helped us greatly.

Lastly, my gratitude to my husband Roland for his patience and understanding while this project continued past the two-year mark!

Sandy Cardy
March, 2005

I dedicate this book to the older generation in our family —
my parents Russell and Margaret Dunn
and my in-laws, Gordon and Bay Cardy.

I also dedicate this book to my brother Stephen Dunn,
the real Michael Hilroy!

Chapter 1

DISCLOSURE

THE CONVERSATION STARTED BADLY; then it got worse. Alfred Hilroy had expected a certain amount of resistance from his children when he told them that he was seeing Mary Beth, but the prolonged silence from his youngest daughter unnerved him.

"Jude?" he said tentatively into the phone. "Are you still there?"

More silence.

Alfred decided to wait it out. Judy's moods were difficult to predict, and he didn't want to say anything that might provoke Judy unnecessarily. As a child, she had screaming, howling tantrums, during which she threw things and spit and tore at her hair. She was like a tiny hurricane; the only thing to do was let it spend its fury and hope that it passed quickly. Judy the adult was still quick to anger, but she'd honed her wit into a sharp-bladed instrument; she wasn't above drawing blood, and Alfred had occasionally found himself on the wrong end of her steel. The matter currently under discussion was a tricky one, and he felt the need to tiptoe very carefully around the subject, allowing prudence to triumph over raw emotion. Still, as he let the silence drag out, he himself was becoming increasingly agitated. He was just about to say something more when he heard his daughter's voice, very faint, on the other end of the line.

"I'm here."

"Are you okay?"

A pause.

Alfred thought he heard a slight intake of breath, the quick, jagged kind that often accompanies tears. Then his daughter's voice came back to him, stronger this time.

"I'm fine, Dad," Judy said. "I just wonder . . . don't you think it's a little soon for you to be dating again? Mom's been dead for only six months."

"I know it must seem sudden, darling. The last thing I want to do is hurt you. You know that, don't you?"

Another pause. Then "What did Mike and Bev say?"

"I haven't told them yet," Alfred said. "I wanted to talk to you first."

Among Alfred's three children, Judy was the youngest at 30 and the one he'd always felt closest to. She seemed to need him in a way the other two didn't and, except for university, had always lived in the family home until recently. Bev had always been independent, able to take care of herself. Alfred thought that it had something to do with her being the oldest, feeling that she had to shoulder every responsibility herself, without recourse to others. When her marriage broke up, she was resolute in her determination to raise her two children, Harry and Megan, on her own. Although Alfred had repeatedly offered whatever assistance he could, he knew that Bev would never accept his help. It wasn't in her nature to ask for favours from anybody, even her closest family members.

In the six months since Joyce's death, Alfred had often felt as though he was the child and Bev the parent. Never more so than the morning three weeks earlier when Bev had insisted on taking him for a tour of the Elmbank Villas retirement residence. "Just for a look," she'd said, "and to get the feel of the place." The feel Alfred had got was one of institutionalization and old age, the smell of vegetable soup in the halls and fleets of wheelchairs waiting patiently for their new occupants. The independent-living concept is fine, Alfred had thought during his visit to Elmbank, but it can last only so long. As you become more feeble, you must confront the idea of a life of what the industry calls "Assisted Living," then possibly "Specialty Care," then the dreaded "Long-Term Care," and finally "Sub-Acute Care." Nursing homes! Home health care! Big bucks! It's like your progress through the school system, only in reverse. Thoughts of kindergarten days, when there were mandatory naps every afternoon, had come back to Alfred. No matter how well managed or nonintrusive these places are (he'd had dreams in which he'd lock himself accidentally in his room closet), he had a need to stay out of a villa or lodge or estate or place or gardens. For as long as possible, anyway.

"I may be well into my old-fart years," Alfred had said to Bev once they'd left Elmbank, "but I'm still too young for that place."

"Okay, Dad," Bev had said. "But just keep it in the back of your mind as a possibility. I don't like to think of you rambling around in that big old house at 75 Delmore all alone."

Alfred had choked down the words that had come bubbling up in the back of his throat. It had been the wrong time to tell Bev about Mary Beth. He'd needed time to decide how best to put it to her. How best to make her understand the ways that the 40-year-old bank teller from Australia, 28 years his junior, made him feel alive and cared for in the wake of Joyce's death. He'd known how it would appear: an older man seemingly in the throes of rebound with a much younger woman. It would have been difficult to explain it to her. When he really thought about it, Alfred found it difficult to explain it even to himself.

Certainly the first few weeks after Joyce's death had been close to unbearable. No one had expected complications when Joyce had gone into the hospital for a routine appendectomy; her death had been so sudden, and it had seemed to throw everyone in the family into a tailspin. Mike had brought his wife, Shauna, and two children, Jenna and Russell, back to Ontario from British Columbia, where he owned and operated his plastics-manufacturing business. They had stayed with Alfred for a week and a half following the funeral. The presence of his son and grandchildren in the house at 75 Delmore Avenue, Unionville, which had been the family home since Mike and his sisters were little more than babies, had been the only thing preventing him from going completely crazy from grief.

In the days after Mike had taken his family back to the West Coast, Alfred had indeed felt wracked with crippling loneliness. In the evenings, he'd sat at the kitchen table, illuminated by the pallid light from the ceiling lamp, eating solitary bowls of cup-a-soup or three-minute microwave dinners, unable to stop staring at the empty chair across from him. Often he'd wake up in the middle of the night, instinctively reaching out for the warm presence in the bed beside him and finding only a tangle of twisted sheets. In his bedroom, Alfred would repeatedly stare at a family photo hanging on the wall, a wonderful windswept cottage dock scene taken years earlier, one with all the Hilroys in various states of half poses and with Molson the retriever caught in midleap chasing a lakeward-bound stick. Each time he looked at the picture, he would feel as if his own life was suspended in midair.

Was it this sense of overpowering loneliness that had made him ask Mary Beth Cain, the pretty blonde teller at his branch of the Empire Bank, out for a cup of coffee, an uncharacteristically impulsive act so out of keeping with his normal demeanour that Alfred himself had been startled to hear the words coming out of his mouth? He'd been even more startled to hear her accept. Then to hear her accept his invitation to dinner. And to the theatre. And. And. Or had he merely been hit by "the bolt," just like 40 years earlier when he'd first met Joyce?

Before he'd even been aware it was happening, Alfred and Mary Beth had become a couple. The day of his visit to Elmbank Villas with Bev, he had instinctively known that it was an inopportune time to broach the subject with his daughter, but in the weeks following it had become apparent to him that he could no longer avoid telling his children about the new woman in his life. But now, listening to Judy's voice on the phone, the initial hurt quickly replaced by a steely resolve bordering on anger, Alfred wondered whether he'd miscalculated.

"What do you think Mom would say about this, Dad?"

"Judy," Alfred said, very slowly and as gently as he could, "your mother is dead." It was not gentle enough.

"I know that, goddamn it!" Judy screamed. "She's dead, and you're traipsing around with some tramp you picked up God knows where. You barely waited long enough for her body to get cold."

"Now, hang on just a minute. You've got no right —"

"Oh, I have no right? *I* have no right? I'm your daughter, for Christ's sake, your flesh and blood. I think I have a right to tell you when you're making a complete ass of yourself."

"Judy Hilroy, you listen to me —"

"You know what, Dad?" Judy said, not allowing her father to finish. "Forget it. I hope you two have a wonderful life together."

Before Alfred could say anything more, there was a click, and he found himself clutching a dead receiver. Gingerly he replaced the handset in its cradle and sat back in his chair. On his desk, another framed cottage picture of himself with Joyce, Bev, Mike, and Judy stared back at him. Even now it made him smile because it showed everyone relaxed and beaming with sunburned faces, with Mike in the background bouncing on the diving board wearing nothing but his summer-league hockey pants and suspenders.

Alfred heard a floorboard squeak and turned to see Mary Beth standing in the doorway to his study. She held a glass of red wine in her hand. "That didn't sound good," she said.

"It's Judy," Alfred said. "As you would say, she's as mad as a frog in a sock."

Mary Beth walked into the room and handed the glass of

wine to Alfred. She stood behind his desk chair and placed her hands on his shoulders. "I don't want to cause any trouble with your kids," she said, slowly rubbing his shoulders. "But I'm afraid I already have."

"Don't worry about it," Alfred said. "It's not your fault. She just needs a bit of time to get used to the idea, that's all."

"I hope you're right."

"Of course I am." Alfred took a sip of wine. "This is delicious."

"Australian shiraz," Mary Beth said. "We're stellar people, and we make the world's best wine — not the plonk you get in other parts of the world."

Alfred tilted his head up and allowed Mary Beth to kiss him softly on the forehead. She gave his shoulder one last squeeze and left him alone again. He looked wistfully at the framed picture on his desk, took another sip of wine, and reached for the phone.

"One down, two to go," he whispered and dialled Bev's number.

Chapter 2

WILSON'S ADVICE

ALFRED ENTERED THE La Gamboni restaurant at five minutes to noon and looked around for Jeremy Wilson, his longtime friend and financial advisor. He didn't expect to find him. Over the years, Alfred and Jeremy had met often for lunch. Alfred had always been early, and Jeremy had invariably bustled in 10 or 15 minutes late.

"Hello, Mr. Hilroy. Anything to start?" asked Jenny, the morose but reliable waitress.

What the hell, thought Alfred, I'll have a smash today. "I'll have a glass of white wine . . . actually, no, Jenny, change that to a half carafe." He knew that Jeremy would have wine: his friend never passed up the opportunity to partake in a few drinks.

Alfred opened his newspaper and scanned the headlines. "Federal Reserve Cuts Fed Funds Rate by ¼ Point." Hopefully that would have a bullish effect on stock prices. On the advice of a friend, he had recently purchased some shares of a high-tech company. Alfred was annoyed at himself for having made this purchase. He'd known when he bought the stock that the price was too high, and he wondered how he'd managed to be duped by an overhyped, unproductive sector of the market. If Joyce had been alive, she would have warned him away from the stock.

Alfred felt himself growing wistful again. He and Joyce had always made financial decisions as a team. With Jeremy's advice and Joyce's willingness to manage a monthly household balance sheet, the Hilroys had built up a comfortable net worth. Alfred and Joyce had debated every potential investment. They had kept diligent track of the progress of their investments and the children's education plans. It had been an effective arrangement. Jeremy had emphasized the importance of goals and the need to ensure that they had money set aside for retirement because Alfred was self-employed. Joyce had developed a savvy for saving, forced herself to learn the basics of record keeping, and made sure that Alfred paid down the mortgage annually with his RRSP refund.

Alfred remembered Joyce practically dragging him to meet with Jeremy to talk about their financial planning; had she not been so persistent, he might never have got around to it. Jeremy Wilson was both a tax lawyer and estate planner. Alfred felt lucky to have had such solid, steady advice from Jeremy over the years on everything from preparing business and personal tax returns to retirement goals, investments, education planning, and estate planning.

"Hey, there you are, old boy!" Jeremy called from the door of the restaurant, causing the other diners in the room to look up in surprise. He marched over to where Alfred was sitting, gave him a quick slap on the shoulder, and threw down his keys with a clank. He lowered himself into the booth with a satisfied exhalation of breath.

"Yes, here I am," said Alfred. "Thanks for joining me. I wasn't looking forward to eating alone again. The noise when the second place setting is taken away always seems inordinately loud. But these days I actually feel like getting up in the morning and doing stuff. Maybe it's the spring — I feel a renewed sense of vitality. I just hope it continues. I guess I'm ready to get on with things."

"Like we all said: you have to give your grief six months, and then you begin to feel better. I'm glad to hear you're getting back to your old self. Golf season's starting, and hitting a pail or two of range balls will buoy your mood as well."

Alfred ordered onion soup and a salad, Jeremy a seafood vegetable wrap.

"So you deposited that insurance cheque to your account?" asked Jeremy.

Alfred was the beneficiary on his late wife's life insurance policy. Two and a half months ago, the insurance company had sent him a cheque in the amount of $50,000. The cheque had sat on his desk for over two months before he'd been able to bring himself to cash it.

"Yes, that's done. It's now collecting a total of about one percent interest per annum."

"Well, let's get it out of there. I recommend that we add the money to your existing mutual funds at Empire Private Trust in the same proportion as you have now. I think that we should invest within your present risk tolerance profile, which is moderate. I wouldn't invest any more aggressively — especially at your age, it's best to stay a bit on the conservative side. With the markets being pummelled in the last while, we may be bottoming out. It's a good time to invest some extra cash. Do you want to invest the entire $50,000?"

"Well, actually, I think I'd like to leave some money in my account — just in case. Why don't we invest $20,000?" Alfred ran his finger around the rim of his wine glass.

"Can I ask what you're planning to do with the other $30,000? That's a lot of green fees. I've known you for 30 years, and you're not exactly a wild spender. Whenever you pick up a lunch cheque, moths fly out of your wallet."

"Very witty. I don't know. . . . I might buy a car, do some house renos, stuff like that. I just feel like spending some dough for a change."

"I think I'm hearing things. *You* spend money? Do you need to see a psychiatrist? A therapist, perhaps?"

"No, no, it's nothing like that. It's just . . . I've been depressed for so long that I think it would do me good to have a little fun. Okay, maybe $20,000 is not enough. Let's invest $40,000. But I want to make sure I have some money available because . . . well, the thing is . . . I'm seeing somebody."

"Aha, so that's it! I knew there was something different about you. No wonder you're so spunky today. Drinking wine and everything. Nothing like a little interest from the opposite sex to rev up the cylinders!"

"Now don't go overboard. We have a good time together, but . . . she's probably too young for me. But you never know. . . . Now, you mentioned on the phone yesterday that there was something else you wanted to talk to me about."

"Right you are," replied Jeremy. "It's your favourite subject: estate planning!"

"Swell, marvellous," said Alfred, rolling his eyes. "This necessitates a refill." He emptied the carafe, the contents settling in his glass save for two drops that glided down the outside.

"Just hear me out. There's a great estate-planning strategy, which was just passed into legislation a few years ago. It allows you to avoid paying probate fees on your assets when you die. It's called the Alter Ego Trust for single individuals 65 or older and a Joint Spousal or Partner Trust for couples, one of whom must be at least 65. Kay and I are implementing a Joint Spousal Trust. In your case, because you're now single, the Alter Ego Trust would be appropriate."

"Sounds interesting," said Alfred. "Doesn't Dr. Freud have a trademark on the use of the word *ego*? Is there an 'Id Trust' as well?"

"No. And you don't have to be Freud to take advantage of this. Basically these trusts involve a tax-planning strategy aimed at senior citizens — that would be you and me, though we still don't admit it. The Alter Ego trust is an Inter Vivos trust which is a trust that is established when the settlor is alive. You can transfer some or all of your assets into an Alter Ego trust and then name your beneficiaries on the trust deed in the event of your death. So really what you can achieve with this scenario is use an Alter Ego trust to replace a will."

"So if I transferred all my assets into that trust, I wouldn't need to have a will at all?" asked Alfred.

"Possibly."

"So what's the advantage of this Alter Ego Trust?"

"The main advantages are confidentiality, protection of capital, for example a spouse in a second marriage situation, and avoidance of probate fees on your death."

Alfred picked the last bit of melted cheese from the rim of his soup bowl. "Probate fees?" he said. "I know the concept, but remind me."

"Fees are paid to have your will 'probated' after you die. The correct term in this province is 'Application for Certificate of Appointment of Estate Trustee with a Will.' But we can just use the lay term which is probate. Basically, after you're gone, your executor goes to court to confirm that you indeed passed away and are not hiding on some secluded desert island somewhere. Also, the executor, here in Ontario called the Estate Trustee, proves that he or she has really been appointed as executor and that there is no other will out there that may appear to mess things up later."

"Why do we even need to go through probate? I didn't have to go through that when Joyce died."

"That's a very good question," said Jeremy. "You need to have your will probated so that third parties, such as banks, can be assured that the executor is the one to whom assets can be released. You didn't need to have Joyce's will probated because you and Joyce had all your assets registered as joint tenants with rights of survivorship except the cottage which has always been registered in your name. Joyce's interest in any asset was automatically passed to you as the surviving owner. Therefore all assets stayed out of Joyce's estate and no probate was needed to transfer ownership to you."

"That explains why all I needed to produce to have

accounts transferred into my name was proper proof of death."

"Exactly," emphasized Jeremy.

"So, getting back to probate, we need to pay for the pleasure of having the courts give the green light," said Alfred.

"That's the simple truth. It can cost quite a sizeable chunk of the estate. The probate fees are really taxes paid to approximate the court costs involved in this process. These fees are normally a percentage of the value of the estate. The majority of provinces in Canada, except Alberta for one, levy fees for this process; most provinces refer to them as probate fees. Here in Ontario the name was changed a few years ago to Estate Administration Tax, or EAT. They really *eat* away at the value of your estate, although it's just one big bite," Jeremy guffawed loudly.

"So what are they, fees or taxes? And how much of the estate do they eat up?"

"Most of the other provinces besides Ontario have passed new legislation. I don't need to feed you the boring details on that. For all practical purposes, nothing has really changed. What they cost varies from sea to sea. Unfortunately a few provinces, such as Ontario, B.C., and Nova Scotia, have discovered that the fees are an attractive way to raise additional tax revenues. Here in Ontario, for example, the fees are $500 on the first $50,000 and $15 per $1,000 thereafter. In rough terms, the total tax is no more than 1.5% of the assets that are probated. As well, there is no cap on the amount we have to pay here in Ontario. British Columbia is roughly the same as Ontario, with no cap on the total amount. So the fees can really add up significantly. In Alberta, on the other hand, these probate fees have recently been reduced to pretty much nothing."

Jeremy finished his seafood wrap with a flourish and instinctively reached for his glass. "Do you want to order another half carafe?"

Alfred hesitated. "I've had all I can handle for now; my head's beginning to spin. Two glasses is enough for me. . . . So the best way for me to avoid paying these taxes is to move to Alberta."

"Har. That's one way to do it. But your moving costs might outweigh the tax savings. Another way to avoid the probate fees is to set up a trust."

"Basically I don't understand why putting stuff in a trust means that I can avoid paying these taxes."

"You and everyone else. Most people are confused about trusts — what they are and what they are used for. There's just one thing I want to mention now. Anything that you own inside of a trust does not form part of your estate at death. So, if you transfer all your assets into a trust, they don't form part of a will and therefore are free of probate fees."

"So how much would I save by using one of these?" asked Alfred.

"Well, let's use an example. Let's say you transfer all your assets into an Alter Ego Trust. You would transfer your house, valued at about $350,000, your cottage, valued at another $350,000, and your nonregistered investments, which are . . . what's the amount again?" Jeremy muttered to himself. "Let's see, you sold half of your business for $250,000 after tax, so you could put that in, and your other nonregistered investments, which come to about $250,000 after we add the

$40,000 insurance money — what does that come to? Ahhh, let's say roughly $1,200,000, give or take several other small amounts. That amount could be transferred into an Alter Ego Trust. The only assets that you can't transfer into these trusts are registered ones. So you couldn't move your RRSP, for example. On the trust deed, you would put your kids as beneficiaries in the event of your death. Then, when the time comes that you're dust, old boy, the total amount, which would be the $1,200,000 plus interest up to the point of death, is passed along to your kids. So let's say your estate grows to $1,600,000 by the time you kick off — that would amount to a savings of about $24,000 in estate administration fees." Jeremy sat back in his chair, almost out of breath.

"You forgot a couple of things," said Alfred. "Remember, I own some shares — not much — in Michael's manufacturing company in B.C. Can those private shares be placed in this kind of trust as well? And what about my condo in Florida?"

"Yes, private company shares can also go in — but not necessary with the Florida condo. There would be no probate to pay on the condo in Florida because real estate held outside Ontario is not subject to probate." Jeremy plunged ahead. "So that's how I get $24,000. If we use the example of roughly $1,600,000 at death, then 1.5% of that figure amounts to $24,000. You can pick and choose which assets you want to put in — you don't have to put everything in the Alter Ego Trust. For someone in Ontario, British Columbia, or Nova Scotia, for example, holding about $500,000 inside an Alter Ego Trust at the time of death, the savings are just over $7,000 — pretty compelling, I'd say."

"Certainly to the ones who are left to see it. I thought you had to pay some tax when you rolled assets into a trust? And how does someone get their money out of the trust?" asked Alfred.

"Those are very good questions," replied Jeremy. "There is usually what we call a 'deemed disposition' when we roll assets into a trust while we are alive, which means we pay tax on the built-up gains on the asset we are putting into that trust. But with these new trusts I'm telling you about, the Income Tax Act allows an exception to the general rule. In this case, you can put your assets in these trusts without having to pay any tax at the time of transfer. Capital gains tax is paid when you die and the assets roll out of the trust to your children. But that would happen anyway; you can never avoid paying tax on transfers of capital assets to the next generation. Also, you can access any of your income and/or capital through these trusts just like you can now. They are transparent in that regard — the main advantages inherent in the use of an Alter Ego Trust are asset protection, control of capital, confidentiality and probate avoidance."

"It sounds too good to be true," said Alfred. "Surely there must be a downside to all of this?"

"Not really. And don't call me Shirley." Jeremy couldn't resist rolling out corny vaudeville lines now and then. "In fact, the only downside is the cost to setting one up. Lawyer's fees can be pretty high, and there would be some annual fees for preparing the trust's tax returns, called T3 returns."

"Still, paying some extra fees today for savings like that in the future is not a bad deal," said Alfred.

"Precisely," said Jeremy. "And there are more reasons why trusts are a great idea in estate planning. For one thing, a trust is protective in that it shields you from others who may want to make a claim against your estate — creditors or wayward spouses. But even better, a trust is very private. You see, one big problem with the probate process is that the will and the value of assets subject to probate must be filed with the court. That means anyone can pay a fee to the court to get a look at your will and the value of those assets."

"Why would I care about that?"

"Let's say you screw up royally on someone's prescription. Say you mess up the dose of someone's heart medication because you're a bit hung over. The customer has a heart attack in the middle of the night. The local media get hold of this. You get charged a fine for carelessness. Then you die from stress. Your kids pick up the newspapers one day after you're toast, and the headline reads 'Pharmacist, Fined for Careless-ness, Dies.' And the subheading says 'Had Large Estate.'"

"Better large than bankrupt. Anyway, it all sounds good, but I think I'll just mull it over for a while. I don't really feel like doing anything too fancy at the moment," said Alfred.

"Fair enough. I just wanted to broach the subject with you. Something you may want to look at doing at some point down the road. Part of the grand pageant of life, eh?"

Chapter 3

INSEPARABLE

MARY BETH AND ALFRED spent all their time together. Movies, walks, dinners, discussions, and intimacy. Mary Beth proudly huddled close to Alfred, arm in arm, as if to show him off to the world in the same way some men might show off a beautiful woman. Mary Beth craved attention, relishing the glances of those who looked twice at the younger woman coupled with a partner whose hair was peppered with silver.

Mary Beth asked Alfred to give her some golfing lessons — another way of garnering some attention from him — so he arranged a few visits to the driving range and enjoyed being the teacher even though his teaching qualifications were meagre. At least he helped Mary Beth to get the ball airborne. He was impressed by her natural swing; she had good coordination and strength. She was a quick learner, and by the third visit she was popping the ball several yards farther than her teacher, which would prompt Alfred to cough and change the lesson to short-game techniques. His diminished strength that came with his age only roused protective impulses in Mary Beth.

Each time she visited the house at 75 Delmore Avenue, her

beliefs regarding Alfred's kindness and generosity were confirmed. In fact, she wanted to believe that Alfred was the most genuine person whom she had ever met. She and Alfred had planned lunch together at his house one Saturday. When she excused herself after three cups of tea for a nature break, she climbed the stairs slowly, taking in the surroundings. His world had been one that she'd always wanted for herself. She admired the well-appointed furniture and paintings and imagined that just here the night before she had been a gracious hostess to a party, prompting compliments and glances from others.

They ate their lunch outside on the backyard deck, the first leaves having exploded from their buds in just the past two days. Alfred produced the family photo albums at Mary Beth's urging. Scenes of the cottage, vacations, pets, birthdays, early Port Hope days, and the U of T graduating class of 1956 in pharmacy. She commented on all the Dick Clark look-alikes in the graduation photo and on how the few women looked like men. She envied the apparent family stability seen in the photos. Alfred didn't dwell on any pictures that had Joyce in them, only once saying quietly, "I miss her." For her part, Mary Beth felt only that this man needed someone to pick up the slack, and she wouldn't mind sharing in such a comfortable and settled life.

∞∞

"Big sister, it's your little bro."

"It's not yet 5 a.m. out there, Mike," replied Bev. "How ya doing? B.C. life agreeing with you?"

"You always ask me that. Thought I'd reach you before you

headed out for work. Got your e-mail about Dad's birthday in July. I'll be at the cottage around that time anyway, so a big party fits in nicely. What's this about Dad meeting somebody? Mom's been gone only six months. Don't you think it all seems so sudden?"

Bev sighed. "It certainly looks like he's been hit by a bolt. I went out for dinner with them the other night — it felt surreal. I mean here was Dad paying a lot of attention to this woman, and she's the same age as me! I suppose we should get behind him. . . ."

"Whoa. Back up. What do you mean she's your age?" Mike was speaking louder than usual.

"Forty."

"You're 40, and I'm only 38 for Christ's sake. What is Dad thinking?" Mike's voice came out higher than usual.

"Dunno, but Dad hasn't been this excited since he won the B flight championship at the club."

"That was 12 years ago. I remember the club had to keep asking for the trophy back — he drove off with it when he wasn't supposed to. What does she look like?"

"Of course you'd ask about her looks first, not what she is *like*. If it's any relief to you, as far as I know, she has no silicone implants anywhere."

"Should I go on 'Bimbo Alert'? Some of the stories I'm seeing in the papers. . . ."

"You can stand down, Mikey. What makes you think Dad would fall for someone like that? He's not rolling in *that* kind of dough."

"He's comfortable enough. You don't think she's a —"

"How would I know? I only had dinner with her, and over-all the night was quite pleasant. She's from Australia, and she's quite chatty — maybe a bit loud — and talks a lot about her-self, but she seemed nice enough, and, you know, this is the first time I've seen Dad smile since Mom died."

"How's Judy handling it?"

"Well, that's another story — you know Judy and her histri-onics. Judy doesn't like her just by proxy, and she has jumped to the conclusion that Mary Beth is either a gold digger or from an escort agency. I, on the other hand, choose to think that their encounter is more than merely a business transaction."

"But you'll keep an eye on things?" asked Mike.

"I'll keep you informed. You know, Dad has spent a lot of time with her, and I have a sense she's about to be awarded a set of keys to Delmore Ave. The last time I called there, she answered the phone."

There was a pause on the line. "Like you said, we just have to let things fall wherever they land." Mike sounded as if he was talking through his teeth. "I'll be coming to town soon. I've got to see this phenomenon myself."

Chapter 4

MOVING
RIGHT ALONG

"THE FIRST HOLE, A PAR FOUR just shy of 400 yards, with an elevated tee looking over the valley, requires an accurate drive in order to lead to an easy lofted iron to a green guarded by two bunkers on the left."

Jeremy was fond of doing imitations of the formal broadcast style seen on old golf exhibitions rebroadcast by the Golf Channel. He performed this routine regularly on the first tee of his club whenever a new player was in the group, which in this case was Evan Temple, a younger member of the golf club. Still competitive by nature, Jeremy either got a laugh or threw the player off his game or both.

"Tell me about a hole that doesn't require an accurate drive," mumbled Alfred as he prepared to hit. He gripped the club loosely, and his right foot was splayed out more than normal when he addressed the ball. He brought back the Ping three-wood into a stiff but sound position, paused briefly at the top, and then uncorked, or rather bunted, a 180 yarder, which fell safely into the valley below.

"Not bad," offered Jeremy.

"Useful," said Evan.

Alfred and Jeremy played golf together once a week. Usually they toured their course quickly in three and a half hours if they got off early, but today looked uncommonly slow since a foursome in front were playing a two-man, best-ball match and thought they could waive the normal etiquette of fast play. There was also a lot of course maintenance under way, with workers in white jungle hats silently raking traps. Today would require patience.

Evan, less familiar with the layout, enjoyed swinging mightily on almost every shot. He played badly but with alacrity.

"How's Mary Beth doing?" asked Jeremy as they waited on the second fairway. Evan was off on the banks of the river looking for golf balls, not just his own.

"Good. Good." Pause. "We had a great evening out last night. Enjoyed one too many drinks."

"So you two have been seeing a lot of each other for just a short time. Do I see a relationship developing?"

"Yes, siree. In fact, she's moving in. We're going to try it for just a while to see how things go."

Jeremy couldn't have raised his eyebrows any higher. "When? What do you mean? At the Delmore digs? Is it that serious?"

Alfred and Mary Beth had agreed that they would keep their pending arrangement under wraps for the time being. He just felt so excited about recent events that he pictured himself cartwheeling down the fairway and singing out "I'm in love, I'm in love, I'm in love, I'm in luuuuuuuve!" For that reason, he couldn't keep quiet for long, and now he started to backpedal.

"Well, no, not exactly — well, kind of. We'll just see how it goes."

Alfred looked over to where Evan was trying to extricate his ball from the hazard without much success. Two thwacks later, a third recovery shot made it back to the fairway, where Evan joined his two partners, who pretended not to notice, in true golfing spirit. His was the first of the three golfers' foreheads to start to glisten.

"Have you told the kids?" asked Jeremy. "How did the dinner and show with Mary Beth go this week? I think you said Bev went along?"

The group in front were plumb-bobbing their putts as if their entire portfolios were riding on the outcome. So Alfred had time to answer. "Yes, dinner was fine — seemed as though they got along well. Bev was quite amiable and chatty. The girls enjoyed the all-singing, all-dancing show, which was great because it was all-boring for me. But, no, I haven't told anyone about Mary Beth living with me — you're the first one to know. It's really nothing to get excited about. I'm just enjoying a bit of fun while the going is good, and it's certainly been good so far. After all, I'm a little on the ancient side for her. What could she possibly want with an old guy like me? I mean, in later years, I'd be Methuselah teaching her golf from a bench on the practice range. Not that there's anything wrong with bench golf. . . ."

Alfred realized he was starting to prattle. He felt uncomfortable about not being straight with the facts. The principal fact was this: he didn't like being alone, and there was no way he wanted to spend the rest of his life by himself.

The second green was finally empty of the group in front. Evan, who had been privy to only the last half of Alfred's soliloquy, was the first to hit. His four-iron from 170 yards started out straight and true before detouring into the scrub, short and right of the green. Jeremy launched a six-iron onto the green with a short, choppy stroke. Alfred hit a five-iron off the toe, and the ball ended up in the greenside bunker. A few days earlier, such a shot would have made him peevish. Not today.

Evan expressed his envy. "Alfred Hilroy — man of adventure! It must be serious if your daughter hung out with you on your date. How old did you say Mary Beth was?"

"On the north side of 40."

"Forty what?"

"Forty and a half."

Evan whistled. "Jiminy, that must get the old blood flowing. I hope your kids are OK about everything?"

"They'd better be; I've got a few more roses to smell." Alfred's ball scudded out of the bunker to within 10 feet of the pin. "She's smart and attractive, and the fact that she wants to look after me in the years to come is a bonus. I can't expect my kids to watch out for me as I approach geezerdom."

"Of course not," snorted Jeremy sarcastically.

They finished the hole quickly and found themselves waiting again for the glacial group in front.

Evan, always forthright, was curious about Alfred's last remarks. "You refer to 'years to come.' Obviously you are thinking long term with this woman?"

Alfred squeezed some suntan lotion onto his hand and applied a generous dose on his face and neck. He flipped the lid shut and tossed the bottle back into the open pocket of his golf bag. "Yes, I am," he finally answered.

"I don't mean to knock the wind out of your sails, but since you're in such a good mood you should be amenable to my having a new will drafted for you," said Jeremy.

"New will? What brought *that* up? I already have a will," said Alfred peevishly. He started scraping away at the grooves of his club with a tee. "Did you know that we have tickets booked for Greece in August?"

"No, you don't."

"Yes, we do. Why, Mary Beth just booked —"

"No, you don't have a *will.*"

"Come on, Jeremy, we can talk about this another time. I just updated my will with you two years ago."

They reached the halfway point, where they had time to get drinks. The groups of golfers were moving with accordion-like effect — moving briskly, then grinding to a halt.

Evan sipped his lemonade and traced the rim of the paper cup with his index finger. He looked at Alfred. "Wills and first-marriage situations can be very different from second-marriage planning. I'll share a not-so-nice story with you. After my mother died 10 years ago, my dad fell in love with Dorothy, who had two kids from her previous marriage. My sister and I were made to believe that, when Dad and Dorothy had both passed away, we would each receive one-quarter of their combined estate, to be shared equally with Dorothy's two sons. But Dad actually died first, which we didn't expect to happen given that Dorothy was older than Dad. Then five years ago Dorothy died, and her will had been changed, leaving everything to her two boys. My sister and I had been completely cut out. All of my dad's stocks, bonds, real estate, everything he had acquired over the years, was given to our stepbrothers through our step-mother's will."

Jeremy shook his head. "I'm sorry. No one should have to suffer setbacks like that."

Evan shrugged. "I know, I usually don't talk about it — only close friends know the story. It's pretty personal stuff."

Alfred frowned. "Knowing that they had inherited your father's lifelong efforts and savings, would your stepbrothers not share the inheritance with you?"

"They would not relinquish one single dollar," Evan said bitterly. "In fact, family heirlooms that originated from my grandparents were passed through to them as well. It was very ugly. My sister and I went to see a lawyer for advice. We were certain that the law would give us our fair share. We were told that there was nothing that could be done because the will clearly stated that Dorothy's two sons were to receive her estate 50-50. Anyway, I've moved on, and at least I do earn a good liv-ing. But my sister, she has not fared so well, and she could have really used some extra cash."

"That's cruel, very cruel," said Alfred emphatically. "I really hate to hear about hostile family situations. I suppose you don't ever talk to your stepbrothers now?"

"Never. The relationship is acrimonious — it riles me to even think about it. Alf, if you plan on making a commitment with this woman, I would suggest you redo your will and com-municate with your kids exactly what your wishes are. Communicate as much as you can about every aspect of your estate. It's also wise to be careful with the handling of family heirlooms — some of them may be more precious to your children than you think. And there's another thing to consider — a prenuptial agreement or marriage contract. This contract, if done properly, can override many aspects of provincial family law — you know, things like the house is one-half your spouse's from the date of marriage and stuff like that. Think about it."

Alfred nodded. "Thanks for the advice. Mary Beth has no children, so in our case at least it's more simple." Alfred stood up and smoothed the creases out of his trousers. "Shall we play golf?"

Jeremy hit a long, straight drive on the par-three 10th hole, with the ball bouncing to the middle of the green just 10 feet short of the hole. "Getting back to my earlier point, you need a new will," Jeremy gently reminded Alfred. "If you get married, it nullifies an existing will, making it void. So, if a will is void, basically that means you don't have one. Then, if you were to expire without a will, it's called dying intestate. This means that the government would decide how to divide your assets between family members."

Alfred chose a club and made two looping practice swings. "If I die without a will and I'm remarried, wouldn't all my assets just pass to my new wife?"

"Nope. Each province has its own laws of how assets are divided when someone dies without a will. The amounts may vary from province to province, but what is common to all of them is that, when someone dies and leaves a family, the spouse and kids share in the estate according to these preexisting rules."

"And how does it work here?" Alfred asked, crouching to tee up his ball with a faint grunt.

"Here the spouse gets the first $200,000, and then the spouse and children share the remainder. Say, for example, that there are two children. Once the spouse peels off the first $200,000, the remainder would be split at one-third to the spouse and two-thirds to the kids."

"Government always has their hands in the pot," said Alfred. He punched a seven-wood and overshot the green. "Don't get me going on government stuff!"

"Even taking potshots at Canada Customs and Revenue won't change the fact that without a will you're doing a considerable disservice to Bev, Michael, and Judy. I can't overstate this. Let's set up a meeting for next week."

"Wait a minute," said Alfred. "Why would it just be a disservice to my three kids? Wouldn't it also be unfair to Mary Beth — assuming, of course, that she is my wife?"

"It depends on how you look at it. Let's say you are married to Mary Beth for less than a year. You get worn out with her nonstop urban lifestyle, and you fall over dead from exhaustion. How do you think your kids would react to her receiving a large chunk of the assets that you and Joyce built up together? They might think of the chunk as their rightful inheritance!"

"Then again they might not. Two of my kids are now financially independent, and it's up to *me* to do what I want with my money," replied Alfred. His tone had acquired an edge.

"Absolutely, old boy. I'm not trying to oil your feathers. I'm just saying slow down, look at all angles, and don't forget to see this from the kids' perspective. Just think about having a new will done, and take Evan's good advice. Consider a marriage contract as well."

Alfred's silence at this remark was enough to get Jeremy off the subject of inheritances, ending his attempt at will and second-marriage discussions. Jeremy considered it prudent not to push his old friend further at the time. They concentrated on golf for the rest of the match, which was uneventful except for Evan's duck-hook drive off the 18th tee, which landed with a thud in the back of a golf cart driven by two very senior members, who did not seem to notice and drove off with Evan's ball wedged between their bags.

"Free drop?" asked Evan plaintively.

After a brief discussion, in which Alfred said there were no free drops in life, and thus shouldn't be in golf, Evan was allowed to finish the hole without a penalty.

Chapter 5

DOMESTICITY
IN THE CITY

THE RENTED CUBE VAN WAS more than big enough to hold Mary Beth's worldly belongings. Four suitcases, a pull-out sofa bed, a dresser, lamps, a life-cycle trainer, three boxes of odds and ends, a lot of kitchen gadgetry, painting supplies. Plus a box for Carling's things. The 12-year-old Border terrier had been acting a bit unruly with this change in his owner's lifestyle. Constantly being left alone or with the neighbour had made him irritable, so it was agreed that the dog would move in only after Mary Beth had settled in with Alfred. All of which happened very quickly, quicker than Alfred had time to tell Bev, Mike, and Judy.

The van's contents were unloaded unhurriedly, Alfred taking care not to wrench his back or anything else. He made a little ceremony of handing Mary Beth copies of the house keys, demonstrating the trick to unlocking the front door, his fingers wrapped around hers. "You just need to get the key in, pull the handle forcefully toward you, and jiggle the key to the left until you hear the click. And the back-door key is this square one, it's not a problem."

Mary Beth was never happier than at that moment.

⊚⊚⊚

Their first weeks together were spent with Mary Beth continuing her job and Alfred putting in his three days a week at the pharmacy and otherwise keeping busy.

Alfred's new partner arrived home early on the second Friday after moving in. "Hi, Alf, how was your day?" she asked, planting a kiss on Alfred's right cheek and simultaneously grappling with a bag of cooking items bought at Sherwin's.

"Fine. Just waiting for you to get home. I planted flowers all day — I never knew how much work it takes to plant impatiens. My knees are a disaster zone. Other than that, pretty quiet. How was work at the salt mine?"

"Okay, the usual boring stuff. I was thinking today, Alfy, I thought I would make us lasagna for dinner — I prepared the meat sauce last night. Is that all right with you?"

"What do you mean is that all right? I've been eating a lot of bagels for dinner over the past few months — anything you make would be a welcome relief. Besides, I think you're a wonderful, A-1 cook!"

"Why, thank you, bugalugs! Why don't you take the newspaper and sit out on the deck? I'll join you shortly — I'll just get dinner started, and then I want to get changed into something more comfy."

Mary Beth hummed to herself as she prepared dinner. Ever since Alfred had told her two days earlier that he wanted her to continue living with him indefinitely, she had been in a euphoric mood. She had practically jumped into his arms at his suggestion of commitment to the relationship. They found they could talk about anything, including plans for marriage — possibly sometime in the late summer or early fall. It seemed so obvious to them.

The previous evening, Alfred had suggested that Mary Beth take some time off work so that she could paint full time and try to establish herself artistically. "I was wondering," Alfred had begun, "what would you think about leaving the bank so we could spend more time together and do some travelling? You must be tired of dealing with those endless customer line-ups, those snaking conga lines of commerce you've got to wait on. You could help me garden, and you would have more time to do the things you love, like your art and cooking."

Mary Beth's eyes had shone with delight. "That would be wonderful. I'd love that very much. But you know, Alfred, if I'm going to give up my income, I'll need some money."

"I'll put you as joint owner on my bank accounts."

"Thank you. I also meant, well, I meant down the road — you know, lifetime financial security."

So Alfred had made promises to Mary Beth.

And she had made promises to him. "I'll always be here," she'd told him, "for better or worse."

The fact that Mary Beth was almost thirty years younger, had lots of energy, and could help out with the more onerous duties was extremely gratifying to Alfred. He believed that he deserved it — he had worked hard all his life, built up his wealth, and cared for his family — now why not have some fun?

Sex and money. Money and sex. The Western world's twin icons. Alfred normally did not dwell on such topics. Certainly not in mixed company. For Mary Beth, though, as their intimacy grew, she was always the first to initiate discussions about each other's assets — the financial ones.

Since Mary Beth now had possessory rights to the kitchen, she moved easily and comfortably around it, leaving items strewn about with the confidence of a longtime resident. She finished prepping the lasagne and put it in the oven, timed for one hour, then glided upstairs to change out of her work clothes. She sat on the bed, looking at a room full of photographs — lined up on his dresser, on Joyce's dresser, tucked into the sides of the dresser mirrors. In fact, the entire house documented Alfred's life in photographs. The pictures were typically of Alfred and Joyce and the children, many of them taken at their cottage. Mary Beth opened the closet and hung up her skirt — while Bev had taken most of her mother's things, Alfred had wisely removed Joyce's remaining clothes from the closet just before Mary Beth moved in. She put on a pair of linen shorts and a sleeveless silk cream short-waisted top, proud that she kept her body toned with frequent workouts — she regularly wore sleeveless tops.

Mary Beth found Alfred outside on the deck, bringing with her two wine glasses and a newly opened merlot.

"Alf," she said, after they had toasted each other. "Alf, I thought, since I now live here with you, I really want to add my touch to the home, so I thought, to make this feel like *real* home, perhaps you could provide some money to me for redecorating and maybe some furniture?"

Alfred tried to recall a word to describe how Mary Beth looked as she asked the question. It came to him as he stretched out his aching knee. *Winsome.* That's how she looked.

"That's a good idea," he said. "Since you'll be joint owner on my chequing account, you can just write the cheques yourself."

"You're a sweetie!" said Mary Beth. She applied a big hug to Alfred from behind his deck chair. "Thanks for being so flexible. I know you'll just love some of the changes I've got in mind. I was thinking today at work about where the best place would be for my painting studio — perhaps Michael's old room. It's very appealing to me — it gets the south sun during the day."

"Whatever makes you happy, M.B." He wasn't surprised to hear himself say that. He felt differently about things now.

Chapter 6

OLD WILLS, NEW WILLS

JEREMY WAGGLED HIS 10° driver and proceeded to propel the golf ball directly under the lip of the fairway trap. "Damn, I'm going to quit this game. Soon."

"You've got to learn to relax a little," said Alfred, going through a more confident than usual preshot routine. He then struck a 200-yard ball straight down the fairway. "Splitsville!" he chortled, grasping his pull cart and setting off toward his next shot. The two men rarely rented electric carts; they enjoyed the much-needed exercise of walking the 18 holes.

"How are things with Mary Beth?" Jeremy asked casually, as if Alfred's use of the word *splitsville* might mean something other than hitting a shot directly down the middle.

"Couldn't be better — I feel pretty young. We discussed the big taboo, the *M* word, last night."

"What, your Maalox dosage?" Jeremy laughed loudly.

Alfred scrunched his eyebrows. "Marriage, you peahead — we talked about getting married — we even went so far as to discuss when it might happen — maybe the end of August. I'm pretty excited — where's my five-iron? I never thought this would happen to me."

"Congratulations, old boy! This certainly is something to celebrate," said Jeremy, rubbing the back of his head. His felicitations were somewhat forced. He didn't really know what to think about this news.

Alfred continued, "I wanted to ask you something. How do I go about adding Mary Beth on the title to the house?"

Jeremy answered without blinking. "Easy. I can just do a new title deed for you if you wish."

"Is there any cost to that?"

"Nope, spouses are exempt from land transfer tax where real property is passed between them. I just need to fill out a land transfer tax affidavit to essentially exempt you from tax."

"Thanks, it'd be great if you could do that for me."

Jeremy approached his next shot and with a six-iron picked his ball cleanly out of the trap to within a few yards of the green. Alfred's five-iron shot was a bit thin but found its way with a good bounce onto the putting surface.

"My game hasn't been this good in years," he gushed. "Mary Beth is really having a ball at the house. Just yesterday she approached me with ideas for renovating the den — 'the smoke room,' she calls it. She guessed the couches and curtains must be from the Beatles era, and she's not far off. When she said 'Either the shag rug goes or I go,' it kind of got my attention. Jeremy, kiddo, she's so full of energy and vitality that I swear sometimes I feel 20 years younger." Alfred stopped and turned to face his old friend. "And you know what else? The libido feels *another* 20 years younger!"

"I'm sure it does," said Jeremy with just a twinge of jealousy.

They reached the ninth tee — a par four with a wide-open landing area. Jeremy was happy for his longtime friend, but his concern was growing. He knew that Alfred, like many of his contemporaries, did not want to talk a lot about wills. But he thought that it was his responsibility to navigate through these rough waters with him. If he couldn't turn Alfred's head around, then no one could. He hated to witness the beginnings of tension or misunderstanding between Alf and the kids. He had to try to insulate Alfred from a potential family snake pit.

"Going up to the lake soon?" asked Jeremy, removing a club-head cover.

"I might take Mary Beth up there for the Victoria Day weekend. The kids probably won't be there. I think they are unsure about spending a whole weekend with Mary Beth at this point."

"Well, that is a bit understandable, if I may say so. You have to give your kids time with this stuff. They might feel disloyalty to their mother if they act too friendly with Mary Beth — at least right now. You know, your kids may also be questioning Mary Beth's intentions. I'm sure she's a fine woman, but think of it from your kids' eyes. They feel protective of you, and it's only natural for them to be cautious. And another thing." Jeremy was now wagging a finger at his friend without realizing it.

"Oh, no, here we go again — Martha Stewart Estate Planning with finesse."

"I think you should give thought to drawing up a marriage contract." Jeremy began to cite several reasons for having a marriage contract.

Alfred, with considerable insouciance, walking two paces ahead of Jeremy, waved his hand. "I don't need a marriage contract. Talk about a surefire way to kill the romance. Now look at this lie. Give me a free drop?" He went ahead anyway and nudged his ball sideways with his foot.

"This isn't about romance. I'm just trying to protect you and your family from possible future claims against your estate."

They reached the halfway house. "Cold beer?" asked Jeremy. They collected two Heinekens plus a hot dog for Jeremy. "Alfy, did you know that once you are married, if you and Mary Beth separate, she has a right to share in the value of some of your property?"

Alfred took a long breath. "I think I know what's going on. It's just not a big deal — she would be entitled only to the increase in the value of my estate since the date of marriage. Once we get married, I'll just put my investments in money markets, and then I won't have to worry about much of an increase," said Alfred sarcastically.

"You're wrong. If in fact you separated shortly after you married, you could be required to pay her an equalization payment of about $350,000." Jeremy slathered mustard on his hot dog. His golf ball rolled off the counter and bounced down the interlocking stone pathway.

"Three hundred and fifty grand? That seems pretty high. How did you arrive at that figure?" Alfred asked, raising his voice a bit while Jeremy pursued his wayward ball.

"Easy — she'll be living in your house. The place where two people live together is known in family law as a matrimonial home. It's always included in a person's family property for equalization purposes — from the day the two of you are married, it technically can become one-half Mary Beth's."

"Maybe I shouldn't be so quick to put her on the title deed!"

"It doesn't matter who has title to a matrimonial home. Whether it is owned jointly or solely, the full value of the home on marriage breakdown, is usually included in what we call the Net Family Property calculation." He took a bite of his hot dog, and a large dollop of mustard landed in his lap. "Oh, bollocks," snapped Jeremy. "Kay just washed these shorts — she'll make me do the next load."

Alfred continued, "Okay, then I'll put Mary Beth on title anyway if it doesn't matter. I have one question. Delmore Avenue is worth $350,000, so half of that comes to $175,000 — how did you arrive at $350,000?"

"Your cottage is also valued at $350,000 — half of that is $175,000," said Jeremy, patiently dabbing at his shorts.

"Oh, no, you're wrong. I don't plan to change title on the cottage. It will stay registered as sole ownership in my name."

"Like I mentioned before, old chum, legal title is irrelevant with a matrimonial home." Jeremy took two short tugs on his beer and checked on the progress of the group in front.

Alfred looked puzzled. "What does the matrimonial home have to do with the cottage? We won't be living there year round — Delmore Ave. will be the matrimonial home!"

Jeremy smiled knowingly as he swallowed the last bite of his hot dog, a sprinkle of mustard peeking out from the corner of his mouth. "This is a very confusing area of family law — most of my clients don't have a clue about this. You mentioned earlier that you and Mary Beth plan on spending time together up there at the lake. You see, you have to understand the definition of a matrimonial home —"

"You have just a leetle touch of moutarde on ze side of your mouth," interrupted Alfred, inexplicably lapsing into a Parisienne accent. It usually was a signal to change the subject.

Jeremy ploughed on. "As I was saying, you need to understand the definition of a matrimonial home under the Family Law Act. There are no limits to how many matrimonial homes one can have. If you and Mary Beth plan to use the cottage then, as your wife, she may be entitled to one-half the value of your cottage as well as the city home."

They finished their beers and got ready to begin the back nine.

"Well, I appreciate your concern, but that's not likely to happen anyway. I'm too loveable — no one would want to divorce me. They'd be considered crazy, right?" Alfred was not expecting Jeremy to answer.

"Depends on the character of the person you marry."

"Just for your info, Mary Beth has a fine character. And you're two shots down after the first nine."

"I'm sure she does — I wasn't referring to anyone in particular. Look, no one *expects* to get divorced. It's just that we can't predict what will happen. Unless . . . are you psychic? Can you read tea leaves, my palm perhaps?" Jeremy held out his palm.

Alfred slapped Jeremy's hand away and spoke softly and slowly. "I'm 68 years old now. I didn't get divorced the first time, and I'm sure as hell not going to let that happen this time."

"Divorce and death are situations often not within our

control," Jeremy said as they made their way to the 10th green.

"What does death have to do with this?"

"Because Mary Beth could be entitled to the same value from your estate on your death as she would if the two of you were to separate. We have to take a step back. All I'm trying to do is convince you that your will and other estate matters must be overhauled. I appreciate how delicate this can be, but I can't stress enough the importance of careful planning here."

Alfred slowly digested this information. "You just stated last week that if I died right after we marry I would die intestate. I'd be a stiff without a will. So why should I bother to draft a new will at all if the presence of one just puts my estate in the hole by $350,000?"

"Alfred, my boy, if you die without a will, the share of your estate that may have to be paid to Mary Beth could be a lot more."

"You have to understand that I don't have a problem leaving most of my estate to Mary Beth." Alfred tossed a golf ball up and down in his hand. "If we marry, she's the one who will get stuck taking care of me in my old age. I don't need to worry about retirement homes anymore. And what an onerous job that will be — having to care for a crotchety, ornery, incontinent old puss like me."

"Yes, it's a frightening thought," replied Jeremy. "But for now let's play golf."

Thus ended the second discussion on the subject of a will for Alfred Hilroy.

Chapter 7

MIRROR, MIRROR, ON THE WILL

WHILE ALFRED WAS THREADING his way around the golf course, Mary Beth was winding her way through Bay Street lunchtime crowds in Toronto's financial district. She could think of better things to do on a day off work than travel downtown to visit her financial planner's office, but her goal was to make every day a day off work, now that she had met Alfred. Now was the time to pay a visit to Susan Turner, a will and estate-planning lawyer. Susan shared the same office floor with Jacqueline Wade, Mary Beth's financial planner.

Shortly after moving to Canada 10 years earlier, Mary Beth was introduced to Jacqueline. Thirty years old at the time, Mary Beth had just arrived from Australia without a nickel to her name and was determined to make a new start in several areas of her life, including an investment plan. She had lived hand to mouth until this point in her life, and she was a neophyte in the areas of investing and retirement planning. Jacqueline taught Mary Beth the basics of concepts such as the time value of money, compounding returns, and market volatility.

At the time of their first meeting, Mary Beth had just begun a job as an assistant to a graphic design artist, earning $25,000 per year. The first step Jacqueline took was to convince Mary Beth that she needed to open a registered retirement savings plan and to begin a regular investment plan in a habit-forming way. Because Mary Beth lacked discipline with her savings habits, Jacqueline set her on an automatic RRSP savings plan whereby she signed a form allowing her bank account to be debited $200 on the first of each month. The money was invested in an RRSP balanced mutual fund that contained both bonds and stocks. Jacqueline helped to define Mary Beth's investment objective of saving for retirement. She also determined other issues, such as time horizon, which in Mary Beth's case was very long because of her young age, and risk tolerance. Jacqueline determined that Mary Beth's risk tolerance was moderate, which meant that she could tolerate the risk of having some stocks in her RRSP but that this risk was best balanced with low-risk investments such as government and high quality corporate bonds.

Mary Beth adopted Jacqueline's recommendations and was pleasantly surprised each year when she received a tax refund of about six hundred dollars. Although Mary Beth's first inclination was to use the entire refund on a spending binge at the shopping mall, Jacqueline was able to convince Mary Beth most years to reinvest at least half of the tax refund back into her RRSP. This was no small feat since she was inclined toward liberal spending habits. Ten years later, her RRSP was worth almost $60,000. As Mary Beth watched her retirement fund grow each year, she developed a deep sense of loyalty to Jacqueline. Jacqueline was able to keep Mary Beth's emotions out of her investment decisions and to guide her through the peaks and valleys of volatile markets. For this, Mary Beth was very grateful.

As she waited at the reception desk for Susan, she recalled one of her first meetings with Jacqueline, in which various investment alternatives for her RRSP were outlined.

Mary Beth was distracted from her thoughts by the sound of Lydia, the receptionist, answering a call. Lydia had the look of someone who'd become bored with her job. In a flat voice, she announced that Jackie would see Mary Beth in the Romeo Conference Room.

"Wherefore art the Romeo Room?" asked Mary Beth playfully.

Lydia remained poker faced and pointed rather than led the client to the conference room.

As Mary Beth entered, Jackie looked up from her laptop. She had a round, expressive face, and her mouth was large, in an American, Mary Tyler Moore-ish sort of way.

"Hi, there! It's been a while. You said something on the phone about being engaged? Super!" Jackie's words came out fast and with apparent sincerity.

"We've kept it pretty quiet." Mary Beth's tone suggested they get straight to business.

Susan Turner appeared in the doorway.

"I'd like you to meet Susan Turner," said Jacqueline.

Mary Beth extended her hand. "It's good to meet you finally." She soon moved the conversation to the matter at hand. "Thanks for seeing me on short notice. I'm living with my fiancé, Alfred, at the moment, and we are planning a wedding at the end of the summer. As Alfred knows, I want to ensure that I always have some financial stability. I would like some legal advice on what Alfred's financial obligations are to me once I'm his wife and how we should best arrange our affairs. You see, Alfred doesn't really want me working anymore. I'm trying to take your advice of being fiscally responsible. Now that my situation is changing, is there anything that I should be doing?"

Jackie wasn't surprised at her client's peremptory tone. She had seen it in others. She indicated to Mary Beth that Susan would handle the meeting from there.

"Well," replied Susan, adjusting her eyewear. "Are you signing anything such as a prenuptial agreement or a marriage contract?"

Mary Beth's eyes narrowed a bit. "No. It hasn't come up. Is that what they call 'prenups' on *Entertainment Tonight?*"

"You got it!" grinned Susan. "Where are the two of you living at the moment?"

"In Alfred's house," Mary Beth said, her voice squeakier than she'd wanted. "Right now the house is entirely in Alfred's name, and I have spoken to him about including me on the title. He hasn't done that yet — dealing with Alfred can be frustrating at times. He procrastinates, but he will get to it eventually."

Susan chose not to respond to Mary Beth's last comment. "What are your assets now, and what assets does Alfred have?"

"I have about $60,000 in an RRSP. That's about it. As for Alfred. . . ." On the long drive downtown that morning, Mary Beth had performed mental calculations of the rough value of his assets. "Let's see now. Alfred is 68 years old, and he has accumulated significant wealth. He just told me he sold half his business for about $250,000 after tax. His house, cottage, Florida condo, RRSP, and other investments, oh, I don't know, maybe one and a half mil?" She said "mil" as though she used the word every day.

As if all of this number talk had made her hungry, Mary Beth extracted an apple from her large handbag and examined it, thoughtfully and deliberately.

Susan thought about invoking the no-eating-/no-cell-phones-in-the-conference-room rule but instead kept quiet and input the numbers in her laptop. "So Alfred still owns part of his business. What would the equity be in that?" asked Susan as she quietly typed in the numerical data.

"Oh, gee, I hadn't thought of that. I'm not really sure."

"Fair enough. Whom has Alfred put as the beneficiary designation on his RRSP forms?"

Mary Beth twirled her hair with her free hand while holding the untouched apple prominently in the other. "I don't know. Probably still his late wife, Joyce. As I mentioned earlier, Alfred doesn't get around to changing anything quickly. So, anyway, not to appear pushy or anything, what do you suggest we do to get on the bandwagon, so to speak?"

She might mean gravy train, thought Susan. "Just a second," she said. "There's one more thing. Does Alfred have a will, and when did he last update it?"

"Alfred hasn't changed his will since Joyce died."

"Whom have you designated as beneficiary on your RRSP form?"

Mary Beth stared out the window. "Jackie and I filled that out just last year. My sister is the beneficiary, but you can check with Jackie to be sure," she said between bites. "Who is the best person to put as beneficiary?"

"First, from a tax point of view, if the two of you were to put each other as RRSP beneficiaries, then on death those RRSPs can be transferred without the taxman coming in and taking almost half of the value in taxes. The most common tax-deferred transfer of an RRSP occurs between spouses. When a spouse is named as the beneficiary of RRSP proceeds, the full fair market value of the deceased's RRSP proceeds can flow directly to the plan of the surviving spouse or to the RRIF — registered retirement income fund — if there is one. This means that the deceased's estate does not have to pay any tax at all on the RRSP."

Mary Beth thought about that for a moment. She had finished the apple and now started to wrap up the core in a Kleenex, neatly like a rug.

"Have I lost you?" enquired Susan.

"Hang on a tick — so does that mean, if Alfred were to put one or all of his three children as beneficiaries of his RRSP, on his death his estate would have to pay tax?"

"Well, I assume, given Alfred's age, that his children are all age of majority?"

"Yes," replied Mary Beth, "although they don't always act like it."

"Are any of Alfred's children mentally or physically disabled?" questioned Susan.

"No, unless Judy's quick temper qualifies as a mental disability," Mary Beth replied with a loud, gregarious laugh. She looked around for a wastebasket.

Susan manufactured half a smile. "To answer your question, if Alfred were to leave any portion of his RRSP to his children, that portion would first be considered full income to his estate in the year of death, and then tax would be paid on that."

"Well, crikey, so the best scenario is for Alfred to leave his RRSPs to me?" Mary Beth was now leaning forward in her chair. "Just so I have this right, it actually makes sense for Alfred to roll his RRSPs to me on death, or else it will actually cost his estate money?"

"Strictly from a tax point of view and presumably because Alfred would be in a high tax bracket at death," replied Susan. "But that may not make the most sense in his situation. Other factors need to be considered. For example, sometimes naming the estate as beneficiary can provide the most flexibility to executors, who can then decide how to split the money up after the taxes have been paid. I can't really answer your question in isolation of other issues, such as —"

"Speaking of executors, wouldn't it make sense, don't you think, for Alfred to put me as executor? Of his will, I mean, and I put him as executor of mine?"

Susan cleared her throat. "Well, yes . . . no . . . maybe, maybe not. What I typically do is draft up what are called 'mirror wills' for many of my married clients. In these situations, each person leaves his or her estate to the other in the event of death. On the death of the second spouse, the assets pass to the children. Typically each individual names the other as executor of his/her estate. And if there's a calamity or disaster that hits both people, the combined estates pass to the next generation."

"So that is the ideal situation, then, no?" said Mary Beth as she attempted to pass the bundle of ex-apple to Susan, who was nearest the wastebasket. The lawyer busied herself with various manoeuvres on the computer keyboard, so Mary Beth rose and strolled across to the waste receptacle.

"Well, it may not be that easy for you. Alfred may feel obligated to leave a chunk of his estate to his children and perhaps name one or all of his children as executors. If he leaves *everything* to you, he may want to ensure that you will leave the estate to his three children on your death." Susan eyed Mary Beth as her client wiped her hands on a tissue extracted from her handbag.

Mary Beth considered this latest information. "Let's say that we decide to go ahead and draft up these mirror wills. If Alfred dies before me, which we expect to be the case given our vast age difference, can I change my will afterward if I want to?"

"Yes," replied Susan. "Many people with children from a first marriage aren't keen on leaving everything to a second spouse. You see, there is no guarantee that the second spouse won't change the beneficiaries of his/her will later in life. In those cases, sometimes a spousal trust can be used."

Susan pushed back her chair, and Mary Beth took the cue that the meeting was over. Susan walked her client to the elevators.

"Just one more thing," asked Mary Beth. "You mentioned something about designations on the RRSP form. Does that mean you don't actually have to change your will to change an RRSP designation?"

Susan answered patiently. "If someone dies, standard practice is for the courts to look at the most recent RRSP designation to determine what the deceased wanted — that means either in a will or just on the RRSP form itself. But I always recommend your wishes also be documented in the will so that —"

"Thank you, here's the lift. I'll call for another meeting soon," said Mary Beth, entering the elevator and pressing *G*.

∽∾

"Where's the start switch on this thing?" Alfred muttered, gazing across a panel of knobs and small symbols on the recently acquired gas barbecue.

"Didn't the distributor go over that with you?" Mary Beth sounded vaguely miffed from behind her issue of *Hello!* She was well into an article on the latest Madonna goings-on and needed to concentrate on the subject.

"Well, yes, but that was last Monday — I think. I can't remember every detail. Where did you put the manual? Maybe it's got a diagram I can decipher without having to take a course."

Mary Beth exhaled slowly as she put down the magazine. She extracted the instruction booklet, wedged into the couch, and passed it to Alfred. He peered at the manual with one end of his glasses in his mouth. He didn't bother with things such as eyeglass holders, which drape around the neck. Mary Beth found his occasional befuddlement endearing, like a lot of male characters in TV sitcoms. She lowered herself onto the couch beside Alfred, using his left knee for leverage.

"It's pasta tonight," she murmured into his nearest ear.

"Pasta night? That's Wednesdays at the Moonglow. . . ."

"No, I'm doing a recipe — tonight — for us. I've been working at ideas from the Food Channel. You can watch MacNeil-Lehrer while I get it ready, and then maybe we can talk during dinner about the 'future.'" She made quotation marks with her two wiggling index fingers.

"Sounds OK. Let me take one more stab at the barbecue. No extra spices, OK? I don't need any more reflux."

Mary Beth was a very good cook. In fact, she could rightfully be called a gourmet cook. Skilfully she sautéed the shrimp and scallops with garlic and onion. She portioned the fettuccine for the two of them and scooped the seafood on top, then lit the candles, all the while deep in thought, mainly about her afternoon meeting.

"Dinner is ready, all hot and steamy! The barbecue can wait. By the way, how was your golf game today?" she asked.

They sat down at the kitchen table, Alfred moving one of the candles laterally so he could see Mary Beth. "Oh, it was great. The drive I hit on the 6th hole — *magnifique!* And I birdied the 11th." He always perked up when he talked about golf.

"That's nice," Mary Beth said, stifling a yawn. She felt tired from her talk that day with Susan Turner. She poured them both a glass of merlot. "I had a very interesting day as well."

"Oh, how's that?" asked Alfred, looking up with his fork poised to deposit the first bite of pasta. "I've sure worked up an appetite playing golf today. You should have seen me today out there. I actually scored lower than Jeremy. I can only remember, in all the games we have played together, maybe five or six times when that happened."

Mary Beth took a sip of her wine and steered the conversation back to where she wanted it. "Good for you. I, ah, had my meeting with the estate lawyer — you know, the one I mentioned to you I was going to see. Anyway, we got chatting about things, and I told her that you and I were planning marriage and that we agreed I would stop working. She has some great suggestions, I think. You know my RRSP? Well, at the moment, I have my niece Janet as the beneficiary. Jackie's advice is to change that and put you as the beneficiary. It really makes sense — she said it's a great tax-planning strategy. She said that couples should put each other as beneficiaries on their RRSPs. Something about the way the money just flows into the other spouse's RRSP, and there is no tax to pay at that time. So I thought that I'd change mine, and I think it makes sense if you do the same."

Alfred was busy enjoying his pasta. "Oh, I know, I have to get around to changing my will. I'll get it done one of these days — Jeremy's been bugging me to do it."

Mary Beth reached over to put her hand over her fiancé's hand. "Sweetie, Susan mentioned that an RRSP designation can be changed on the actual RRSP form itself — it takes two seconds to do. You still have Joyce as beneficiary on your forms. You know, honey, it would make me feel a lot better about us being a team if we addressed some of these things. I feel like I'm living with ghosts everywhere. You've been driving our relationship quickly, and now we're engaged. It's wonderful that we are committed to each other — what's important to me is not just an emotional commitment but also a financial one. What do you think, bugalugs?" She pouted her lips and blew

Alfred a kiss, with one of the candles fluttering as it sailed by.

"I know, I know, you're right. Jeremy is coming over tomorrow to watch another playoff game with me. I'll ask him then how I should make a beneficiary change with my RRSP."

"You make me so happy! We'll have to do a little celebrating later tonight. What do you say?" Mary Beth said in a sugary voice and with a wink across the table.

"Sure, dear. The dinner is outstanding. What did you add to it?"

"It's the best-quality seafood from the market. I grated fresh parmigiana cheese, and I used extra-virgin olive oil — just for you."

"What, do you think I have a thing for virgins? I'm living with you, aren't I?" Alfred laughed loudly at his own remark.

Mary Beth smiled broadly back at Alfred.

Chapter 8

THE LION'S SHARE

"I'VE DECIDED TO LEAVE just about all of my estate to Mary Beth," announced Alfred with authority.

Jeremy blinked. His friend's sudden earnestness caught him off guard. "Why is that?" he asked, not taking his eyes off the whirling hockey players on the television.

"Because I love her, and she's very good to me. For God's sake, *shoot!* I mean, you've got to drive to the net!"

"Is that really a good idea? Why not split things up between Mary Beth and your kids?"

"Because I want to make sure that Mary Beth is well taken care of after I go. I've taught my children to be self-sufficient, to take care of themselves. Mike is independent now money-wise, so I wouldn't need to leave him anything. As for Judy, I do help her out from time to time, so, yes, I guess I would leave her something in my will, but. . . ."

Jeremy put down his glass of iced tea, muted the sound of the hockey game on TV, and looked directly at his friend. "Alf, hear me out. When it comes to dividing your estate at death, an unequal distribution can cause a lot of problems with your kids. Fights over estates are likely to rip a family apart more than any other event."

Alfred nodded as he listened. "I know, I know. But just listen to my viewpoint for a sec. I often help Judy by supplementing her rent payments. With Bev, even though she never asks for help, I insist on contributing to her kids' education plans every year, and I like to pay for their camps in the summer. I haven't given any money to Mike in ages — haven't had to. I don't think an unequal distribution is unfair to Mike since he has a mortgage-free home, a thriving business, and a wife who doesn't need to work! So why should I leave him anything?"

"Great question. There is no simple answer to that. But I have noticed that sometimes, when there is an uneven distribution of the estate, the children may accept the parents' reasoning, but on a purely emotional level they view a smaller legacy as less love."

Alfred looked at Jeremy for the first time and raised his eyebrows. "These issues and others are reasons why I can't tackle my will yet. Do you have a solution to the 'equal/unequal' dilemma?"

"Not a solution — but I have some advice. There is no right answer or wrong answer, and every parent must make his or her own determination. My suggestion to you is that, if there is to be anything but a strictly equal division of your estate, you let your children know about the plan in advance."

"You mean a family meeting?"

"You could, but better yet don't call a family meeting. Bring the subject up casually over a dinner and raise the hypothetical issue of equal division or division based on need and see what happens. I guarantee you the result will be very interesting."

"I understand what you're saying, and I know that your advice is sound. But I'm not ready to discuss my estate and will. Nor my last colonoscopy, my bedroom habits, or my opinion of the seal hunt."

"Well, just think about it. Now to point number two!"

"I knew there'd be more," winced Alfred as he turned his gaze back to the screen.

"You know, Alfred," said Jeremy, "I don't wish to sound patronizing, but you might wish to think again about leaving the whole kaboodle to Mary Beth — that is just asking for trouble. There are ways that you can provide for her without having to leave everything to her outright. Remember I told you about different kinds of trusts? Trusts in general are a great tool in estate planning. You can leave assets to someone inside a trust, and they can enjoy the income from those assets without necessarily depleting any of the capital. The beneficiaries of the trust can be anyone that you name. In this way, you ensure that at least the capital stays within your family." Jeremy took a sip of his iced tea.

"Mary Beth is the same age as my kids, roughly," emphasized Alfred. "So what good would that do? My kids would never see the capital anyway."

"Good point, you're absolutely right. You then make your grandkids the beneficiaries of the spousal trust. You already mentioned that Mike is financially independent and that Bev isn't far behind."

They paused to look at the hockey game and its closed captioning on the screen. *"Oh, baby, things are heating up now!*

Down the ice comes Mogilny! The Leafs are storming the Devils' goal!"

"Stuff it! Yes! Two to nothing! How about a beer?" Alfred pressed the button to turn off the TV mute. "That's the other thing. I don't really want to complicate my estate at my age. Trusts, alter egos — all this stuff sounds expensive and complicated. Besides, Mary Beth will take care of me when I really need it."

The old friends looked directly at each other for one of the few times since the start of the afternoon third-round Stanley Cup match 30 minutes earlier.

"Think about it, Jer." Alfred talked above the loud commercials airing just prior to "Coach's Corner." "Think about the advantages of my being able to remain in my own home late in life with my younger wife. I won't be lonely. I really want to remain in my own home, in my own neighbourhood, for the rest of my life. I'll have full control of the channel changer and keyboard mouse. That's more privacy than any retirement residence or long-term-care facility."

"Alf, when that time comes, you can always elect for Home Care anyway!"

Alfred shook his head. "Thanks but no thanks. Costs of private care are big, big, big — I'll bet it would be up to six grand a month, including normal living costs. Having a Home Care worker who may or may not be compatible would make me feel like I'm institutionalized in my own home. I don't want to be on a regimented schedule, you know, laundry days, counting bowel movements, going for regular walkies. Also, health-care workers today are stressed out, and I don't think they always have the best interests of an elderly fart or fartess in mind."

Jeremy smiled. Don Cherry could be heard shouting from his TV hockey soapbox, but for once no one was listening. "Remember Evan Temple's story? Alf, how can you be sure that Mary Beth will have your best interests in mind 20 years from now or whenever?"

Alfred smiled. "Because I just know. We've had frank discussions about our needs, our fears — we've really opened up to each other. I never thought I'd be talking this frankly with anyone. But she really makes me comfortable, and she's told me several times that she will always be here for me right through to the end. I know you think I'm gullible, but basically we each fill a need in the other."

"What is *Mary Beth's* need?"

"To not have to live alone with just a succession of dogs for the rest of her life. To be financially secure. Besides, she really loves me — I know that. Cheezie?"

Jeremy didn't respond. There was only the crinkling sound of the Cheezie bag as they watched the replay highlights. "If you bequeath everything to Mary Beth in your will, then how do you feel about her remarrying after you're gone and letting some schmo live in your house, spend all your hard-earned money, and inherit Mary Beth's assets?"

Alfred was ready for Jeremy's question. "Because Mary Beth promised me that she would include my children as beneficiaries of her will — even if she doesn't for some reason, my kids are financially independent. She doesn't yet have a will, though her lawyer suggested that, when we do get around to our wills, we prepare them together. Such as you did for Joyce and me a couple of years ago."

The period started with a series of icing calls that ground the hockey game to a standstill. Jeremy decided to wade in. "Don't be gullible. You can't count on Mary Beth staying true to her word. You don't know how common this is. First spouse dies. Surviving spouse meets someone new. Surviving spouse feels really young again. Before you can say 'Baba-lou!' they move in together. Children become annoyed and perplexed." Jeremy, a skilled raconteur, stood up as if to command more attention from Alfred. "Recently I had a client whose husband had died last year. She met someone new, and he made her feel young and beautiful — you know how women are — anyway, he romanced her right to the altar. Since the wedding, she has changed title on all of her assets to 'joint' with her new husband — all bank and investment accounts. The result? When she goes, all of her assets go to him. I think he was putting the screws to her — the guy doesn't hold down a stable job. Anyway, the kids really dislike the man, and they called me to talk about their mother's situation and her will. I said they had better speak with their mom, even though I know that tensions in this family are high. They see this guy as nothing but a phoney upstart. They want to know what they can do to stop him from cleaning out their mom's finances, not to mention their inheritance. One of the kids is wondering if he should use his power of attorney, behind her back, to put his mother's assets in a trust. I don't think that the mother has even told her kids that the assets are now held jointly. So you see it can get messy." Jeremy sat down.

"Golly, these two teams have come to play! Have we got action for you today! That'll be icing against the Devils!"

Alfred had been listening to Jeremy, though his gaze had been fixed on the TV screen. He watched as the camera zoomed in on the linesman, who was carrying the puck back to the other end of the rink, weaving in and out among the exhausted players.

"Well," said Alfred, throwing one hand up in a dismissive gesture, "I'm sure there are lots of stories, some of them good, some of them pretty ugly. But I'm no King Lear. I trust my kids, and I'm sure they trust me. I know that you're looking out for my best interests. But what Mary Beth and I have here is a special relationship. And that's the way that I want to leave it."

"Your call," said Jeremy. "How are you going to tell Bev, Mike, and Judy?" His tone was mild, but the words had a cutting ring to them.

Alfred popped two more Cheezies into his mouth and wiped the orange residue on the sports section of the newspaper. "I won't right now. Maybe later when the kids begin to like Mary Beth — when they get to know her and start to admire her good qualities. I think their suspicion of her will die down over time. I just want everything to be easy and everyone to be happy."

"Alf, keep listening. Parents tend to be very secretive with their children about this kind of stuff, and secrecy is not the route you want to take. Consult your children first — they are the ones who will have to live with your decision. Don't assume that your kids will always treat each other with goodwill."

"I hear ya," replied Alfred casually. "In the meantime, at

Mary Beth's suggestion, we would like to talk to you about RRSP beneficiary designations. We need a refresher on RRSPs and how they are taxed — can we come and meet with you together to talk about that?"

"Why just your RRSPs?"

"I told you that I don't want to do my will just yet — I'm not in the frame of mind for that. But in the meantime, Mary Beth met with her lawyer yesterday to discuss RRSPs. I gather that they can be handled outside of a will. I promised Mary Beth that we could address our RRSP beneficiary designations together."

"Sure, I'll help you with that," said Jeremy without much conviction. "But promise me one thing."

Alfred bounced up from his chair. "Why does Quinn play that Belak guy so much? He skates like his jock's on backward."

Jeremy's bank of patience was fast being depleted, but he pressed on. "You two can meet with me on Monday morning to discuss your RRSPs, but —"

"I'm at the pharmacy Monday. How 'bout Tuesday morning?"

"Okay, Tuesday morning, but do me a favour and read just one article I'll send you by e-mail when I get home. It's on the benefits of a trust and in particular the advantages of using a spousal trust. Will you read it before you hit 'Delete'?"

"Will do, old boy. I hope we don't have overtime; M.B. is stopping by on her way back from the gym soon, and she finds hockey baffling. She only knows field hockey, and so far I can't get her interested in what she keeps calling ice hockey."

They watched the end of the game, a 3-2 win for the Maple

Leafs. As Jeremy got up to leave, a Viagra ad blared its message for the fifth time in the program. He had now broached the subject of wills with Alfred on three separate occasions. He had no idea if he'd made any headway at all.

⌾⌾

Alfred watched admiringly as Mary Beth prepared cream of celery soup, straight from the pages of the *Joy of Cooking*. She had found the well-worn 1972 edition (47th printing) in a box in the basement and had restored it to a place on the kitchen counter. She had unearthed it a few days earlier, by chance opening it to the foreword. A Goethe quote appeared by itself on the facing page:

> *"That which thy fathers bequeath to thee,*
> *earn it anew if thou wouldst possess it."*

Strange quote for a cookbook, she'd thought at the time.

"A little nutmeg and cornstarch, and Bob's your uncle," offered Alfred. "By the way, we can meet with Jeremy this Tuesday morning to address the RRSP designations you suggested. Okay with you?"

"Perfect. I'm meeting with my lawyer again on Tuesday after lunch. Now, why don't you go watch a bit of TV? Dinner will be a few minutes."

Alfred padded out of the kitchen, and instead of turning on the TV he fired up the computer. Jeremy's message was already waiting for him, the fifth in line after two jokes, a quick solution for restoring one's waning sex drive, and an offer to strike pay dirt with European currencies. He'd already forgotten Jeremy's advice, but he knew he'd promised to read his message.

Alf,

Thanks for having me over today to watch those pesky Leafs. Six more wins and we'll have our first Cup since the middle part of the past century.

Here are my notes on spousal trusts (also known as testamentary spousal trusts):

- It is set up in a will and is formed as a result of someone's death.
- Passing property on death to a surviving spouse or a proper spousal trust will not trigger any taxes.
- When assets are left to a spouse or spousal trust, there is a deferral of tax on capital gains until the spouse disposes of the property or dies.
- A spousal trust entitles the deceased's spouse to all of the trust income. As long as the spouse is alive, he or she will be the only person entitled to any capital from the trust.
- You can specifically indicate in the trust deed that you either allow or disallow capital distributions to the surviving spouse.

Why would you set up a spousal trust instead of giving assets directly to your spouse?

1. A spousal trust is commonly used when the person making the will has remarried and there are children from the previous marriage. A spousal trust can provide for your spouse

and ensure that your kids will receive something fom your estate.

2. A spousal trust is protective. If your spouse remarries after you are gone, the assets in the spousal trust are protected from claims in the event of divorce.

3. There may be concerns about the ability of the surviving spouse to deal with property — what is his or her financial acumen? A spousal trust would be appointed a trustee who has the responsibility for investing the money in the trust in a prudent fashion.

As always, I'm available to talk about how this relates to your situation.

Cheers,
Jer

The Lexmark printer announced "Printing started!" in its androgynous computer voice, and Alfred mused about what he had just read. This is all very nice, but it can wait, he thought and placed the message in a drawer reserved for longer-term projects. The aroma of celery soup wafted into the room, prompting Alfred to head back to the kitchen, back to the brand-new love of his life.

Chapter 9

CLASH OF THE BOOMERS

JUDY STEERED HER CAVALIER into the driveway of her child-hood home on Delmore Avenue, keeping left to avoid the area where the asphalt had crumbled. She didn't want to jostle the three decks of black-eyed Susans and the pots of impatiens that occupied the back seat. It was the first May since her mother's death, and she wanted to continue the tradition of spring planting that her mother had observed. Judy also intended the flowers as a means of making amends to her father for the harsh words she'd spoken to him in their previous conversation. As soon as she'd hung up the phone, she'd begun to feel guilty about snapping at her father. Her mother's death had left her almost completely bereft; she could only imagine the pain her father must be experiencing. She couldn't deny her feelings of animosity toward his new girlfriend, but she wasn't really justified in taking those feelings out on him. In the end, she only wanted what was best for him.

There was no answer at the door even though her father's Buick was parked on the street. He's probably at his new girl-friend's place, Judy thought as she walked back to her car. No doubt he spent the night there. She wrestled the flowers out of the car, taking the impatiens around to the back door and leaving the decks of Susans temporarily on the car roof. When she returned to the back door of the house, she found that it was unlocked.

The first thing Judy noticed when she entered the kitchen was the mess. Bottles of olive oil and vinaigrette dressing lined the kitchen counter. Pots and pans sat in a sink that was half filled with dirty dishwater. Cookbooks lay open on the counter. Judy knew that her father's new girlfriend was an expert cook, but she was still startled by the general disarray. It was such a contrast with the days when her mother kept the kitchen completely organized. What Judy found most striking was the disappearance of all the Hilroy artefacts: the decorative plates, the delicate hand-painted glasses, even the corny wooden sign that read "Bed and Breakfast — Make Your Own." And where was the brown teapot, which Mike had broken years before in a fit over not being allowed to watch *The Mod Squad* and which his father had painstakingly reconstructed with epoxy glue?

Judy felt a twinge in her stomach. What other Hilroy family possessions had disappeared or been moved? She entered the adjoining den and immediately noticed that the curtains were gone. Molson, their golden retriever, had chewed the fabric almost to pieces. Judy remembered how she and Bev had talked their mother out of replacing the curtains. They'd thought they were part of family history. Any item the girls thought had family significance was not thrown out or given away. At worst, such items were sent to the cottage.

The sound of voices brought Judy back to the present. She turned and headed back to the kitchen. Try to keep an open mind, she thought. Dad is happy and well fed. Keep thinking that way. Dad is happy and well fed.

Alfred pushed open the front door, fumbling with the key in one hand and a bag of muffins in the other. Mary Beth breezed by him, balancing a cardboard tray of Tim Hortons coffees.

"Hi there," Mary Beth said, hoisting the tray in greeting.

"Hi, Dad, hi, Mary."

"That's Mary Beth. Nice to meet you."

"Ah, right. I'm Judy. Nice to meet you too." Judy looked back at her father. "Just thought I'd bring you some plants I picked up at Tucker's."

"So I see, yes, wonderful," said Alfred. "Want to split this coffee with me?"

"Sure, though I should start planting some of the flowers," Judy said. She reached for the cupboard to the left of the sink where the coffee mugs resided. Instead of the familiar array of mismatched, chipped, and faded mugs that the family had accumulated over the years, she found a large collection of vitamins and tablets in white plastic containers.

"Oh, those are my greens," said Mary Beth, seeing Judy hesitate. Alfred's new mate was wearing black gym tights with a cropped black spandex workout top. Her blonde mane was pulled back into a ponytail.

Judy watched Mary Beth as she rinsed out a coffee mug that had been left on the counter the night before. Any woman can have well-defined calves, a flat stomach, and a tight rear end if she's never had kids, thought Judy as she sucked in her stomach. So what's my excuse?

Mary Beth was going on about her greens. "Because greens have chlorophyll, derived from alfalfa and clover, which is good for absorption of iron and —"

"I get enough iron from eating red meat," Judy said. She turned to her father. "What are you up to today, Dad?" She couldn't bring herself to say "What are *you two* up to?"

"It's the gym for Mary Beth, and I think I'm playing tennis with some of the guys at Jeremy's club. I can still play a damn good game of doubles, you know."

"Just don't overdo it."

"Your dad is in*cray*dibly fit." Mary Beth's Australian accent was occasionally quite pronounced. Judy found it annoying. "He can still stay up late at night and answer the bell really early the next day," Mary Beth said, poking at Alfred's midriff and wiping a muffin crumb from his upper lip.

Judy couldn't look Mary Beth in the eye. "Yes, especially with Mom's help over the years, Dad's remained in decent shape."

"Do you work out at all?" asked Mary Beth.

"Sure, I run two or three times a week. That's about all I have time for. You know, work can be very demanding. I guess you don't have to worry about overtime at the bank. . . ."

"Not anymore," said Alfred. "Mary Beth's leaving her job in a couple of weeks. She's going to take some time off to decide what she really wants to do. For now, she'll do some painting, and I have big plans to put her to work at the cottage this summer. There are a lot of projects waiting to be done up there."

"Yeah, I'll put my bathers on and get to work up there. I can be real creative," Mary Beth added with a smile.

Judy felt her stomach begin to churn. "Um, are you spending the whole summer up there?"

Alfred put his coffee down. "Well, Jude . . . actually, now is as good a time as any to tell you. We were going to invite you and Bev for dinner. But since you're here now . . . Mary Beth and I are engaged!"

Judy's increasing discomfort now turned to near nausea. Judy felt hurt and angry and had to consciously bite her tongue to keep from saying something she would later regret. She tried to remember the good manners and poise that her mother used to emphasize, but she was unable to summon them up now. Not smiling, she said, "Isn't this all very sudden? What's the hurry?"

Alfred beamed; he looked like a freshman candidate running for political office. "Mary Beth and I have been together for some time now, and it's been great. At my age, things happen quickly. What's the point of extending a courtship when you just know it's right?"

"What about Mom?"

"Your mother would want me to be happy, and I am."

"I've never understood why people your age bother getting married," Judy said. "When do you think you'll have the, ah. . . ."

"Wedding? We're thinking sometime at the end of August — not a big shindig."

"I don't think I want to be a bridesmaid," said Judy in a trancelike state. She sometimes wished she could control her remarks, but today she didn't really care.

Mary Beth laughed nervously. "How about the maid of honour?" She often said silly things when she was uncomfortable.

Judy didn't find Mary Beth's remark the least bit amusing. She couldn't wait to get home and call her siblings. "I'll just use the loo, and then I really must get going."

Judy left the newly betrothed couple to finish their coffees and made her way upstairs to the washroom. As she passed the door to her old bedroom, she casually glanced in, and what she saw froze her to the spot. A new Cybex fitness Stairmaster sat in the middle of the room, gleaming with all its metallic promise of a healthy lifestyle. Five- and ten-pound free weights surrounded the beast, sitting on the new grey carpet like escorting destroyers. In the corner were a medicine ball and a wicker basket half-filled with gym clothing. Track lighting and a floor-to-ceiling mirror completed the decor. A $3,000 price tag hung from the rail of the Stairmaster. I've heard lots of gold-digger stories, Judy thought, but I never thought I'd see one in my father's house. Grimness set in. She backed out of the room, dazed, and slowly made her way back downstairs.

In the kitchen, Judy found Mary Beth standing behind Alfred with her arms wrapped around his middle, giggling. Judy glared directly at Mary Beth. Her resolution to attempt to control her anger lasted only until she opened her mouth. "When you said you were going to the gym this morning, I had no idea you meant it was *upstairs*. What is all that crap in my bedroom?"

Alfred untwined himself from Mary Beth and offered to

explain. "I was going to tell you soon — I didn't expect you to come over this morning, and —"

"Where's the bed and my chest of drawers?" interrupted Judy, her gaze now fixed on her father. "Where's my stuff?"

"They're in the garage for the time being. I wasn't going to throw them out. I thought you could take them, or we could ship them to the cottage."

Judy turned her glare to Mary Beth. "Do you find your time constraints so severe that you are unable to drive to a gym like ordinary people? Especially now that you're leaving your job?"

For a moment, Mary Beth's glittering eyes suggested that she might challenge Judy, but she seemed to think better of it.

Alfred intervened. "Look, let's not argue. I just bought Mary Beth some gym stuff so that she could feel comfortable in this house. Think of it from her point of view: she doesn't want to be confronted with family ghosts everywhere. I told her to fix up a couple of rooms with her own furniture."

"Fine, fine," Judy said with her arms crossed tightly across her chest. "I just hope it gets lots of use. That's a nice shopping spree you went on. Next I guess we can expect a sauna installation or perhaps a tennis court out back?"

Mary Beth smiled weakly at Judy, then looked at Alfred, who said nothing. "Right, then. The fitness club beckons," said Mary Beth. "The big one, I mean." She grabbed her purse and stepped hastily out of the room.

Provoking Alfred was next to impossible; he hated confrontation. On the other hand, he wouldn't retreat into complete silence. "Did you really have to react that way? You can berate me all you like, but you have no right to talk to Mary Beth that way. I'd like you to show just a little respect the next time."

"Respect? *Respect?* Dad, do I have to paint a picture for you? She comes in here like a Hollywood diva without any respect for what Mike, Bev, and I might feel. Don't you think this spending is a little — no, a lot — frivolous? Obviously she doesn't have respect for your hard-earned retirement savings!"

"Now calm down. I just put a little money in an account for her and told her she could renovate the house a bit. Judy, this house hasn't had any work done to it in over 20 years."

"And you call thousands of bucks of fitness equipment 'renovations'? Dad, with all due respect, she's got her talons on your wallet, and you don't even get it, do you?"

Before Alfred could assemble an answer, Judy grabbed her keys off the counter and stormed out, stepping over the impatiens in the doorway. Alfred watched his daughter jump into her car and, before he could sound a warning, saw one black-eyed Susan container after another slide off the roof of the car as it gained speed down Delmore Avenue.

Chapter 10

SIBLING SUMMIT

"ENGAGED? THE OLD man's engaged? Holy shit! What's the rush? Is it the blonde bank teller?" Mike's voice echoed from the speakerphone in the den at Bev's home.

Bev and her still agitated sister were on a call to their brother in British Columbia. Judy had just arrived, breathless and flustered, and Bev had suggested they hold an impromptu "sibling summit." She found the three of them could solve family problems easier by getting together once in a while and talking things through.

"Yes, it's the teller all right, and I think she's bad news." Judy recounted the events of the morning. Listening to herself tell the story, she was surprised at how she was still getting stirred up. "Once I saw my room transformed into Cain's Gym, I should have left without confronting Mary Beth. It's lucky I didn't just climb out onto a window ledge and do a swan dive to the patio."

"That's one way of attracting attention," said Mike. "Look, even if she's up to no good, what can we do? It's Dad's call. She probably really loves him — we shouldn't really be surprised that he's found a girlfriend. He still has a lot of charm, right?"

Judy snorted. "Yeah, but I thought he might have hooked up with one of the women on the casserole brigade, someone like Mom."

"What are we really worried about?" asked Mike.

"Dad's welfare, of course. That he doesn't make a fool of himself — that he doesn't get hurt," said Bev.

Judy bit her thumbnail. "But it's our house, our cottage, our stuff. . . ."

"Jude, I'm sure he's thought out the financial side of things pretty thoroughly," said Mike, calmly but unconvincingly.

Bev jumped in. "Um, Mike, I wouldn't be so sure. We need to get Dad to talk about his money situation, including his will, before it's too late."

"Half of it is Mom's," Judy interjected. "I'm sure she would-n't want to see it go to some tart —"

"Mike, who is the executor anyway?" asked Bev.

"Well, if you don't know, I sure don't."

There was a pause.

Bev looked at her sister, who was now worriedly chewing the nail on her right pinkie. "Mike, I thought you and Dad might have talked about all this at some point in the past, no?" asked Bev.

"No, not at all. You know Dad. Back when I was 11, he was a bit shaky talking to me about the birds and the bees after he caught me staring at Delores Shamess's large boobs all week-end, that one time they were invited to our cottage. (I mean the Shamess family, not the boobs.) I remember him coming into the bathroom when I was having my scheduled eight o'clock bath. He closed the toilet lid, sat down, then asked, 'Mike, you know how to, um, give a girl a squeeze?' 'Sure,' I said, and with that he stood up and walked out. Same thing when it comes to talking about money — you know Dad, and Mom was like this too. 'One does not talk about one's will while one is alive!'"

"But we should find out," said Judy. "What if one of us calls Jeremy and asks him — like right now?"

"No, that won't work. Jeremy can't pass on confidential information. It's up to Dad to tell us that stuff if he wants to. No use sweating about it — his executor is probably one of us, and we'll worry about that when the time comes — which hopefully isn't for quite a while!"

"Michael, we have to ask him. I won't stand by watching some. . . ." Judy was close to spluttering her words.

"We can't change the old man."

"But what if he puts the Blonde as executor?" Her fists were clenched, and Judy resented her brother's more philosophical approach.

Bev took this as a cue to step in as mediator, a role she often resorted to during their childhood years. "ok, let's step back a minute. Mike, since you'll be here next week, I'll suggest to Dad that the four of us get together for dinner. Jude, are you ok with this idea?"

"Sure, the sooner the better. We need to plug the flow of money before she sucks him dry —"

Mike interrupted, "Jude, you're getting worked up probably at nothing. I'll bet he hasn't done anything silly with his will."

"You guys always tell me not to get worked up," Judy said

with exasperation. "How do you know there isn't a problem here? We don't even have a clue about the executors. I smell a big rat, at least a sizeable mouse. And how are you going to make it a Blonde-free dinner? They live together, don't they?"

Mike laughed. "We'll pry him loose for a few minutes. Look, Jude, the best thing you can do is to feign indifference when Mary Beth's around. No more getting indignant, OK? What happens, happens. It's important to Dad that we keep the peace."

"You've been out on the West Coast too long, big brother."

Mike laughed. "And don't expect Dad to be forthcoming about any money matters. He'll just tell us that what he's doing is right or that he's taken care of everything, you know, standard Dad-speak. He would've been excellent on Parliament Hill. As for me, I don't like having to deal with the fact that Dad won't be here forever. We just lost Mom not too long ago."

"At least one of the men in our family has noticed," quipped Judy.

Chapter 11

RRSPs PLEASE

JEREMY PULLED OUT A photocopy of Alfred's RRSP application, opened several years earlier at Empire Wealthline, the brokerage arm of Empire Bank. Jeremy kept copies of all of Alfred's financial records. He handed the form to Alfred.

"Your beneficiary designation you will find on page 4," instructed Jeremy.

Alfred looked over the form quickly. "I just need to change the beneficiary on this from Joyce to Mary Beth," he said, all businesslike.

Mary Beth smiled over at Alfred from the corner of Jeremy's office, where she was examining the goldfish tank.

"Yes, sir," responded Jeremy, not minding his friend's drill sergeant demeanour. Alfred had stressed earlier that the RRSP designation was the only topic he wanted to discuss. Jeremy really wished that he could convince his friend to address all of his estate planning, not just one small piece. But he accepted that he would have to let it lie for now. "You will need to make changes with a service rep at Empire Wealthline. I cannot do it for you. But I will help you understand what your options are.

Mary Beth, have a seat and let me go over some pointers with respect to RRSPs and beneficiary designations."

Mary Beth sat down beside Alfred.

"Do you both know what a terminal return is?"

"Yup," responded Alfred. "It's the last tax return done after someone has died."

"That's right," said Jeremy. "And in that terminal or final tax return, as some call it, your executor is responsible for filing the final income tax returns on time and ensuring that all the income taxes due to CCRA are paid. I know that sounds like a Russian hockey league, but it is just good old Revenue Canada with a new name: Canada Customs and Revenue Agency. All assets held in the deceased's name are deemed sold on the date of death, at full fair market value, even though they actually haven't been disposed of. Then the tax is paid on the incremental value of those assets over and above what they were acquired for. OK so far?"

The betrothed couple nodded in agreement. Jeremy thought he was still keeping his friend's attention, even though Alfred now had his legs stretched out in his chair and was fiddling with the loonie and toonie change in his pocket.

"Your current RRSP, Alf, as you pointed out, still has Joyce named as beneficiary. Just because Mary Beth will be your new wife, don't assume that your RRSP will automatically transfer to her on your death, if that is what your wishes are. You need to specifically state that on the RRSP form itself."

"Agreed," responded Alfred. "So, refresh my memory, what would happen if I did nothing? That is, if I didn't change the name from Joyce and then died?"

"Well, the rule is, if an RRSP is payable to a deceased individual, the monies are paid into the estate at death of the RRSP holder. So, if you didn't change the designation from Joyce, your RRSP would be payable to your estate on your death and handled according to the divisions in your will. But. . . ." Jeremy paused. "But you have no will, so that RRSP would form part of your assets at death, which would be subject to division based on Ontario laws of intestacy. It gets complicated."

"Well, let's assume that my will is done, for the purposes of this discussion," said Alfred.

Jeremy held up his index finger. "Fine. Then option number one — you can leave an RRSP to your estate. If you do, the full value of the registered plan at the time of death is included as income in the terminal or final tax return. Also, the market value of the RRSP would be added to your other assets in your will to arrive at a final calculation of probate fees."

"So why would anyone leave their RRSP to their estate, then?" asked Mary Beth.

"Good question. If you do not have a spouse, a disabled child, or a child under 18, you can name your estate as the beneficiary if the estate needs money to pay bills. Or someone may expect no other income in the year of death, and thus the tax bill may not be too high."

"I guess that one's not for me," said Alfred.

"Also, there is a little-known area of estate law that allows the executor of someone's estate the discretion, after death, to elect to have part of or all of a deceased's registered assets pass on a tax-deferred basis to a spouse, if one is alive. This can be considered only if the RRSP proceeds are left to the estate *and* the spouse receives the proceeds under the will directions."

Mary Beth raised her eyebrows and looked at Alfred. "But then you are leaving decisions up to your executor, who may or may not make the most logical choices."

"Perhaps not," conceded Jeremy. "On the other hand, if a beneficiary such as an individual or a charity is appropriately designated on the RRSP, then no probate fees are payable on the amount."

"Can an RRSP be held jointly?" asked Mary Beth.

Jeremy shook his head. "No. RRSPs and RRIFs cannot be registered jointly."

Alfred nodded. "So what are the other options you wanted to discuss?"

Jeremy held up his index and middle fingers. "Options number two and three. You can make a beneficiary designation to a dependent child or grandchild *or* to a mentally or physically disabled child or grandchild. In both of those situations, you can have the RRSP taxed in their hands. Now, Alf, you don't have any dependent children or grandchildren, so this scenario doesn't apply to you."

"Certainly not in the case of Mike. Maybe" — Alfred looked up at the ceiling fan — "maybe Bev's kids. Since she split up with Stan a couple of years ago, I've been funding their education plans and giving them money every year toward their camps and living expenses."

Jeremy put his hands behind his head and gazed directly at Alfred. "That *could* be one of your options. I'd need to talk to CCRA to get a decision as to whether or not that constitutes 'financially dependent.'" But because Bev is working and also

supporting the kids, I don't think this is an option for you."
Jeremy drummed his fingers on the desk. "You see, if you leave
it to a financially dependent child or grandchild, the registered
funds can be used to purchase an income-producing annuity
that matures when the child is 18. This can be a tax-effective
way to get money into the hands of a child."

"I don't understand. Then who pays the tax?" asked Mary
Beth.

"I'll use an example," said Jeremy. "But first do you understand the tax rate structure and how it works?"

"Maybe you should go over it again," volunteered Mary
Beth.

"No problem," said Jeremy. "We have a progressive tax rate
structure in this country. The more money you make, the more
tax you pay on each additional dollar earned. Someone who
earns $20,000 each year will pay tax of about 26% for each
additional dollar earned. On the other hand, someone earning
over $100,000 in this province pays tax at about 46% on each
new dollar made. But each province has slightly different
provincial rates. In Alberta, the top rate federally and provincially is about 39%, in Saskatchewan 45%, and in the
Northwest Territories about 42%. OK so far?"

Alfred gave Jeremy a thumbs-up sign, and Mary Beth followed suit.

"Now let's talk RRSPs." Jeremy took a pen and notepad and
wrote down "$200,000" in large numerals, then held it up for
everyone to see. "Alf, your RRSP is worth more, but let's say it is
worth $200,000 and at the time of your death you leave it to
your grandchild, who is 14 at the time. Two things can happen.

The full $200,000 can roll to the child and be included in that child's income all in that one year. This would probably still result in less tax than if the $200,000 were included in your terminal tax return. Or, by purchasing an annuity for the child, the income can be spread over several years. In this example, if an annuity were purchased at 14, then the $200,000 could be spread over four years, resulting in income to that child of only $50,000 each year. So, overall, the total tax paid on the RRSP is less by spreading the income over the child's remaining years to age 18."

"I reckon that there still is *some* tax to pay by leaving an RRSP to a child, no?" asked Mary Beth.

"Right you are. But it is still a good option to consider," said Jeremy.

"What happens if the child beneficiary has already turned the age of majority and then the grandfather dies?" asked Mary Beth.

"You have good questions, Mary Beth. The trustee of an RRSP, for example, the financial institution, will usually pay the full market value of the RRSP directly to a designated beneficiary. In the case of an adult child, the full value of the RRSP would pass to that child, and the estate would pay the tax on that value. It's only with minor dependent children that the tax bill can be rolled down and included as that child's income. That's why we refer to it as a 'rollover.'"

Mary Beth was deep in thought. "My only asset is my RRSP, worth about $60,000. My sister is the beneficiary. Has tax been avoided by leaving her the full amount?"

Jeremy smiled. "You're a quick study."

"I like to find the loopholes. Like the times I knew how to get cigarettes at less than, um, full market value."

"Hush," said Alfred, looking mildly shocked.

"To answer your question," said Jeremy, "the taxes will be paid somehow. The CCRA has armies of workers with all the time in the world, and they will collect from anyone they can find to pay up the tax owing — do you have an executor?"

"No. I don't have a will. I was told I don't need one because I only have the RRSP."

"Maybe, maybe not. To avoid confusion, it's still a good idea to have a will to indicate that the RRSP is going to your sister, *net of tax*. Also, you may have some cash in your bank accounts and some other nonfinancial assets that can be addressed in your will."

Jeremy stood up and strolled over to the fish tank. "If you have a will, your executor can be personally responsible for the tax if he or she distributes the RRSP before paying the taxes. CCRA will approach your sister in this case for the additional tax due. Let's hope that it hasn't already been spent, because otherwise CCRA can pursue any person who has received gifts prior to your death." Jeremy sprinkled fish food into the tank. "And if that doesn't work, then the executor may be personally liable for the tax because she or he distributed assets before getting clearance from CCRA."

"And another option for RRSPs?" asked Mary Beth, anticipating the response.

"Leaving assets to a spouse. When a spouse is the named beneficiary, RRSP assets can be passed to him or her with no immediate tax due. The assets are transferred right into the spouse's plan. This allows the registered funds to continue their tax-deferred status and preserves the value of the RRSP or RRIF."

"And if we don't get married, but we live together, am I considered a spouse after three years?"

"Another good question, Mary Beth, but that's not true. The three years you're referring to is the definition of 'spouse' under the Family Law Act of Ontario. There's a separate definition of 'spouse' for income tax purposes. The Income Tax Act, by the way, is federal legislation and therefore applies to all provinces. In the act, common-law spouses are defined as two individuals who have been living together for at least 12 months or, if less than 12 months, are parents of the same child."

"Can I get a word in here?" asked Alfred, who'd been doing his best to heed his friend's instruction to listen.

"I think we'll let you," answered Jeremy.

"I'm turning 69 this year. My RRSP will convert to a RRIF. Because I'll be leaving my RRIF to Mary Beth, does she continue to receive the income?"

"Yes," said Jeremy. "Both RRSP and RRIF assets can be rolled over to a spouse. With a RRIF, the spouse becomes the annuitant and continues receiving RRIF payments without having to transfer them to a new account. The advantage here is that, if Mary Beth does not require the annual income from the RRIF, it can be converted back to an RRSP. This shelters the investment income from tax until the RRSP matures. This can be done provided Mary Beth is still under 70."

"That's the only way it could possibly happen," laughed Alfred.

Both Mary Beth and Jeremy looked blankly at him.

"I mean, I hope Mary Beth will be under 70 when I die. Figure out the math. If she's 70 when I go, that means I've lived to be nearly 100. The only good thing about that is at some point I'll be able to shoot my age at golf, if I stay healthy."

They all laughed, Mary Beth the loudest. "If you live to be that old, you could be a great-great-grandfather and leave your RRSP to lots of dependent grandchildren."

"I won't have any money left if I live that long. I plan on spending it."

"On what, I wonder?" asked Mary Beth, blinking rapidly.

"Hmm, yes, that could be —"

Jeremy interrupted Alfred with a sudden movement in his chair and started shuffling his papers.

"So I will call Empire to change the designation to Mary Beth, then," said Alfred.

Jeremy was worried that Alfred was acting precipitously, so wherever he could stall his friend he would try. "No rush, Alf. Since you are turning 69 in a couple of weeks, you must convert your RRSP to a RRIF by the end of this year. Do it then."

"Shouldn't we do it now?" said Mary Beth with a look of concern. "Doesn't that complicate things by waiting?"

Jeremy coughed. "Not at all. A conversion to a RRIF creates an entirely new plan. Tax officials won't allow a designation made for an RRSP to be automatically carried over to a RRIF, even if the account number is the same. Since you'll need to open a RRIF by December at the latest anyway, you might as well wait until then to change your beneficiary designation."

"Well, that saves me one trip — might as well do both at once," responded Alfred cheerily.

Mary Beth looked deep in thought. "And are there maximums on how much can be withdrawn from a RRIF?"

"There are no maximums to how much can be withdrawn from either a RRIF or an RRSP. But whatever you take out is added to your income and taxed accordingly."

"Oh, well, that's good to know," commented Mary Beth.

"Having a young wife has several benefits," said Jeremy, writing a note to himself on a piece of paper.

"It sure does," agreed Alfred with a wink and a smile.

"I'm still referring to your RRIF, smarty. When you convert to a RRIF this December, you can use Mary Beth's age to make the minimum withdrawal calculation."

"What is the difference using her age versus my age?" asked Alfred, leaning forward in his chair, an earnest look on his face.

"The minimum amount you must take from a RRIF yearly is set by the tax authorities and is based on age. Each year's minimum withdrawal is based on the plan's fair market value at January 1st of that year. So let's use the same $200,000 value from our earlier example. Alfred, if you use your age for the minimum withdrawal next year, you'll be 70, and you are looking at the minimum being about five percent of the plan's value or roughly $10,000. Using Mary Beth's age to determine your minimum withdrawal next year, the rate would be approximately two percent or about $4,000."

"So I am an asset to you after all, in more ways than one," Mary Beth proclaimed proudly. "Without me, you would have to pay so much more in taxes both during your lifetime and after."

"That is if there's anything left at the end," said Jeremy, who immediately wished he'd said something else. He quickly changed tack. "That's not all. There are more things that can be done with a younger spouse."

"Yes, incredible things," said Alfred.

Jeremy ignored Alfred's latest innuendo, calculating how he should surreptitiously launch into the will topic again. He had an idea. He leaned forward in his chair and spoke clearly and authoritatively. He sensed that his old friend's attention was wandering to thoughts of chip shots or something else. "Because you still have employment income, you can contribute each year to a spousal RRSP on behalf of Mary Beth and get an annual tax deduction each year that you do this. Furthermore, in your will, you can have a clause that authorizes your executors to make a final spousal RRSP contribution to use up any RRSP room that you still have available. Because you plan to continue working part time, you will generate RRSP room for several more years. The rule for a final spousal RRSP contribution is that, provided you have a spouse, the executor can make one final contribution up to 60 days after the end of the year of death. This contribution will generate a tax deduction for your terminal return. But you need a will for that."

"That's right, bugalugs, we really do need to have our wills done," piped up Mary Beth.

"In due course," stated Alfred with a sudden movement of chair legs scraping and papers shuffling. "Gotta go now. We have places to go, people to see. . . . Many thanks, Jeremy."

Chapter 12

JOINT OWNERSHIP 101

MARY BETH HOVERED AROUND the reception desk, waiting for Lydia the receptionist to look up.

"I'm here for my one o'clock appointment with Susan," Mary Beth announced, ignoring the phone headset attached to Lydia's round, rather large head and the fact that Lydia was otherwise busy with another customer.

Lydia held up her right index finger while holding the headset to her ear with her left. With impatient customers, Lydia often wished she could employ her middle digit instead. Mary Beth didn't sit down to wait but instead fixed her gaze on Lydia while remaining totally motionless, as if to cast a spell over her and compel her to do her immediate bidding. Lydia drew out her phone conversation for another few minutes, with Mary Beth rooted to her place in front of the desk. The waiting room impasse finally ended with the appearance of Susan Turner.

"Hi, Mary Beth, come on in, I'm actually running ahead of schedule today."

"Terrific! What weather, eh? It's hot enough to boil a

monkey's bum, as they say back home! I can't wait to hit the lake next weekend."

Susan smiled bemusedly and pointed to a client chair. "That will be nice. What's Alfred doing today?"

"Well, he works at the drugstore Monday, Wednesday, and Friday, so today being Tuesday he's off for the day."

Mary Beth plopped down and proceeded right to business. "Joint ownership of the house for me and Alfred. Good idea? I mean, if we hold property jointly, isn't it possible to avoid paying death taxes or whatever they're called?"

Susan put up her hand as if to direct oncoming traffic. "Whoa, slow down — that's a loaded question. I should clear up a common misconception. There are no death taxes in Canada. No inheritance taxes either."

"Oh, right you are — I knew that we didn't have inheritance taxes, but I'm just not sure what other taxes might be lurking about."

Susan listened politely to her client. "What you're referring to are 'estate administration taxes.'"

Mary Beth, who had started to root about in her handbag for something to eat, raised her eyebrows. "And they are. . . ?"

"An estate administration tax is an amount paid when someone's will is probated. They are also called probate fees. You've probably heard of the term 'probate' — it's a 'proving' of the will by the court. It's the court's confirmation that the will is the last will and testament of someone who has just died. The amount of the probate fee varies from province to province, but essentially the amount you pay is based on the value of the deceased's estate stated in the application for probate."

Mary Beth absorbed this information while chewing on an old mint she'd found in her bag. "Alf and I had a meeting this morning about beneficiary designations, and I learned a few things. So, just to make sure I understand, if I die tomorrow, I pay no probate fees since my only asset is my RRSP and I'm putting Alfred as the beneficiary?"

"That's correct. You see, naming beneficiaries on RRSPs, RRIFs, and insurance policies means that these monies pass directly to the beneficiary. They aren't part of someone's estate at death. You can also avoid probate fees by holding property in joint ownership with rights of survivorship."

"Why is that?" asked Mary Beth intently.

"When ownership of property is registered between parties as joint tenants with rights of survivorship, the deceased's interest in the asset is automatically on death passed on to the surviving owner. This transfer is not handled in the will. So, because the asset stays out of the estate in this instance, it is not included in the calculation of probate fees."

Mary Beth made a crunching noise with her mint and nodded, indicating that she understood. "I mentioned to you at our meeting a couple of weeks ago that the house we are living in now is in Alfred's name only. Wouldn't it make sense, then, for Alfred to put me as joint owner on the home and, well, other assets as well — you know, the cottage, bank accounts, stuff like that? I mean, in this way, he could avoid having to pay those estate taxes." She looked in her bag for more mints but couldn't find any.

Susan spoke slowly. "Not estate tax. We need to use the proper terms here to avoid confusion. Let's keep it simple and just refer to these fees as probate fees, since that is still what most people call them. The quick answer to your question is, yes, from purely a technical viewpoint, we can avoid probate fees by holding assets jointly. But there are a lot of other things that need to be taken into account before you think about joint ownership."

"Well, I need to know whether or not it makes sense in our case to consider doing this," said Mary Beth.

Susan was silent for several seconds, then leaned forward in her chair. "Part of my job as an estate lawyer is to be aware of the emotional issues that can affect my clients and the importance of communication — it's an integral part of the whole estate-planning process. Have you spoken to Alfred about your thoughts on this matter and other financial issues?"

"You bet. We're very open with each other, and we have spoken at length about our financial matters. I always have to start the conversation because Alfred doesn't like discussing money and stuff — he would rather keep putting it off. In my family, these topics were dinnertime talk. We were always very open about money — and sex too!"

"I'll bet getting a word in edgewise in your house was a challenge," added Susan.

"We just talk over one another. Listen, I also want to apologize. In our last meeting, I realize that I was a bit abrasive — I know my assertiveness and pushiness with questions must look suspect and make others believe the only reason I'm with this guy is for the dough. You must believe me. That's very far from the truth — it's just my nature to be forthright and direct —"

Susan interrupted, "You don't need to apologize. But I must

caution you — your particular situation isn't that straight-forward. You will soon have stepchildren. By putting you as joint owner on all of his assets, Alfred will effectively be cutting his kids out of the value of his estate. There are many ways in which probate fees can be minimized and tax rollovers can be benefited from, but you and Alfred should really come in to see me together for proper estate planning."

Mary Beth became fidgety and stood up, making her way to the window. "Alfred's kids, my stepchildren — yikes, *stepchildren!* — wouldn't necessarily be cut out of his estate! Couldn't we just agree that I will leave everything to his kids equally when I check out?"

Susan smiled. "Yes, but that's something best discussed privately between the two of you. The other side of the coin is that Alfred may want to consider putting some of his assets into joint tenancy with his children today."

Mary Beth looked nonplussed. "He could do that?"

"Absolutely," replied Susan. "You can convey a joint interest in financial assets or real estate with anybody — doesn't have to be a spouse."

Mary Beth went back to her chair and sat down, making doodle marks as she gathered her thoughts. "But if Alfred put his assets in joint title with his kids, then isn't he cutting me out of his estate?"

"Yes, that's right."

"But don't I have rights as his spouse?"

"Yes, you will, once you're married to him."

"But don't I now have rights since we're living together?"

"Not entirely. It's not that simple. You must separate income tax law from family law. Under the federal Income Tax Act, common-law spouses have rights with respect to tax-free transfers to each other similar to married couples but only after 12 months of living together. At the moment, under family law, which is what you are referring to, common-law couples are not recognized as having *automatic* property rights upon marriage breakdown or death. They have to make a claim to the courts for property and ongoing support — stuff like that. It's a very complex area. But basically married couples are entitled to split the growth in the value of an estate, which is basically determined by formula, in Ontario anyway."

"What are the automatic rights of married spouses?"

"Most provinces have laws that protect a spouse's right to a just and equitable distribution of property, including the matrimonial home. Spouses cannot just be written out of a will, for instance."

Mary Beth gazed down from the window at the midtown gridlock. "That's good to know. Now, getting back to joint assets, because we plan to get married, Alfred really shouldn't put any of his assets jointly with his kids, then, no?"

"Mary Beth, it's not that simple. The whole picture needs to be looked at by both you and Alfred as a team to decide how equitably his estate should be split between you and his children, should he pass away before you."

"But Alfred's children are already financially successful — well, the first two anyway — so is there still an obligation for him to leave money to all of his kids?"

"That's a very good question. The short answer is no — there's no moral or legal obligation in most provinces to leave

money to financially independent children. That's the strict letter of the law. But this is about more than just the law. Death,
taxes, executorship, joint property — it's important to understand these issues, but that's not all you need to be concerned
with. People aren't robots who make decisions based only on
technical data — well, most people anyway. You will really need
to understand the emotional issues facing you and Alfred as well
— and, as we all know, emotions aren't rational. You say Alfred's
kids are doing well financially? It's really irrelevant. To be fair to
everyone, Alfred may very well feel obligated to leave a portion
of his estate to his children. Also don't forget that he has grandchildren. If Mr. Hilroy's children want to extend their kids'
education, such as grad school, they may need assistance."

Susan paused in order to let Mary Beth finish compiling her
notes.

"Is it possible for both you and Alfred to come to see me
together?"

Mary Beth shook her head. "No, I don't think so — Alfred
already has a lawyer. But getting back to joint ownership —
what do you usually recommend to a couple who don't have
any kids from previous marriages?"

Susan continued patiently. "As I've said, it's really not that
straightforward. Most couples in first marriages hold property
jointly."

"You mean jointly with each other, not with any of their
children," exclaimed Mary Beth, a bit ahead of herself.

A little knowledge is a dangerous thing, thought Susan.
"Yes, with each other. While joint ownership does have its
advantages, such as reduction of probate fees, there are also

disadvantages in putting assets jointly with someone other than a spouse, such as children."

"Oh? And those disadvantages are, um, what?" asked Mary Beth. She blinked several times during the silence.

Susan removed her glasses and gently rubbed her eyes. "Well, there are tax issues to be concerned with and also legal issues. First, from a tax viewpoint, when you add another person *who is not a spouse* as a joint owner, you are effectively disposing of a portion of that asset at fair market value. For example, if you add one other person to the title on an asset, you are disposing half of that asset; if you add two other persons, you are disposing of two-thirds of the asset; and so on. This could lead to a tax hit if the asset has appreciated in value. A lot of people are unaware of this."

Mary Beth was listening vigilantly. "So, if someone places an asset jointly with a child to avoid these probate fees, they may in fact be inadvertently triggering a bigger tax hit today."

Susan put her glasses back on. "Exactly. You've got the gist of it."

"You mentioned legal problems too. What might those be?" Mary Beth uncrossed her legs and leaned forward slightly in her chair.

Susan looked at her watch. "I'll list them briefly — I have another appointment in five minutes. First, you are subjecting the asset to the potential claim of any creditor of that child. Second, you are subjecting that asset to matrimonial issues of that child. Third, if the parent puts a principal residence jointly with a child, and the child does not live there, the parent may lose half of the principal residence exemption on the growth of that home after the transfer. I've just listed three problems that can occur with joint ownership and children. I always recommend seeking professional advice before anyone considers putting assets in joint ownership with children." Susan closed the "Cain" folder in front of her. "One more thing — do you have a power of attorney? Are you familiar with it?"

"Oh, yes, somewhat. Although it is less important than the will," Mary Beth stated matter-of-factly, stuffing her notepad and pen into her purse.

"Actually, you should give as much attention to the power of attorney as you do to your will. A 'P.A.' is a document that legally provides a trusted individual with the power to act on your behalf if you are unable to do so yourself — for example, if you are incapacitated for any reason."

"I know what it's for — Alfred probably needs one, but I might wait until I'm older. I don't have much power right now to give to someone."

Susan smiled at Mary Beth. "That's a common misperception as well. Even younger people with a very modest estate should consider executing a power of attorney. The chances of someone your age being disabled far outweigh the likelihood of dying. Along a similar vein, I have many young clients who have life insurance but neglect to take out disability insurance. Healthy people in the prime of life can be suddenly disabled by an accident or serious illness, and their misfortunes become doubly hard when there's not enough insurance."

"That's a cheery thought."

"No, indeed. But it's something that should be thought about in case bad fortune strikes."

"So whom do I appoint as an attorney?"

"You don't actually need an attorney. The person you appoint to act as your agent is called an attorney, but this individual can be anyone you choose."

"And when should I get one of these?"

"Soon, when you do your will."

Mary Beth remained deep in thought as she walked through reception toward the elevator, not noticing the farewell wave offered by Lydia.

⌈∞⌉

Later that afternoon Mary Beth vacuumed, did some laundry, and otherwise tidied the house. She padded into the kitchen and flipped through the cookbooks for ideas. She expected Alfred to be home soon and wanted to get started on making him a superb meal. Mary Beth was always trying to please Alfred, and she loved to take care of him and his home. Her mind wandered back to her meeting with Susan. Mary Beth planned to discuss the details with Alfred later that night. She had deliberated the past three days about making further changes to the former Hilroy-clan house — she felt uncomfortable at being the source of conflict and ruminated continuously over Judy's recent reaction.

Mary Beth recounted in her head the discussion she and Alfred had after their run-in last Sunday with Judy. She began with "Alfy, I'm sorry about the barney this morning with Judy. She was mad as a cut snake. I know how much it upsets you to get into a tiff with your kids. If you like, why don't we change

Judy's room back to its previous state to placate her. I can put the gym stuff in the basement."

Alfred shook his head. "My kids just have to accept the fact that my life won't remain static in order to accommodate their wishes for things at this house to remain unchanged. It will just take them time, but they will soon come around and see the wonderful and kind person that you are."

"You always have such kind words, bugalugs, but I just wonder if we are moving too fast — I mean, for us it's not too fast, but maybe your kids need us to slow down a bit."

Alfred enveloped her in his arms. "It's not up to my children to mandate an appropriate courting period for us. We will be the ones to feel the pain of unfulfilment if we live our lives according to the dictates of others. And, in the end, my kids will respect you more for living your life the way you want."

Mary Beth switched her thoughts back to the task at hand. She prepared the "Pork Medallion in a Demi-Glaze Sauce" that she had selected for this evening's feast. As she stirred the sauce, she thought about how she loved Alfred. He was a wise man by virtue of his age and intelligence. He was everything she had dreamed of in a relationship. Above all, Alfred had the two qualities that were most important to Mary Beth in a mate: kindness and generosity. And Alfred was certainly fitting the bill.

The front door opened, and Alfred entered with a bottle of red wine tucked under one arm and a 12 pack of beer under the other. Mary Beth greeted him at the front door with a loud smack on the cheek. "Maybe you should stock those items at the drugstore — it would save you trips to the liquor store. What's the slab of beer for?"

"For the kids tomorrow night. Mike and Judy like beer. Bev usually just drinks wine. Smells great in here — what's cooking?"

"You'll see. Get yourself a coldie and let's go sit out back on the patio — I'll join you in a divvy. It's too beautiful to be inside on a night like tonight."

They wandered out back to the patio. Mary Beth sat down beside Alfred and put her hand on his knee. "Alf," she began, "as you know, I had my second appointment with Susan Turner today. She asked if you and I had discussed how we are handling the wills and your property and the like. Wanted to know if we'd had open and frank chats about everything."

"And what did you say?"

"Oh, I mentioned that we had discussed it all even though you don't care much for the topic." Mary Beth grinned as she rubbed his back.

"Did you come out of there a bit clearer on some of the issues?"

"Yeah, we talked about the need to have our wills done, joint ownership, and other issues." Mary Beth relayed the details of her dialogue with Susan. "I know this isn't an easy topic for you, but Susan said that we really should have our wills prepared, and of course before that we need to decide how you plan on splitting your assets between me and your kids. Have your thoughts changed any since the last time we discussed this?"

"As I said to you a couple of weeks ago, and I also said this to Jeremy, I still feel comfortable passing most of it to you. My kids are pretty much independent now, except for Judy. I would have to leave something for her, I would think, because she doesn't have much — she really should buy herself a town-house or something, you know. All that money being wasted on rent."

"Whatever your decision, we need to get into the specifics and have the wills done. But, at the same time, I realize that we need to address how to best handle your kids' inheritance — whether it be at your demise or later at mine."

Alfred sighed. "Today I had one of my oldest customers, Mrs. Blanche, come into the store. She is 88 and has Parkinson's disease. She has received Home Care in the past few years, but just last year they were going to discontinue all of her home services because of budget cuts. Her daughter raised a real stink, so her Home Care services were only halved. Just this year they were halved again, resulting in her receiving about one-hour homemaking visits each week — basically just for bathing. Well, one hour just isn't enough, so her daughter is forced to put her mom into a long-term-care facility."

"I reckon that would be a dreadful decision to have to make. I'm so glad that my mom had me when she was 22 — being only 62 now, she is still so young and hearty. I'm thank-ful that I don't need to worry about that just yet. Why did you bring that up?"

Alfred turned and faced Mary Beth directly. "I don't want my kids or you to have to face that decision with me. I don't plan on getting old for at least another 10 years, but when I do need regular care the absolute last place I want to be placed in is an old-age prison."

"I agree. Plus, in 10 years, what will the state of our health care be compared with now?" added Mary Beth.

Alfred ran his hand through his thinning hair. "Right you are — it's already abysmal. So I really do want to make sure that we have enough money in order that my last years are spent living comfortably in my own home. And of course I want to ensure that you are also well taken care of after I go. With that said, my kids will receive some financial assistance, but I don't want to address the specifics just yet."

Mary Beth continued, "Financial security is a hot button of mine, and I have always admitted it — people can call me what they may."

"Don't worry, I'll take care of things for you on that end," said Alfred, leaning over to give Mary Beth a peck on the cheek, delighting her with his comforting reassurance.

Chapter 13

A BARBECUE
AT ALFRED'S

THEY STARTED UP THE stone path to their father's home.

"Looks like Bev's already here; she said she'd be cabbing it," said Mike, fuelled by nervous energy and walking ahead of Judy. "Should I roll out some Aussie jokes, you know, just to build rapport? Like the one about the three Irish professors and the kangaroo and —"

"Oh, knock it off," said Judy, grabbing her brother by the sleeve before he could barge into the house. "We'd better do the doorbell thing."

"Go ahead, but I'm heading in anyway. Yoo-hoooo!" boomed out Mike, resurrecting an old Hilroy arrival salute that their grandmother had started.

Bev emerged from the kitchen. Alfred appeared next, looking tanned and relaxed. Mary Beth loomed in the background.

"Hello there! Mary Beth, come on out! You know Judy," said Alfred, waving his hand toward his daughter, though Judy had already disappeared into the living room. "And here's Mike, the middle one, he's in from B.C."

"Great to meet you! And who's this?" asked Mike doubtfully, looking at Mary Beth's elderly terrier clacking its way out of the kitchen.

"Nice to meet you too. This is Carling. Down, Carling! He's just a bit blind, don't mind him," said Mary Beth chirpily as the dog took an interest in Mike by brushing his wet nose several times along his Dockers.

The introductory chatter continued, save for Judy, who was quietly going over old family albums in the living room. The rest of the gathering hovered in the kitchen, letting Mary Beth handle the bulk of the food prep.

Mike used the condition of his trousers as an excuse to head upstairs to use the washroom and see for himself the home gym phenomenon. Judy wasn't exaggerating this one, Mike thought as he looked at the Stairmaster, Lifecycle, and Universal. He made his way down the hall to his own former bedroom. It had not been left untouched. His old bed had been removed, and a sectional brown leather couch ran lengthways along the wall where the bed once stood. Carling's blanket lay on top. Clearly his room now belonged to the aged canine. An antique desk about six feet by three took up almost the entire other end of the room. He examined the old oak, wondering if his future stepmother was planning to be another Hilary Clinton or whether the desk was just for show. A book on estate planning lay on the desk, the only book. Mike reached to pick it up, and a piece of paper that had been stuck to its back floated down faceup on the desk. He put the book down, looked around, and then read what he could see, bent over with his hands behind his back like a curious museum visitor:

To: Mary Beth Cain   May 15
75 Delmore Avenue

> For services rendered $400.00
> Please send payment to:
> Susan Turner
> Estate Lawyer

"Where there's a will, there's a lawyer," thought Mike. He replaced the book on top of the invoice and rejoined the group downstairs. His mind wandered several times as he sipped his beer and traded stories about Australia with Mary Beth. He quite liked listening to her. Her loud, distinctive laugh made him smile. He convinced himself that his dad knew about Mary Beth's meeting with a lawyer. He tried to put it out of his mind.

"Might be an idea to light the barbie, bugalugs, or your kids may not be able to drive home legally," Mary Beth suggested. Judy, who had rejoined the group but was keeping quiet, offered only a weak smile.

With that cue, Mike grabbed two more cold ones and accompanied his father to the patio, leaving the three women sipping wine in the den. "So, Dad, how are things at the drug-store?"

"Not bad. My partner's doing a great job, and business is as good as always."

Mike began his probe, trying to sound nonchalant. "Have you thought about when you might sell the remaining equity you hold in the business — you know, the other 50%?"

"Not sure. I feel pretty good these days. I'd say I'm good working there for at least the next year if not longer. Why do you ask?"

The gas barbecue gave off a whumping sound as the gas ignited, making them both jump slightly.

"Just curious. You'll be busy with Mary Beth and stuff — I just want to make sure that you want to handle it all." Mike was calculating where he could introduce the *w* word — the will.

"Oh, sure, I'm still youngish. Mary Beth will be an asset, you know. She feeds me like an emperor, and I was thinking that she could help a bit at the drugstore. I can pay her a bit of a salary. Jeremy would agree to that idea, from an income-splitting point of view anyway. We can even split the remaining equity that we'll get when my partner, Jim, pays for the other 50% of the business down the road. You know as well as me that it makes sense for the income from that capital to be split between two people rather than just earned in my name at high tax rates." Alfred scraped away at the grill.

Mike thought about the information he'd seen upstairs. "Yeah, right. Of course. Uh, Dad, speaking of equity, have you changed your financial affairs, you know, your will and stuff?"

"Don't worry, son. I know what I'm doing, everything is fine. Do you think the grill is hot enough for those steaks?"

Mike wouldn't be thrown off his topic. "Hot enough. I think putting equity in Mary Beth's name can be risky — that is, if anything happens to the marriage in the future. Also, have you considered, if something happened to you, your partner at the pharmacy would have to deal with Mary Beth, and vice versa, if something happened to your partner, you could be dealing with his wife."

"Nothing unfortunate is going to happen." Alfred increased his busyness with the steaks, looking only at the grill.

"Dad, with all due respect, you don't know that. We never expected anything to happen to Mom, did we? I have to think about that with Shauna and me — I mean, we'll be doing our wills soon. My partner and I have had some legal advice, and we need to arrange a buy-sell agreement for our business. This is put in place in the event that one of us dies the remaining partner can buy the business at a fair price from the estate. You see, we want the first rights to buy out each other's shares in the event of death or disability; otherwise, a surviving family member will become the new partner, and we don't want to end up in that awkward position. Life insurance can be used to buy out the deceased's interest in the business, and —"

"You're much younger. That's different."

"Not really. Why is it different?" Mike realized that he might be pressing the issue too much.

Alfred became quiet and poked at the meat with the prongs, then flipped the two steaks in the middle. Only sizzling sounds.

Mike repeated his question. "Dad? Why is it different?"

"It just is. Things are different at my age. The steaks are almost done. Why don't you go in and see if the gals are ready?"

Mike saw that he wouldn't get far with his father. He retreated to the kitchen, thinking that at least he'd tried to get the will discussion started. How can I bring up the fact that

Mary Beth has obtained legal advice? he thought. Does Dad know about it? Is this woman exerting undue influence over him? Maybe Judy isn't the only one who should be concerned with this woman. Mike looked back at his father piling up the sirloins on the platter.

The Hilroys and the Hilroy-to-be sat at the pine dining room table, Alfred and Mary Beth on one side and Mike, Bev, and Judy in a row facing them on the other. Carling, despite a problem with his saliva glands, which periodically created pools of drool, was allowed to hover around and under the table, at least until Mary Beth caught hold of the steely glare Judy was giving the aged animal.

"Carling, dear, you're more damp than usual tonight, lovey! Let's get you outside."

"He can be a real pain sometimes." The terrier lay down on its stomach in protest as Mary Beth dragged him by the choke chain to the patio. "Lie down, old boy, you stay here," she said, leaving the sliding screen door open a foot.

"Tell me, what are you two planning for the wedding?" asked Mike, by now well fortified with wine, having passed his rental car keys to Bev.

Mary Beth brightened considerably. "We originally thought August would be a great time, but we're now thinking that maybe early fall is better by the time we get everything organized."

Bev asked a question of her own. "How many guests do you expect to have?"

"Oh, three to four dozen, I'd say."

Judy stared at her plate, one of the prized collection of hand-painted porcelain items her parents had received decades ago as a wedding gift.

"Have you chosen a venue? And have you thought about a place for the reception yet?" asked Mike.

Alfred and Mary Beth looked at one another. Alfred cleared his throat. "Well, actually, Mary Beth would really like to get married back home so that her family could attend. . . ."

"Australia?" Bev looked at her brother and sister.

"Australia!" echoed Judy, sounding as if the place might be the planet Jupiter.

"Yes, that time of year is beautiful in Melbourne," said Mary Beth. "I thought that, if we plan well ahead, you all would be amenable to coming 'down under' for the wedding."

The sounds of cutlery scraping on plates seemed to grow louder.

"Are you paying for our airfare and hotel?" Judy asked, folding her used paper napkin. The question was loud enough for everyone to hear, though it was clearly directed at Mary Beth.

Mary Beth laughed reached for the salad bowl, trying to think of an answer.

Alfred pushed back his chair. "Can I get anyone more steak? Veggies?" he asked, then disappeared into the kitchen to get more food whether the guests wanted more or not.

Mary Beth plunged ahead. "Well, it's just a thought now. If it's too far, the other idea we talked about is to have the wedding in Australia and then to have the reception here later in Canada so that —"

Alfred reappeared in the doorway holding a gleaming empty platter. "Steak I can understand," said Alfred, "but I didn't know Carling likes asparagus as well. Look, he's devoured the whole lot. I caught him moving on to the hollandaise sauce bowl."

Mary Beth, after waving her salad fork in the unrepentant terrier's face and putting him on his leash on the patio, returned to the gathering profuse with apologies. "I don't know what I'm going to do with that dog."

"A forepaw injection at the vet's might work," offered Judy.

Mike quickly reverted to the main topic. "Now there's an idea — I mean having two receptions. You still have a lot of time. I'm sure it will all get figured out."

Mary Beth brought out a blueberry pie that she had made from scratch that afternoon, and the group retired to the patio with pie and dishes of ice cream.

Other than one more episode with Carling, in which his flatulence got out of hand and he had to be dragged away once again, the group managed to get through the rest of the evening by sticking to nonfamily topics.

On the drive home, Judy was eager to revisit the family situation. "What a selfish twit. And she just thinks that we all want to drop everything, including a few *G*s or so, to wing our way to Australia, money no object."

"Yeah, that one floored me a bit," agreed Bev, adjusting the seat in her role as relief driver for Mike. "I guess she thinks that we can just leave our kids at home with sitters like it's no trouble at all. I'm not sure she thinks about those little details."

"It is a bit extreme," added Mike. "But brides do want to get married in their hometowns, I guess." Mike broke into song. *"That's all they really waaaa-a-aant, brides just wanna have fuh-un!"*

Judy almost smiled. "Sure, but common sense would suggest that you don't ask an almost 70-year-old person to endure that arduous 20-hour flight."

Mike laughed. "Maybe you could look after her dog while she's gone."

Judy looked at Mike from the back seat. "Aren't you the least bit offended by all this?"

"Jude, you have to learn to lighten up sometimes. I'm just trying to use humour to make light of a difficult situation. Sure, I'm concerned." Mike recounted his attempted dialogue with their father at the barbecue.

"Should I be surprised?" asked Judy.

"Well, I've got to keep trying. A little persistence, if done right, will pay off. And I'll need you two to help me."

Mike decided it was best to keep to himself what he'd noticed on Mary Beth's desk.

"I'll drag it out of him if you won't," said Judy. "I'm serious."

"No, listen to me, Jude," said Mike. "We have to stick together as a unit. You can say what you want to Dad. But try to be patient with him, ok?"

They arrived at her apartment, and she let herself out. "Not to worry, I'll keep the phone lines open," she said and headed up the steps of her building.

Mike said to Bev, "I'm a bit concerned about Dad splitting the equity of his business with Mary Beth. There must be a solution that will keep everyone happy."

"I agree. Sure, he has to support her financially," said Bev, "but I know there are other ways to do this, such as trusts and other tools that basically can preserve capital for the next generation. But we need to get at this soon."

Mike nodded. "There are indeed lots of strategies out there, but in the end it's Dad's decision to make. And estate-planning seminars are as ubiquitous as diet doctors. I just received another invitation for one in the mail last week. The real challenge will be getting Dad to listen to us."

"You've just brought up a good point. . . ."

"Yeah, Dad doesn't like to discuss this stuff at all."

"No, I don't mean talking to Dad. It's too soon for that — we haven't done our homework yet. Think of what Mom's advice would be to us before we try to sell Dad on anything. We need to research some of these techniques first, and then, armed with well-thought-out information, the three of us can take him out to dinner and discuss this like adults. Mike, I think you should go to that estate-planning seminar in Vancouver you were telling me about. It's free, and you'll get some useful handout material. They'll answer any questions too. I'll go to one here as well. Then you and I can talk, share notes, and take it from there."

"It's a deal," said Mike. "I guess we have to start somewhere. What about Judy?"

"For now, let's not say anything. We'll bring her into our discussions later when we have a plan for what we're going to say to Dad. She says she doesn't have any interest in this kind of stuff anyway. She'll listen if we have a specific plan. If we don't, then she's more likely to get sarcastic."

They rode along in silence for a few minutes.

"What else are you thinking?" asked Bev.

"Well, I wasn't going to tell you this, especially Judy, but I found something upstairs tonight that may mean a lot or a whole lot of nothing." Mike described the Turner legal invoice.

"I'm glad you brought this up. This is how easily family rifts can start. One person assumes one thing is happening without getting the proper facts. Dad may very well know about her meetings and may even be encouraging them for her own independent legal advice. That's even more reason why we need to start our homework soon. Does your schedule bring you to Toronto before our July 1st trek up to the lake?"

"I'm not sure, but I can always arrange another stop before then," said Mike. "Why?"

"Because after we've attended the seminars, maybe we should go together to see an estate person, someone like Jeremy."

"That might be a good idea," said Mike. "And there's another angle we seem to have overlooked in all this. We seem to think we're indestructible ourselves. We need to take time to look at our own estate situations. For the sake of the four kids — Megan and Harry and Jenna and Russell."

Chapter 14

GOTHIC NOVEL NIGHT

Bev looked around the room at her eight fellow book club members. Normally she would have devoured the assigned novel in a few sittings and have been ready to talk about it at the monthly meeting. Not tonight. She had read only a few chapters of Daphne DuMaurier's gothic novel *Rebecca* and was quietly sitting trying to remember scenes from the various movie and TV versions. But her mind was wandering back to thoughts of the previous night's estate-planning seminar.

"What do you think, Bev?" asked Vi, the evening's leader of the discussion, blinking her eyes and pursing her lips.

"Uh, I. . . . I'm sorry?"

"The implied relationship between Rebecca and the house-keeper Mrs. Danvers. How important do you think it is to the resolution of the story?"

"Well, I don't know," said Bev, flipping through the paper-back's pages as if an intelligent answer would appear. She decided to bluff her way through. "Maybe Mrs. Danvers just resented her boss bringing an upstart second wife half his age to the mansion, where she could get her hands on the de Winter fortune."

"That's an interesting tack," said Patricia, another participant sitting next to Bev. "But I don't get the impression that Max's second wife looks like a gold digger."

"Maybe not. But Max would certainly be thinking about executor services, wills, insurance, taxes."

The others looked at Bev blankly.

"OK, OK, he wouldn't be thinking such stuff in a 1930s gothic novel. But I was at an estate-planning seminar last night, and I thought of our hero Max. What if he doesn't have a will or hasn't changed it since Rebecca's passing? If he doesn't have a proper will, then the second wife, whose name I can't remember, might be entitled to the lion's share of the estate. This might tick off someone like Mrs. Danvers, a lifelong family servant."

"I hardly think so," sniffed Vi, "but let's move on, shall we?"

At the break, Bev explained herself to Patricia and Marcy, the two participants she'd developed friendly banter with over the past several meetings. "I don't know why I went on about that will idea. I guess it's because I have a lot on my mind tonight."

"All right," Patricia said, "why don't you tell us about it? I could see when you first walked in here tonight that something was troubling you. Is your dad okay?"

"Well, yes, it *is* about Dad. He's fine, thanks," said Bev, seeing her friends' concerned looks. "His health is great. In fact, he's so fine that he's taken up with another woman. And they've gotten engaged even faster than Max de Winter did." She laughed at the others' startled looks.

Marcy, an observant woman, spoke first. "Let me guess.

Not everyone in your family has taken a shine to the new member. In fact, one or all of you find her intrusive and annoying."

Bev smiled at Marcy's candour.

"What's she doing to annoy you?" asked Patricia. "Leaving her dentures and knitting needles all over the place?"

"Hardly!" Bev snorted. "More like her miniskirts and sports equipment. The only thing old about her is her dog."

Marcy laughed and continued. "Let's see now — and, if that isn't enough, you may be worried about your inheritance."

"You've guessed it. Sounds like you've been through this before," said Bev.

"Almost every day," responded Marcy.

"I don't understand."

"As you know, I'm a psychologist. I actually specialize in linguistics and family mediation. Many people who come to see me are dealing with family conflict of one kind or another — conflict between children and a stepparent is very common. The children often have problems adjusting to a new partner in a parent's life. Some of them perceive a potential threat to their inheritance. It's a complex situation that is becoming more frequent."

Bev nodded. "That's exactly my own case. My brother Mike, my sister Judy, and I don't know what, if anything, Dad has done with his will. My brother tried last week to ask Dad about his affairs — his will and stuff — and he just brushed him off. It's a little disconcerting about their age difference. I mean, is she seeing stars or dollar signs?"

Patricia offered her own story. "My father remarried a couple of years ago. He plans on leaving everything to his new wife, a high school acquaintance he hadn't seen in 40 years but ran into on the Internet. He moved out of the house to live in his sister's basement until the new wife could uncouple herself from her own marriage and fly here to live with him. It's caused, shall I say, just *a bit* of dissonance in our family. We tried many times to talk to Dad about his plans, but he would just shrug or change the subject."

Mary, a large, ample-chested woman helping herself to sponge cake, couldn't help but hear the group chatting and weighed in with her own story. "That's as bad as when your father meets someone new, changes his lifestyle so drastically that he sells the family cottage because his new wife doesn't like it, and forgets to tell anybody. 'I didn't think you'd care' was my father's response when I challenged him."

"It's certainly a tricky subject. Sorry to bring all this up in the first place." But Bev could tell from her friends' understanding looks that everyone felt better for having talked about it.

Vi could be seen at the other end of the room, waving her paperback and calling the book club meeting back to order.

∞∞

Bev and Marcy sat across from each other in a Tim Hortons booth. They were seated at a table for two, next to the window. "I haven't had an apple fritter in ages," Marcy gushed. "It's an item off my list of banned foods for today only."

"Of course," said Bev. "Thanks for taking the time after the book club to talk to me about my situation. I guess you can tell my father's on my mind a lot these days."

Marcy saw the glum look on Bev's face. "It's OK to be concerned. I'm sure your father isn't stepping into a snake pit. If he's at all like you, he's not the type to fritter away his assets."

"Hold that thought. I do need another fritter." Bev looked down at her stomach. "No, maybe I won't. No, I'll get one on the way out and throw it in the freezer at home. All right, back to reality. It's just that we don't really know Mary Beth, and we aren't able to pin down her true intentions. It seems that she really has no other agenda except to marry this wonderful man. But some of the things she's bought already and how she's converting our family home into her palace. She likes to spend money. Only she doesn't seem to have a lot of her own, if you know what I mean."

"Ah, yes, families and money — this topic alone accounts for more than half of the issues that people see me about," said Marcy, shaking her head. "Again the family that one grows up in provides the foundation for one's attitude toward money."

"Surely within reason, though," Bev snorted. "I mean, the way Mary Beth spends money is suspect to me."

Marcy shrugged. "Maybe, maybe not. You see, from what you have told me, spending money frivolously was always frowned upon in your family — in fact, would you agree with me that extravagances in the Hilroy family were considered morally suspect?"

Bev smiled at Marcy's accuracy and nodded.

Marcy paused momentarily and looked out the window, gathering her thoughts. "As children, the way you three heard your parents talk about spending planted assumptions in your mind at an early age that now determine how you judge others. With memories of your parents' beliefs dominating your brain, I would venture to say that you regard Mary Beth and her spending as a grave character defect. But possibly, in Mary Beth's family, spendthrift periods could have been a form of celebration — one to be relished. Mary Beth may associate spending with happy childhood memories. We can release others from blame by getting to the heart of understanding these differences."

"That's an interesting point of view," conceded Bev. "I suppose we need to keep an open mind before we pass judgement just yet. It always helps to have another perspective on these things. Yet the same man who never spent money before doesn't even seem to notice it flying out the window now."

"Hmm, fair point." Marcy took a sip of her coffee. "And how are you, Mike, and Judy getting along with each other, what with all these changes?"

Bev shrugged. "There's tension even though we lead different lives and don't see each other a lot. We are all different personalities. Judy can lash out when she's stressed. Her sarcasm can be hurtful. She is very upset about Mary Beth converting her old bedroom into a gym. Myself, I feel edgy, and now I've noticed it especially at work."

Marcy patted Bev's hand. "This can be a very emotional issue. As for Judy, she is now being treated as a stranger in her old home, and it is violating her connection with your father. That connection may be more pronounced than perhaps with you and Mike because Judy has no kids and is more attached to your dad. So, when she came upon her old bedroom no longer there, I can understand why it hit her hard. People, really all of us, object when our old bedrooms are turned into offices or dens, or in Judy's case a gym, because we want to keep our rightful place inside the family — it represents nurturing and comfort. Your dad's house is her security blanket. If her job didn't work out, she thought she could always go home."

Marcy took the last bite of her fritter and looked out the window at the pelting rain. "And what about your brother?" she asked.

"Oh, Mike will mask his feelings, but at least he doesn't have his head in the sand. He avoids conflict — kind of like Dad. When things get tense —" Bev began to laugh, an alleviating kind of laughter.

"What's so funny?" asked Marcy.

"Well, when things get tense, Mike just sings," said Bev, rolling her eyes.

"Been there," said Marcy, laughing. "My brother is the same. It's a guy thing. Making a joke of disaster is a way to ward off evil, and it's much more common among men than women. Mike's singing, in his mind, creates rapport with you and Judy by sending a message of 'We're in this together.'"

Bev dabbed at her eyes with the napkin. "Sorry, with all the stress right now, I just need a good laugh."

Marcy grinned. "These things can certainly leave you tied in knots. Talking effectively with your dad is just one part of the solution. You and your siblings also need to keep things in perspective and not let any rifts spiral out of control."

"I know, but Judy is sometimes hard to talk to. Whenever I offer advice about anything — her job, her relationships — she gets annoyed and tells me not to interfere."

Marcy fingered the rim of her coffee mug with her index finger. "If there's anything more certain to fail, it's giving advice to an upset person when she's not asking for it. Even if she asks for advice, you can often expect an 'I've tried that' response. You must make sure you understand the other person's values and listen carefully to her point of view. Open-ended questions and empathetic responses get people to open up more, and then the chances of a productive discussion are more likely. In your case, you're the older sister. Birth order often can play back in families, over and over again. Being the eldest, do you find yourself needing to be the peacemaker in the family or to be the take-charge type?"

Bev looked startled. "That's right."

Marcy continued, speaking with authority. "So, as the oldest, you offer advice and express concern about everyone. You attempt to maintain the harmony. But often your concern can be interpreted as criticism and interference by your younger siblings. These patterns, forged in childhood, can persist throughout our lives. Often they can lie unnoticed, but when under strain, as the three of you are now, the patterns can resurface in a more powerful way."

"Interesting. So what is to be done about it?"

"If family conversations are causing a lot of discomfort, I would be happy to talk to members of your family together. This could be just the three of you, or we can include your dad and his partner."

"Thanks. If things break down to the point where that becomes necessary, I'll do that."

"Don't wait until things break down," emphasized Marcy. "Any time is a good time for understanding and improving family relationships. As for talking to your father about his estate, you'll require effective communication tips. Trying to get him to talk about his will, investments, and other assets just focuses on technical issues. Your real underlying challenge is to use proper communicating techniques with your dad to help him to open up, and then the technical topics may follow."

Bev sighed wearily. "You're absolutely right, but I guess none of us really knows how to get through to him so that he will understand our position. It's as if there's this iron gate around his mind that's both rusted and padlocked."

"My expertise is in the field of family communication. I'm not a specialist in communicating effectively with older individuals. So here's my idea," said Marcy, folding her napkin into a small square. "I'm taking courses at university working toward a master's in communication. Occasionally we have guest speakers come in, and next Thursday night we have a gentleman from Penn State University, Dr. Don Helfenbaum, addressing the class. Why don't you come along and listen?"

Bev raised her eyebrows. "How can I just slip in unnoticed?"

"Oh, it's easy — people do it all the time when we have speakers. Especially Dr. Helfenbaum. I've heard him speak several times before, and he's dynamite. He's written three books; one is called *Intergenerational Communication*. Don't let the dry title fool you. This guy's not a fast-talking spin master. His expertise is in the art of communicating with ageing people. His lectures are always full, and he's great to listen to. You really should come — I guarantee it won't be a waste of your time. I can meet you right outside the classroom a few minutes before the seven o'clock start, if you like."

"Fantastic. Thank you. I never expected gothic novel night to work out so well!"

Chapter 15

BIG CHILLS
OVER WILLS

"THIS IS THE SUMMER OF Exterior Painting," said Mike. It was his way of announcing the tackling of another annual chore at the Hilroy summer cottage. He and his sisters had just tackled the Friday-afternoon traffic to get up there in time for a dinner party. Mike looked at the faded white-trimmed windows and veranda railings and the old green-stained board and batten siding. "Doesn't look like Dad's got started — no, look here, some scraping's been done."

"Not a heck of a lot," said Bev, running her fingers along the wood windowsills, which for her were at eye level at one end of the cottage before the ground started sloping away toward the other end. "I guess he did the bits where you don't need a ladder — that'll be for you, little bro."

"I'm sure the old man can still hang off a ladder, but these days I think he's more interested in Mary Beth's paint chips than the ones he gets at the hardware store."

Bev's two children, Harry and Megan, and Mike's two, Jenna and Russell, had already run straight down to the beach and could be heard shrieking in delight. Giant soap bubbles were being launched from the dock using a big wand presented years ago by Alfred to his own kids. Chet, the neighbour's Portuguese water dog, paced silently back and forth along the dock, watching the bubbles hover over the water in the hot, still air.

"It's nice to have everyone here for once," said Bev. "Splitting up the summer weeks between us and Dad is fine, but it'll be great to have everyone together. I think Dad said he and Mary Beth would be up Sunday morning. That gives us all day Saturday to finish off any chores."

They approached the front door with its wood-framed screen. Mike, with the key in hand, went in first and adopted a formal, documentary-like tone. "All right now. Close your eyes, take a deep breath, and let's all once more reenter the world of Hilroy Cottage, a world of pine scents, old comic books, mouldy cupboards, bat droppings, what the heck?"

Mike stopped in mid-sentence, and Bev and Judy knew that their brother had seen something not expected. They peered inside.

The long pine couch with the faded red- and green-striped fabric was nowhere in sight. In its place were two chunky matching armchairs, upholstered in a tawdry pea-green and ochre fabric. A brand-new area rug dominated the centre, a neutral wool sisal weave with dark brown bordering. Mike said the new furnishings reminded him of some of the older hotel lobbies he visited on his business travels.

"She has a lot of nerve doing this," said Bev, recovering her tongue. "But I've got to remember our pact from this morning — we're going to let minor nuisances from Mary Beth roll off our backs. And this is only that — small potatoes — and those new chairs, well, they're just chairs." She examined them more closely.

"The chairs are one thing," added Mike's wife, Shauna, a petite woman with long, bluntly cut, pin-straight blonde hair reaching just to her waist. She adjusted her wire-rimmed glasses, which framed her large blue eyes and thinly arched brows. "What was that you were saying, Mikey, about Mary Beth not doing any painting yet?" She jerked her left thumb twice in the direction of the far wall.

An immense, unframed watercolour took up much of the wall. Spring flowers in vivid orange and yellow pastels. The bottom right corner displayed the swirling four-inch-high signature of M.B. Cain.

Judy appeared in the doorway, a pained expression on her face. "Having Cain's Gym back at Dad's place is bad enough; now she's got most of the boathouse as an art studio. Mike, your fishing tackle and bait are stuffed in a corner. What's next, a cable TV cooking show from the kitchen?" She saw Mike examining the new painting. "Mary Beth's, no doubt?" She stood squarely in front of the artwork, hands on hips. "No wonder Dad hasn't done any house painting. It looks like she's used his favourite oil-based exterior brand — and with a very wide brush."

"Well, it's a bold piece of work, but c'mon, Jude, let's not get bugged — we just got here. Myself, I'll wait until cedar shakes are done in a hot fuchsia before I get ruffled. Now, who's for a dip before dinner at the Duggan's?"

∞

They moved in single file down the path from the cottage. Mike, as usual, was in the biggest hurry even though he was loaded down with a large cooler stuffed with appetizers, wine, and dessert. He switched the cooler back and forth from each hand as he navigated over rocks and pine needles. Bev, Shauna, and Judy trailed behind, Judy thankful that her brother no longer let the pine branches slap back in her face as he often did in long-ago summers.

"It's always a treat to see the Huggin' Duggans," said Mike, referring to his old friends Brook and Janine Duggan. "If ever there was a model couple, they're it. Married straight out of high school, no seven-year itch. Heck, I even saw them making out on the dock the other day. You'd never guess they just had their 20th anniversary."

As they climbed a rocky series of ledges that drew them closer to the Duggan cottage, they could hear the children's delighted howls from the water's edge. Apparently the kids were still energetic after a full day of water sports. The air was humid and still; screen doors could be heard banging shut and then the voices of their hosts and other guests. It was time for the annual kick-off dinner party, held on the July 1st weekend. The event rotated among a small group of neighbouring cottagers, and now it was the Duggans' turn.

Brook was the first to spot the Hilroy brigade as they approached the viceroy cottage. "Mike, you old sea dog, get over here! Bev, your kids are happily running amok with ours. Judy, Shauna, great to see you!"

The other guests had already arrived, including Brook's sister Stephanie, John and Sue Bertussi from directly across the bay, and three of their four children in tow. Roy Finstadt and his son Zak completed the group.

The sun was still strong, and the children were content to remain down at the dock. Performances of their best cannon balls and frog dives kept the children's laughter at an ear-piercing high. The assortment of water noodles, kayaks, and the famous water trampoline also guaranteed well-entertained children until sundown.

The adults quickly fell into easy conversation. John and Roy were at the far end of the deck comparing notes on their respective annual rates of hair loss. Roy, an economist, would always say, with a watery grin, "The loss is growing, but at a declining rate."

Brook saw to it that everyone had a drink, then clapped his hands together, rubbing his palms up and down as if to ignite a spark. He was a handsome man in his mid-40s with reddish hair, a matching bushy moustache, and a freckled forehead etched with a trellis of horizontal lines. "Hey, everyone, a toast to another great summer, good friends, good food, it can rain only overnight, fewer bugs, no jet skis, and great health!"

The three Hilroys raised their glasses with everyone else but simultaneously felt a twinge of sadness since this was their first get-together since their mother's death the previous fall. Mike remembered his numb feelings mixed with confusion and anxiety and his concern for his father and sisters. He also remembered how Brook and Janine had phoned and offered to help with some of the arrangements.

"I was just recalling how much you guys helped us last fall when Mom died," Mike said to Brook. "It was terrific how you supported us through an emotional time, and only you could get away with some of those funeral home jokes."

"I'm glad we could help. And still have a chuckle." Brook was contemplating other thoughts as he watched Mike throw his head back and adroitly drain the last few drops from his Heineken bottle. "Hey, Mikey, what's this I hear about your old man having a new squeeze?"

"Yep, it looks like we're going to have a stepmother in the family."

"You've got to be kidding!" said Janine, who'd joined them at the dock along with the others. "They're engaged?"

"What's she like?" asked Brook.

Judy sucked in her stomach, thrust out her breasts, and strode across the dock, swinging her hips from side to side. "Ooooh, bugalugs, you are one fair dinkum mate!"

The group hooted, with John remarking, "Wow, I never knew your dad had it in him. When can we come over for a peek?"

Bev scowled. "Not!"

"She's got things pretty stirred up in our family right now," said Mike.

"Like spending all of Dad's money," said Judy from the end of the dock, gazing out over the bay.

Roy nodded. "When my Mom first started dating Fred a couple of years ago, my sister and I were worried. The problem was we didn't know his motives. Was he in the relationship for the right reasons or the wrong ones?"

Judy smiled. "I know what you mean. My father's a great guy, but this woman is only 40. What does she want with someone 28 years her senior? It makes me suspicious."

Roy lowered himself into a canvas-backed chair, popping half a dozen peanuts into his mouth. "I hate to bring up the business side of things, but have you talked to your dad about his affairs?"

"He's having only one affair that we know of," suggested Bev.

"It's not *really* an affair. It's two adults having a good time," said Mike.

Judy looked at her brother coldly.

Roy kept going. "You know what I mean — his will."

Judy gave out a half snort, half laugh. "Dad is more likely to go hang gliding nude than talk about wills. He very much keeps his own counsel in these matters."

"That's for sure," said Bev. "We'd probably get further asking him to divulge the details of his sex life."

"Maybe not," said Mike. "You'll remember he never gave me the old birds-and-bees talk."

"Oh, now I see," said Shauna.

Roy the economist's high-pitched laugh carried across the bay. "My mother was a noncommunicator as well. Never said anything about her estate at any time. Until she saw a close friend's family disintegrate over poor will and inheritance planning. It scared her because she didn't want to leave a bitter legacy to my sister and me. She called us one night last winter, and we hashed out all topics — everything out on the table. It required four meetings and a lot of compromise and understanding, but in the end it was that openness that will allow us to avoid a series of donnybrooks."

"How did your mom include her partner, Fred, in all of this?" asked Shauna.

"He was included in all of the family discussions — which I resisted at first. Turned out he's a good guy after all, and he also wanted family harmony. My sister and I quite like him now — but it took a while."

"So, if I may ask," enquired Bev, "what type of compromise did you arrive at — I mean in terms of your inheritance?"

"Well, Mom and Fred have had their wills done together, and he has two children from a previous marriage as well. So, in the event of death of either of them, they will act as each other's executor, and the bulk of each estate is to pass to their respective children. Mom's estate is considerably larger than Fred's, so my sister and I are pleased with this arrangement. Except the house — they own that jointly. It's an expensive home in a high-end neighbourhood. It was Mom's money that was used to purchase the house — that's where my sister and I at first didn't see eye to eye with Mom's strategy. I mean, why should this guy get the house if Mom goes first? But Mom really wanted it that way — she loves Fred, and it's important to both of them that the other is able to keep the house and continue to live in it indefinitely without any strings attached. We had to accept their wishes — for the sake of harmony."

John Bertussi, an arbitration lawyer, jumped into the conversation. "Roy, you're one of the few lucky ones. I've seen dozens of disputes over the past five years since I moved into the estate law area. Most don't turn out for the better. Where there's a will, there's a skirmish, if not a war."

"John, if we knew whether Dad even had a will, that would

be a good start!" Mike had his hand on his friend's shoulder to emphasize his point.

John shook his head. "You must keep trying. You may need to try different tactics before you're able to open up the lines of communication. I stress this, not for money reasons, but for keeping the family peace. Siblings, even those who are very close, like the three of you, can often turn on one another. I once had a client throw a book at her brother's head because he'd sold an old painting that had been earmarked for his sister, but no one knew about it. The book missed and knocked over my tropical fish tank."

"Holy mackerel! Must have been a copy of *War and Peace*," said Mike.

Shauna rolled her eyes. "We were just talking about that very issue yesterday. I'm proud to say that, as of last night, Mike, Bev, and Judy have begun to communicate among themselves."

"That's right," said Bev. "Yesterday we talked about inheritances."

"Yeah, like how badly I want mine," said Judy.

"We all want our inheritances," said John. "Keep those sessions going, and attempt to include your father in those discussions — eventually he will comply. It's not really money that can ruin families but the lack of communication and understanding. I remember a case last year that involved a home-made will. You know, those will-kit wills that you can purchase at the drugstore. One of the gifts expressed in the will referred to 'My personal monies to be divided equally between my three sisters and one brother. . . .' Unfortunately this wording had different interpretations. The deceased's siblings argued that the term 'personal monies' referred to all nonregistered investments, including bank accounts, term certificates, GICs, and other securities held in the safety deposit box. The deceased's husband, on the other hand, who was to receive the residue of the estate after specific gifts, argued that 'personal monies' related only to the two bank accounts."

"So what was the final outcome?" asked Mike.

"After a lot of fighting, the court decided that the term 'personal monies' meant just the two bank accounts. The court believed that the deceased woman's wishes were to leave most of her assets to her husband. So, in the end, we had a situation where the deceased saved on lawyer's fees by preparing a homemade will, but the costs of the lengthy court battle far outweighed the savings advantage of using a will-kit will. And that ended any family cohesiveness or affection between the deceased's husband and her siblings."

Everyone was quiet for a moment, looking at a pair of loons as they took turns diving in search of their supper.

John's wife, Sue, who had been in the kitchen wrestling with a recipe, joined the conversation. "I have a friend whose sister had a joint bank account with her mother, worth about $25,000. It was set up that way to avoid probate. The will left all other assets to the two daughters equally, but the sister with the joint bank account cleaned it out shortly after their mother died. My friend asked her sister for half of the bank account money by suggesting that it had been their mother's intention to split that money between the two of them. Her sister refused. My friend said that her mother had never understood the true meaning of a joint bank account, and she was very upset at her sister for taking advantage of their mother's ignorance. So, needless to say, my friend felt betrayed. For that amount of money, she wasn't prepared to invest the time and money to go to court. The sad thing is that she'll never see her sister again, voluntarily anyway."

"John, tell them the story about the six siblings who visited your office," said Brook.

"Ah, yes, the Fairbrothers. At the office, they became known as the Badbrothers. One day five brothers and their sister came in to talk about the estate of another sister who had recently died as a single woman with no will. There was one take-charge, type AA brother who said that the late sister's only assets were a house, a car, and a bank account. The sister referred to the late sister's jewellery. The brother replied 'What jewellery?' The sister demanded that he disclose the contents of his briefcase, but he refused. Lots of shouting and pounding on the desks. One of them grabbed the glasses off the nose of the youngest one and shrieked, 'You don't need these, you can't see two feet in front of you anyway!' They yelled for half an hour in our parking lot, lots of insults and offensive gestures. We never heard from them again."

"Fights over the family cottage can also be really ugly and drawn out," added Sue.

"Remind me to add 'cottage' as an item we need to discuss," said Judy, looking at Bev and Mike.

"I remember the Sims cottage," said Janine, pointing at a red-roofed boat slip across the bay. "It now belongs to some guy from the Toronto pro lacrosse team."

"What did happen to the Simses?" asked Stephanie, who'd also appeared from the kitchen.

They half-expected to hear a story of an ageing axe-wielding cottager driven crazy by jet-skiing relatives.

"Their father had bought the cottage in the 1950s. The Sims brothers, like a lot of kids in the area, grew up with hours of swimming, fishing, jumping off high rocks, building bonfires, all the stuff we were lucky to have. They were as inseparable as the Cartwright brothers on *Bonanza,* but that all came to an end when they inherited the family cottage. They started sharing the cottage three or four years ago. By the next spring, the lawyers' letters were flying. Apparently one of them wrote 'I no longer consider you my brother.'"

"That kind of line will get attention. How did it get out of hand so quickly?" asked Mike.

Janine continued. "The eldest, Peter, has a wife and baby daughter. They saw the cottage as a retreat where they could revel in the wonders and silence of nature. Jack, who has no kids, has a much more driven style, both working and playing. Jack would always arrange to meet friends up here, stay out late, careen home at midnight in his 200-horsepower Black Max outboard. Peter was tolerant at first but gradually lost patience. Jack apparently couldn't see any problem. Rather than work it out, he ran to a lawyer as soon as Peter challenged him. The end result was a 'For Sale' sign on the cottage."

John had been sitting on the edge of the dock peeling off the entire label on his beer bottle. "It's one thing to try to share a cottage with siblings. Put spouses and kids in there too, and all of a sudden you're in a slow cooker."

"Wait a minute," said Bev. "I think that we three Hilroys, thank you very much, happen to be handling cottage life together in total harmony. You don't have to assume that it's always going to be fights!"

John disagreed. "I think you have to assume that anything can happen. So you need to constantly work at communicating and being prepared to handle any problems."

"I agree with John," piped up Stephanie. "Remember the Worthingtons, about 10 minutes up the lake? Maybe it's just because they were never very close to begin with, but the three sisters ended up in a series of disputes over scheduling time at the cottage, bill payments, the replacement of rugs, furniture, bug screens, you name it. Two of the sisters wanted to sell the cottage, but the third sued them to block the sale, saying that she was willing to draw up a shared schedule to keep the cottage. But the judge saw no possibility of working things out, so he ordered the cottage sold. I just saw the cottage listed yesterday."

"Why didn't she just buy out the other two sisters?" asked Sue.

"I don't really know, but with some foresight I know they could have worked it out in everyone's favour with just a little bit of creativity, such as the parents leaving the cottage to the one child who liked the cottage and equalling up the estate with other assets for the other two kids."

Judy nodded. "I know — there's that kind of stuff all the time. You do need to understand the family dynamics. I suppose wills can be used as a weapon to correct past grievances, real or otherwise. I agree with Bev. It's unlikely that would ever happen with us."

"Your father may have the best intentions in the world," admonished John gently. "Not only should those intentions be expressed clearly in his will, but also the ideal situation would be for your father to communicate his wishes during his lifetime to avoid different interpretations between the three of you versus Mary Beth."

"We're trying," said Bev. "But Dad is too tightlipped and unwilling to discuss anything."

"There's still time," said John. "And trying to share a cottage is another challenge facing you. You three now have to deal with another person in the equation — your dad's new partner. Having her around will seem like a forced marriage. You may find that there's always something festering. And when all is revealed, it can be like a bad divorce. No matter what, someone may feel like he or she got shafted."

"Maybe so," said Mike. "At least we're going into this Hilroy adventure with our eyes open."

The group went up to the cottage for dinner. Judy was the only one to hear the first rumble of far-off thunder, like distant artillery.

Chapter 16

BOATING MADE DIFFICULT

"MOMMY, A BRIGHT RED CAR is coming down the lane. Whose is it?" Harry, Bev's seven year old, looked up the hill hesitantly and then back at his mother for an answer.

"It's a bit early for Pappy to be here. Um, no, it isn't," Bev said, spying the personalized 'MB' licence plate and Carling the terrier's head peering from the driver's-side window.

"It's a convertible!" said Mike, appearing from the kitchen.

"I guess that little purchase siphoned off a nice chunk of Dad's dough." Judy's tone was resigned.

"Hello, Dad, Mary Beth!" Mike grinned expansively at the new arrivals. "Very nice vehicle there. Still got your Buick, Dad?"

Alfred could barely nod yes before he was swarmed by a rush of four grandchildren led by Harry, with Megan, Jenna, and Russell close behind.

"Want some help unloading?" Bev smiled at Mary Beth, deciding to refrain from any new-car comments.

Judy hung back in the kitchen, sweeping the floor for the second time that morning.

"Why, thanks!" replied Mary Beth, slapping at the backs

of her knees. "Mozzies! The little buggers like me."

"Let's get unpacked and to the dock, then," said Alfred, eager to get settled in.

⟨⟨◦⟩⟩

Mary Beth, in her one-piece, high-cut ruby-red bathing suit with matching sari, staked out a sunny spot on the dock. Alfred decided to start work on scraping and refinishing an old deck chair. Judy, Shauna, and the children were up in the cottage playing board or video games, and Mike and Bev sat in a shady area of the dock reading.

Fifteen minutes passed. "*Much* too early for a nap!" Mike bellowed suddenly. "Let's get those kids out here! Time for a spin on the water, I'm talkin' water skiing!"

The older children knew the drill — ropes, life jackets, ski-fitting, gas level, and so on — and before long most everyone had had a quick turn around the bay, tugged by the *Punch n Judy*, a 10-year-old outboard co-owned by Mike and Alfred.

Judy, who had been doing most of the boat driving, looked over at Mary Beth stretched flat out on the dock, snoozing. Then at her brother, one eyebrow raised.

"Okay, *next!* Mary Beth!" shouted Mike.

"What? Not me, lovey, I'm not worth a crumpet in the water." Mary Beth listened to the grumbling sound of the idling outboard and looked at Judy, perched on the top of the driver's seat, impassive behind large sunglasses, looking at Mary Beth like a prison warden on an inmates' outing.

Mike persisted. "We'll take it slow for you — come on, it's

a riot." He was reeling in the towrope, and to Mary Beth he might as well have been an Old West vigilante about to string up the latest outlaw.

Yet her nature was never to turn down an athletic challenge. "I'm a sailor, not a skier. I'd rather tame a shark than stand up on those boards. I'd like to drive the boat instead, but . . . oh, what the heck, show me what to do."

Alfred looked up from his scraping. "Way to go, hon! I'll let you take the boat for a spin later on."

Judy spoke from behind her tempered sunglasses. "And the kids love to see new ski tryouts every year. Megan, will you please show her the drill?"

"Yes, strap me in, or on, whatever," Mary Beth said, removing her hat and sari and grinning gamely.

Megan provided a quick tutorial on how to start from sitting on the edge of the dock, the use of hand signals, and how to stay within the boat's wake.

Mary Beth sat stiffly, watching Mike pay out the rope as the grumbling boat slowly bobbed farther away from shore and listening to more instructions from Megan. Carling stood trembling beside his owner, looking as if he would be required to perform a canine equivalent of skiing.

"Looking good," said Mike. "Let me know when you're ready."

"Anytime, I guess. . . ."

"Hit it!" commanded Mike of Judy, punching his fist in the air like a music conductor.

Judy pushed the throttle forward, there was a surge of water, and Mary Beth lurched face first into the lake and out of her skis. She soon reappeared corklike, in a jumble of rope and skis, sputtering, "This is certainly different than serving tennis balls!" Carling retreated from the dock in alarm and confusion.

Mike swam back to Mary Beth and helped her to reattach the skis, putting her back in the ready position and using sports terminology — "Stay with it," "Stay within yourself," "Focus now!" — that Mary Beth found amusing but less than helpful.

Four tries later, each attempt looking more dignified than the previous one, Mary Beth had successfully been launched as a skier ("We have traction!" shouted Mike with glee, switching to business metaphors) but had trouble standing straight on the skis. She remained content to hang on to the rope with both hands, bum thrust out, legs spaced widely apart, thinking that water skiing was no more difficult than handling a sailboat off the Great Barrier Reef.

"Aunt Judy," said Harry, quietly carrying out his spotter duties, "she's trying to signal, but I don't think she can take either hand off the rope. Her mouth is opening and shutting a lot."

Judy stared straight ahead.

The skiing party approached a large taxi boat coming in the opposite direction, with an equally large garbage scow in its sizeable wake.

Judy shouted at Megan. "Did you remember to give M.B. the 'How to Handle Big Waves' lesson?"

Megan put an index finger to her lower lip and shook her head sideways, eyes wide. At that moment, Mary Beth attempted to stand up straight, guessing wrongly how to tackle her first group of big waves. The force of the first one caught her with her legs stiff and locked in place, unable to absorb the impact properly. Her skis became like slippery banana peels. She fell backward, slapping the water loudly, bitingly, with her behind being the initial point of contact. She bounced once and did a half pinwheel before letting go of the rope.

Embarrassment was quickly replaced by pain. Mary Beth bobbed about as the scow's wake washed over her, its pilot pretending to be oblivious to the antics of the nonlocals.

Alfred's grandchildren, in the bow of the boat, howled with delight, clutching their stomachs. For them, this was the height of summer entertainment.

"Do it again, Mary Beth, puhleeeese," they clamoured as the recovery operation began.

"That was cool," gushed Harry after they had dragged a sore Mary Beth into the boat.

"You go, girl!" said Megan appreciatively.

If falling down a lot is important to these kids liking me, then so be it, thought Mary Beth, her tailbone aching and her body hurting more than from any gym workout she could remember.

⬥⬥

I love this cottage, thought Mike. Here I feel most at peace. Especially at the time of day when I'm up before the others and can hike up to the road for a run before breakfast. Then head down to the water, peel off the running gear, and plunge in. No mess, no stress.

Just float for a while, wait for the delivery of the morning paper by the stringy-haired student in a 20-horsepower boat, hurled with varying precision to the same spot on the dock every morning. It's great being able to dress like a slob and go unshaven, at least until Shauna calls a halt.

All this is worth the trouble. It's worth the time you need to take to manage a second property, despite living across the continent and being able to use the cottage only for three weeks of vacation plus tack-on days at the beginning or end of a business trip. And it's worth the effort to make sure that my father and two sisters can manage the summer schedule of who does what and when. As our kids get older, though, there will be more demands on scheduling, something that will have to be worked out. Add Mary Beth to the picture — where will she fit in?

Mike ended his morning reflection with a two-handed belly slap, grabbed his towel, and headed for the kitchen. He loved to cook bacon over the ancient Gunn and Company stove, drink coffee, and watch the "sleep-inners" drift into the kitchen, drawn by the aromas.

Alfred and Mary Beth sat at the kitchen table, the first two early risers besides Mike.

"Hot again, looks like," said Mike, dropping the newspaper in the middle of the table.

"The heat will help your backside, muffin, in addition to your first-aid supplies," said Alfred, who'd risen early to drive into town for ointment and a heating pad.

Mary Beth picked out the newspaper's health section. Mike noticed her fingernails, done in a French manicure, white

defining the half moon at the tip of the nail and underneath.
The look was meant to be clean and precise — like her hair.
No doubt she would have to schedule extra appointments to
restore some of the damage caused by her skiing expedition.

Alfred was musing over his monthly bills. He always set
aside a holiday morning to examine his expenses.

Mike stopped flipping bacon for a second and looked up at
his father. "You know, Shauna and I went to an estate-planning
seminar in Vancouver a couple of weeks ago."

Alfred looked up. "Did you find it interesting?"

"Yeah, so much so that we are now in the process of preparing our wills. I didn't think that we needed wills until we went
to that seminar."

"Why did you think that?" asked Bev, who had just
appeared in the kitchen, followed by Shauna and then Judy.

"Because Shauna and I hold everything together jointly. But
we soon realized that we need wills to distribute our assets into
trusts for our kids in the event that we die in a joint disaster —
you know, an accident that takes Shauna and me simultaneously." Mike placed pieces of bacon on paper towels. "It's kind
of an unthinkable topic, for sure, but we see the need to
address it."

Shauna added, "There's so much to think about, things like
guardianship issues, executors, taxes, trusts."

Alfred looked up at Mike and Shauna. "You've got that
right." He remembered the discussion he'd had with Jeremy
recently about equal versus unequal division to children. He
decided to try Jeremy's suggestion of bringing up the topic.
"Um, well, there are lots of things to consider. I have a friend

who is trying to figure out whether or not he should leave his estate to his children equally or unequally based on financial need. Tough call, I'd say." Alfred drummed his fingertips on the edge of the table, then picked at a small piece of candle wax stuck on the edge.

"Hmm," said Mike.

Bev took the bait. "At the estate-planning seminar that I went to a few weeks ago, one of the overwhelming messages that came through was how the subject of inheritance can really cause conflict between siblings — and how, if families had communicated long before the problems arose, they could have staved off hostilities."

"That's a very good point," remarked Shauna. "I've heard often that fighting over a deceased parent's estate is the most likely cause of family members never speaking to each other again."

"Even worse than the debates over where Christmas will be held each year?" asked Mike.

Bev smiled. "Almost as bad as that. And we'll hear more about estate battles. The current generation of retired Canadians is expected to bequeath nearly one trillion dollars of assets to the next generation over the next twenty years — people like us."

Judy, who'd been half-listening with her head leaning back in the big chair, felt her stomach begin to churn with anxiety. She was still pondering the subject of equal versus unequal division. She tried to pinpoint her sentiments. "Well, getting back to Dad's point of equal or unequal division, if a parent helps out a child financially from time to time, then I don't think that a division in the will based on financial need is inappropriate."

The air was so still that the lake flawlessly reflected the trees on the shoreline. The children could be heard easily from the woods as they debated the rules of their prebreakfast games.

"I agree it's okay to help out children in unequal amounts during one's lifetime. The problem as I see it is how do you arrive at a division based on need in a will?" asked Bev. "A will is drawn up at a certain point in time. But if the will distributes a parent's estate based on the children's respective financial circumstances at the time it is drafted, what happens when that will remains unchanged for, say, five years or more? I mean, when the parent dies, it could very well be that the estate is being distributed unequally but that financial circumstances among the family have altered dramatically since the will was drawn up."

Judy grabbed the wide arms of her chair and drew herself up so that she was now perching on the edge. "But what would your view be if financial circumstances among the heirs do not change since the making of the will?"

"Well, then I might be able to accept the idea of unequal distribution, I guess, but on a deeper level it still perturbs me — just don't ask me why," said Bev.

Alfred leaned back in his chair, coffee cup in hand, amused with the discussion.

"The will could be reviewed and updated yearly," suggested Judy. "In that way, it's adjusted for any significant change in circumstances."

Mike shook his head. "That's sensible but maybe a bit too

labour intensive. I believe that the estate should be divvied up even-steven."

Judy looked at Mike. "Why? I just want to play the devil's advocate here. Let's say that, as an example, someone really doesn't need an inheritance. What does it matter how much someone else in the family gets?"

"That's purely my gut reaction to the issue of our inheritance," said Mike. "I understand what you are saying, and on a logical level I can agree with your viewpoint, but on an emotional level I don't buy it. The child getting the least amount may interpret that as though he was the least-favoured child."

"That's true, but I do see Judy's point," admitted Shauna. "If one person or family needs more money than the other, there's nothing morally wrong with an unequal split."

"No, of course there's nothing morally wrong. But if parents take the path of unequal splits, they may inadvertently be setting the kids up for failure," countered Mike. "Humans are visceral creatures, and emotions, not rational thoughts, are what drive many people. A family goal should be to *prevent* sibling contention or at least to minimize it. Unequal distributions are too subjective. I think you're asking for nothing but squabbles when you go that route."

"I agree," said Bev. "Imagine trying to arrive at some arbitrary unequal formula. How do you get to a division such as 40, 30, and 30% or 40, 40, and 20%? Discussing percentages lends itself to greed because then you have to get into specific values."

Judy bobbed her head. "I suppose I see your point," she conceded.

Mike helped himself to a handful of blueberries that Bev had just washed for their dad's favourite breakfast dish: blueberry pancakes. "If I may be so bold as to swing the discussion to the three of us here, remember that, if at any time one of us were destitute or down and out for some reason, God forbid it happens, it's our responsibility to help out the other, financially or otherwise. I think families need to have an element of trust and just act accordingly."

Judy smiled. "That's true. If I win the lottery big time, I'll gladly concede my inheritance."

With the discussion edging dangerously close to the Hilroy home front, Alfred was relieved when his four grandkids came racing into the kitchen, out of breath from their games. He'd heard enough, interesting and revealing though the topic was. "That was an illuminating discussion. Now let's eat, I'm starving."

"Let me make the pancakes now," suggested Bev.

Alfred forgot about his pile of bills. "That sounds like a marvellous idea — blueberry, right?"

"No! You stay out! No!" Carling's paws clattered on the porch floor outside the kitchen as he tried to muscle his way into the kitchen, using Judy as an escort. She tried to keep Carling out using only her right leg but failed; the aged dog could still pick the right spot to make his move past certain obstacles.

"Relax," said Mike. "He's not in the way."

"Mike, remember the rules we had with Molson — not inside except in bad weather. Why should it be any different now?"

"Jude, I think you should get a dog," teased Mike. "You might actually appreciate having a mutt of your own."

"Molson was enough of a handful. I remember how one of our neighbours never talked to us again after he knocked up their Shiatsu at the annual street fair. How he managed that with a dog a quarter his size impressed a lot of people. Mom called it a doggedly determined impregnation."

"I'll take Carling out," said Mary Beth. She rose from her chair slowly, holding both hands against her lower back. It took her several painful seconds to fully straighten up. She reached down to grab Carling by the choke collar. "Arrrggg," Mary Beth reacted as a muscle spasm spread pain to the left side of her sacrum. She paused, resting one hand on the counter, listing to one side. Alfred immediately stood up to assist her, and she mustered a weak smile as she pushed a reluctant Carling out the door.

Judy retreated outside to refill the kindling box.

Alfred drained his coffee mug, grimacing when he realized that only the grounds remained at the bottom. "I have some chores lined up today — at least for myself, that is."

"Like maybe retrieving those golf balls you hit from the dock to that shoal of rocks yesterday?" asked Bev.

"Yes, there's that. But this is a real chore, something I've been putting off for a while now. I'm finally going to rip down that sagging bunkhouse."

"The bunkhouse?" Mike looked up from the newspaper with a surprised look.

"That old pile of green planks has been an eyesore for a long time. Like 50 years. It needs a rebuild. We're planning some renos to the kitchen as well. I have Josh Forrest from Creative Contracting stopping by tomorrow."

Mary Beth kept her eyes focused on the second round of bacon she was cooking at the stove.

"What renovations?" asked Bev.

"Dad, why tear down the bunkhouse?" Mike asked. "Just leave it. All it needs is a few new shingles, paint, new screens, and a cleanup inside."

"*What* renovations to the kitchen?" repeated Bev, not waiting for her dad's reply.

Alfred answered Bev's question first. "The kitchen hasn't been done in donkey's years. Mary Beth and I are looking at renovating it — not now — maybe start in the fall."

Bev stared at her father. She had stopped mixing the buttermilk pancake batter and was clutching the bowl tightly in both hands. "What sort of renovations are you thinking of?" Her voice had taken on a distinct edge.

"Everything. Put in a brand-new kitchen with an island and. . . . You can help choose colours."

"Like yank out the whole kitchen — oh my."

"Why the resistance? I thought you kids would be happy to see some changes. You're always complaining about how everything is falling apart around here."

"There's a difference between repairing something and tearing something down," said Bev. "I'd like to hang on to memories here — childhood memories. A big part of that is our surroundings, more so now that Mom is gone."

The pancakes and bacon were consumed with hardly any

attention as Mike, Bev, and Alfred fell into impassioned debates over alterations to both the kitchen and the bunkhouse. They reminded Alfred of past battles among members at the golf club over design changes to the course. Judy observed the heated exchange silently, feeling satisfied that her two siblings were finally not masking their feelings.

"Dad, with all due respect, some things can't just be wrenched apart. For instance, what would you do with *that*?" Bev pointed at a two-by-four fake supporting beam that Joyce had put up when the children were little.

"Mom used to mark our heights every summer as we grew," pointed out Judy. "See, look at these lines here. The lowest one says 'Bev, three years old.' And here's where Mike's height was marked at age 12 and where Mom wrote in the height in centimetres and you crossed it out and put it back in feet and inches."

"Why is that so important to you?" said Alfred. "You keep telling me I have to fix up the kitchen at Delmore. When I decide to do some renovations to the cottage, now you're all up in arms. I can't figure you three out."

"Don't include me," said Judy breezily. "I'm not complaining about anything."

"For a change," said Bev before turning back to her father. "Dad, you can't just go and tear down stuff around here without talking to us first."

"I can't? Last time I checked, title to this place was in my name."

Alfred had a point, but Mike refused to acknowledge it. "Dad, you're sounding trite," said Mike. "It's just that some things are important to us around here, and . . . the bunkhouse, the post, the Gunn stove right here — they provide some continuity."

Alfred was not buying this appeal to nostalgia. "Why should you care about an ant-infested eyesore — unless you want to make it into an outhouse? Otherwise, I don't see the issue here."

Mike paused with his hand on the refrigerator door. "Because they are childhood shrines, and they should remain that way." He pulled open the fridge door, and the handle snapped off in his hand. "OK, not everything's a shrine."

"Childhood shrines — what are you talking about? How can that barn out there that hasn't been used in 20 years be elevated to mystical status? Not even the grandkids use it."

Mike examined the old Frigidaire handle. "Metal fatigue. Like Bev said — memories, Dad, memories — that's how." Mike sat down across from his father.

"Like what memories?"

Mike leaned back impatiently in his chair. "The details aren't important — I'm just asking that you not rip apart the joint, that's all."

Bev pressed the issue further. "Same with the kitchen, Dad. I don't mind a paint job or, ahem, a new fridge or some basic carpentry — just the basic layout should remain the same. After all, this is only a cottage — spend the money on Delmore instead."

"I'm not tearing down the joint; I'm only saying that the cottage needs some fixing up."

"More pancakes?" asked Bev.

There were no takers. They were now feeling anxious and out of sorts, especially Alfred. Disagreements within his family put him off. When Joyce was alive, Alfred used to allow her the pleasure of sorting out routine family quarrels. "Time to put on the striped shirt, dear. You handle this one," he'd say and leave the room. Often referred to as "the control tower" or "JOC" (Joint Operations Command), Joyce would relay and mediate information between Alfred and the three kids. When Bev, Mike, or Judy would call home from university, Alfred would get on the phone at the end of the conversation, usually to talk about business — tuition payments, loan documents, savings, and so on. In fact, Joyce often talked *for* Alfred, with remarks such as "Your father is very pleased about your marks" or "Your dad wants me to remind you not to drink and drive."

Alfred said it was his turn to clean up and take care of the dishes before the wave of grandchildren washed over the kitchen. Mary Beth remained uncharacteristically small and quiet and in her chair. Judy followed Mike out of the room.

"You feel really strongly about that bunkhouse, don't you?"

"Yes, ma'am."

"Do you think Dad will leave it alone?"

"He's still the boss."

"Don't worry, he'll relent — he often does when one of us feels impassioned about something."

"I guess. It sure was a lot easier when Mom was around. She always knew how to talk to Dad — he's just so obstinate some-times that it drives me nuts. I didn't want to get into it, but that bunkhouse has great memories. It's where I got my first kiss, from Sharon Bearnarth. In fact, it's where I got a lot of firsts — my first beer, my first smoke ring, my first. . . . Where is Margie McCracken these days, I wonder?"

⊙⊙

"Better batten down the hatches!" exclaimed Judy from the edge of the dock. The late-afternoon oncoming storm propelled the Hilroys into their well-practised routine of shutting windows and putting away lightweight things. They always loved the thunder and lightning. Judy remembered her mother's hot chocolate with marshmallows while watching the storm theatrics. The power supply was often interrupted, and out would come the candles and the worn copies of the Nancy Drew or Hardy Boys mysteries.

"Bev, can you give me a hand with the boat?" asked Alfred as the wind picked up in intensity and the lake became greyer by the minute. "We also need to get the canoe up onto the dock before it gets blown away to Oz." The two set off down to the dock and began the task of putting the cover on the boat.

"How was your party Friday night?" asked Alfred.

"Terrific, always my favourite weekend of the year — I start to look forward to it from about March. The usual people were there. Did you know Roy Finstadt's mother married her boyfriend Fred last fall?"

Alfred fitted the cover over the bow of the boat. "Oh, really — I always liked her," he said. "She always was a spunky one. We used to play croquet together years ago."

Bev tightened the knots on both the stern and bow lines. "Your spunkiness is showing too — you have your own marriage coming up. Speaking of which, are you, um, getting your affairs in order, you know, I mean before the marriage?"

Alfred struggled to get the cover buttoned down at a tight spot. "Like what? Give me a hand with this darn thing, will you?"

Bev helped him to snap the cover buttons into place. "Well, your estate and all that."

"My affairs *are* in order," Alfred said. He secured the back of the cover over the engine area and tucked the corners in tightly around the stern. "There, that should do it, Bev. Now let's retrieve the life jackets and noodles from the dock."

Bev dreaded having to force the discussion, but she soldiered on, this time more directly. "I think we need to hold a family meeting." The rain started to patter on the boathouse roof.

Alfred straightened up and looked directly at Bev. "A family meeting? Why?"

"To talk about how your estate is being divided. God forbid anything should happen to you. I know this sounds greedy, and maybe it looks that way, but Mike, Judy, and I want to be prepared. In case there is anything that we should know."

"You need to be very patient. I don't plan on dying for a long time."

"Dad, stop being presumptuous — this isn't about dying."

"Sure sounds like it to me."

"Mike and I have attended some estate-planning seminars. Your will, I mean everyone's will, needs to be bulletproof against challenges."

"Challenges?"

"From someone making a claim against your estate — if things are not spelled out properly."

"You're worried about Mary Beth making a claim, you mean?"

"Well, no . . . yes . . . there's that and other consequences of not having a proper will — you know, the provinces have set formulas if someone doesn't have a will."

"I have one. That's all I can say. I don't intend to discuss the details now — that would be a surefire way to cause problems."

"Dad, not talking about it will cause more problems."

Alfred took a deep breath, a weary look coming over him. "I inherited very little money from my parents. I worked hard for everything that I have. Therefore, my wealth is my business, and I can decide what I'd like to do with it."

"Of course, Dad, but I think —"

A loud clap of thunder interrupted them.

"Looks like we're going to get wet," said Alfred. "Let's get that canoe out of the water. I don't enjoy dodging lightning bolts."

⌒⊙⊙⌒

"Alfie, let me drive. For goodness sake, I've sailed off the Great Barrier Reef, what can this little lake do to me and you? Besides, I've been watching you guys all week. Forward, neutral, reverse, throttle up, throttle down, bumpers in, bumpers out." Mary Beth fixed her blue eyes on her betrothed.

"It's a powerboat, dear. With a 165-horsepower engine. On a lake with big rocks and things hiding in it. Sailboats are a bit different to manage. Maybe I'll let you drive when we're in the middle of the lake."

Mary Beth decided not to talk anymore about wanting to drive the boat. Direct action was now required. She slid into the driver's seat, wedging herself around Alfred, who was standing behind the wheel about to sit down. She grabbed him playfully around the waist and pulled him onto her lap.

"We can both do this! Start 'er up, mate! You point, I'll steer." Mary Beth wriggled coyly, arms threaded around Alfred's middle, hands guiding his on the steering wheel. "Oooh, cheek to cheek, shall we dance?" she whispered breathily.

"Shucks, Miss Cain, a man's gotta drive when he wants to drive. But since you seem set on giving it a whirl, here you go. But let me back her out first. Actually, let me back you out as well." Alfred disentangled himself from his fiancée and began the routine of getting the powerboat under way — safety checks, fluid levels, tie lines, et cetera.

Mary Beth sat quietly observing.

"You just have to pay attention to details, and then it's quite easy," said Alfred in his official pharmacist voice. "See, I'm going slowly backing out, especially when the other boat's alongside here. Try not to bang the sides. Now, when you put it into forward gear, you push the throttle this way. Here, you ready?"

Mary Beth wasn't expecting to take the helm so soon, but she wasted no time switching places with Alfred. He'd backed the boat out to a point where it idled perpendicular to the boathouse.

Alfred cupped his hands to his mouth and bellowed toward the cottage, "We're heading out for a spin, everybody! Back in a jiff!"

Before he could resume his instructor duties, he was jerked back in his seat by the force of the engine responding to Mary

Beth's pushing the throttle well forward, just as she'd seen Judy do with the skiers. Alfred had time only to yell "Hey!" as the bow rose. Mary Beth was puzzled why they were headed back into the boathouse, remorselessly and in what seemed to be slow motion. Alfred was a great deal less puzzled as he realized he hadn't straightened the steering wheel after backing out. Mary Beth was wide-eyed as Alfred could only hang on. The boat retraced its path out of the boathouse in perfect reverse order, only faster. Alfred wondered why they hadn't hit any-thing as they churned into the boathouse, neatly bisecting the slip space between the right side of the jetty and the left side with the other boat moored in its place.

Neither of the engaged boaters was ready with any new ideas on how to reverse the tide of events, so the *Punch n Judy* did its best to continue its journey on dry land. With the bow still well up in the air, there was no initial sickening crunch. The hull used the end of the slip as a kind of ramp, the rubber strips on its edge acting as a weak but not useless first line of defence. Alfred remembered the cost of this boathouse, put in just a couple of years earlier. He tried to recall the strength of the beams that had been hoisted into place. Particularly at the top end, because now the bow pranged into the corner where roof met wall. The engine made a belching noise, like a 20-year-old man having just chugged a 12-ounce mug of draft beer. An old propeller, belonging to *Punch n Judy*'s predecessor (the *Maggie*, a wooden inboard) was clipped off the nail it hung on and pinged in the air menacingly before exiting the side door. And then they stopped.

Mary Beth remained frozen in place, looking up at the cobwebs on the ceiling. Alfred had put his hands out instead of hanging on and was hurtled at a two o'clock angle into a pile of life preservers, right shoulder first. It's just like the movies, he thought. Slow motion. He didn't feel the knock on his head at first. Someone began to laugh, startling him. Then Alfred realized he himself was laughing.

With Mary Beth still clinging to the wheel, the *Punch n Judy* was held back from further progress by the connecting beams. Perched briefly 90% out of the water, the boat began to slide back into the slip, looking like a miniature *Titanic*, the engine still running although knocked back into neutral. Mary Beth remained mutely in place as the boat settled at a 70° angle, the engine gamely bubbling away in the water.

"Might as well turn off the engine, if you can find the key," mumbled Alfred from the jumble of life jackets. The shock of pain came in from his shoulder 30 seconds later, in baked spasms, hot and terrible. When he shifted, a bolt of agony flew in from his head also. Alfred passed out.

Mary Beth remained frozen in place, yelling or screaming or both.

Chapter 17

HEIM'S HARROWING STORY

TEN MINUTES LATER, without any protest, Alfred, who'd by now partly regained consciousness, allowed himself to be walked very slowly to the car for the trip to the local hospital. He spent the trip lying on the back seat, his feet elevated because that's what someone had heard should be done in the event of possible concussion. Dizzy from the bump on his head, numb from the shoulder injury, he tried to focus on the sight of the treetops and power lines whizzing by. Mike and Shauna sat up front, anxious but in control. They tried to keep Mary Beth and Bev in sight up ahead in the convertible. Judy sat keeping a watchful eye over her father and giving him regular sips of water. A neighbour was watching the kids at the cottage.

Amid the general hubbub caused by the accident, Alfred had made sure everyone heard at least one thing before heading out. "You know, it's my fault, not Mary Beth's. I didn't set the wheel properly, and waving my arm like Lawrence of Arabia in a cavalry charge made her push the throttle too soon. If there's to be any finger pointing, point it at me."

Ninety minutes after arrival, Bev, Mike, Judy, Shauna, and

Mary Beth stood in a knot in the emergency area. A pink-cheeked doctor approached them.

"I'm glad you got Mr. Hilroy here so fast. He's been in and out of consciousness from the concussion, which I expect will only continue for a short while. He's also broken his clavicle. He should be OK, but obviously we need to keep him here for a couple of nights. I really don't believe there is anything to be alarmed about, but I need to know which of you has a power of attorney entitling you to make decisions concerning Mr. Hilroy's health care."

The five adults looked at each other. Mary Beth, already rumpled and tear stained from her worry about Alfred's condition, burst into a fresh round of sobs. "Oh, I never want to see a boat again! I'm such a noodle! I'll never forgive myself."

Shauna put her arm around Mary Beth and ushered her to a chair. Bev, Mike, and Judy looked at the waiting doctor and then again at each other.

Mike spoke first. "It just struck me that we don't know if Dad has drawn up any powers of attorney, do we? Neither medical nor financial. Who wants to ask Mary Beth if *she* holds the power?"

"I'll do it," said Bev.

Mike heard the subsequent stifled wail from Mary Beth and had his answer, shortly confirmed by his sister.

"No, Mary Beth says Dad never talked about or granted her a P.A. I guess it's still with Mom."

"Terrific," said Mike, sounding more sheepish than sardonic.

"I don't think it will be a problem this time," said the doctor. "Since he's beginning to stabilize, I don't expect he will have a relapse, but a valid, up-to-date power of attorney is something your father should be looking into. Otherwise, you're pretty helpless in being able to make decisions regarding your father if he is incapacitated. You'd be relying on the courts to make decisions for you. I'll reinforce the importance of this document with your father before he leaves the hospital."

"I'd say luck's been on Dad's side, thank goodness," Mike said. "But he's got some housekeeping to look after when he gets well."

∞ ∞

Between visitors, Alfred tried to rest as best he could in his semi-private room. His shoulder caused him severe pain, and he could only lie in his bed, imagining himself playing famous golf courses. Beside him in the other bed lay a very old person, with the classic sunken features of the centenarian. Everything about the man looked collapsed except his nose, and frequent moans came from the bed, their tone signifying to Alfred all the indignities of the last days of old age. If the complaints from his neighbour became too loud, Alfred would concentrate more on his imaginary golf games.

Seven-iron, please, he'd say to his fictitious caddy, preparing to make his third shot of the hole from among the cypress trees at the famed Pebble Beach Golf Links.

After carding a 36-hole score of 195, Alfred found he could sleep for the first time since the accident. And, when he awoke, his more unfortunate neighbour's space was now occupied by someone else, a much younger man who smiled over at Alfred.

To Alfred, much younger meant about 50 years of age.

"Jimmy Heim's the name, bad knees are my game. I think they keep moving me from room to room because I talk too much. You just let me know if my yakkety yakking bothers you."

Alfred looked over at his new roommate. Jimmy was a large man, bullet headed. His head and hands seemed to be out of proportion with the rest of his body. They exchanged their "What you in for?" information.

Then Alfred told Jimmy all about Mary Beth and his three children. Soon Alfred was listening to Jimmy's life story. It was a lengthy but interesting story about lots of travel, work, antique gun collecting, and a big family that was harmonious in all but one respect.

"My older brother Larry and I have not spoken for five years," said Jimmy, becoming reflective for the first time in his narrative. "We grew up close and remained close all the years leading up to then."

"What happened?" asked Alfred, finding himself enjoying his bedside story.

"Things fell apart shortly after Dad had his stroke. And he was always the communicative type — always spoke to us about his will. He even suggested we attend the meetings with his lawyer, a friend of his, to draft up his will. The estate was modest, and both my brother and I were named executors. The will left everything to us equally. So really there shouldn't have been any problems — there weren't any foreseeable ones to us anyway." Jimmy became silent and pensive.

Alfred's curiosity was piqued. "How did things unravel, then?"

Jimmy turned his head and looked at Alfred. "Two things.

First problem appeared right after Dad became gravely injured from a car accident. There was no hope of recovery. Unfortunately he hadn't prepared a power of attorney for personal care, which would have given Larry and me guidance as to his medical wishes, including what he would have liked done in the event of a major incapacity. Anyway, we disagreed on the handling of this situation. I wanted to prolong Dad's life because I thought there was a chance of recovery. Larry wanted Dad to avoid further pain and suffering. Neither one of us was right or wrong, and we both loved Dad very much. We had numerous arguments that escalated in intensity. And, of course, Dad couldn't express his opinion on the matter. That was the beginning of the end. If Dad had filled out a proper power of attorney for personal care, we would have avoided this first strain in our relationship."

"I'm sorry. I can't believe it gets worse from there."

"Oh, yes, indeed. It wasn't until Dad finally died that the serious acrimony began. You'd never guess what caused things to implode."

"I'll bite. What?" said Alfred, who by now was sitting upright in his bed looking earnestly at his roommate.

"The funeral."

"You're kidding. How?"

"I wanted to have a full-frills funeral for Dad because I thought that is what he would have wanted — he always enjoyed a good party and liked formal ceremonies. My older brother wanted to have a simple funeral. He said that a fancy funeral was a waste of money and that we would inherit more if we went the cheap route."

Alfred poked at the green Jell-O on his lunch tray. "So what happened?" he asked, motioning with his good arm.

"Anyway, my older brother, always the take-charge type, had his way in the end because I gave in. I was worn out and fed up. I just felt that Dad deserved a high-end funeral, if you will. If only Dad had included his funeral wishes in his will, we could have avoided the big fight. That was the one clause that Dad didn't mention in his will. So, you see, it isn't always just money that can cause disputes in families."

"What a terrible story. It's frightening the stories I hear about all that can go wrong."

"I've lived through hell with both my father's incapacity and his death. Dad had a will, but if he'd only talked about his funeral wishes with us we could have avoided a family brawl. Plus he completely overlooked the granting of powers of attorney."

Alfred looked down at his food tray. "Gee, I don't have one of those documents either, at least not an updated one. And, given my accident, it could have been a lot worse. I sure don't want to be kept on life support if I have no chance of recovery."

"Well, my story shows how important family communication is. If Dad had clearly stated his wishes in his will, or if we had gotten him to talk about them, I mightn't be estranged from my brother. I can see why a will should be done thoroughly with a proper professional, not a homemade or kit will."

Alfred answered sombrely. "I don't think of what I own as being that important. I just don't picture my kids living with hatred. They have my love, and I have theirs."

"You don't have to be rich and unloving to leave fights among your children. One feature of the will that's full of potential for family battles is the handling of personal items. My cousins staged an undeclared war over cabinets full of china. You know what — the fighting is usually not over money, it's over memories."

Alfred looked over at Jimmy, a startled expression on his face. He was about to speak, but he just nodded his head and remained silent. He looked down at the hospital sheets and thought about how upset Bev had been over discussions about changes to the cottage kitchen and Mike's reaction to tearing down the bunkhouse. "Memories, Dad, memories," Mike had said emphatically. Alfred began to understand.

Jimmy looked over at his roommate. "You don't mind me talking about all this? Sometimes it can get a bit heavy."

"It sure can," said Alfred. "But about a year ago, I wouldn't have listened to you. And now this bump on the head may have woken me up."

"I'll say just a couple more things. Wills that have been made without considering all the circumstances can be ticking time bombs. The rifts that can occur may last for generations. You may have the best intentions in the world with your kids and . . . what's her name? Maribel? But the only way to avoid the big family fight is for you to communicate your wishes now — your wishes in the event of your incapacity and your wishes after death."

Alfred didn't feel much like talking anymore. "I will," he responded wearily.

"And don't forget to discuss your funeral and burial desires too."

"I won't."

Jimmy flipped through his *TV Guide*. "Look what's on in five minutes. *Six Feet Under*," he said with a chortle.

⬦⬦

Alfred lay there listening to Jimmy's rhythmic snoring, thinking about his roommate's story. Should I discuss my plans with Mary Beth? With the kids? What should I do about the cottage? How do I handle Judy? How do I split my estate between Mary Beth and the kids so that everyone is happy? Alfred gradually fell asleep, dreaming of himself hosting a TV roundtable discussion show. His guests included Queen Elizabeth and actor-comedian Will Smith, with whom he chatted pleasantly about their latest projects. Another round of guests appeared with much applause, this time his children and Mary Beth. He heard everything they were saying. They heard everything he was saying. On wakening from his dreams, Alfred usually suppressed most of the content and thus didn't remember much, but this time he awoke in the hospital the next morning knowing exactly what he had to do.

Chapter 18

HELP FROM HELFENBAUM

"Everybody take a seat! Let me get this tape recorder set up, just a second. . . . Michael, *sit!*"

Judy, Mike, and Shauna could see that Bev was anxious to share her findings.

"ok, some background here," Bev said, after the others had made themselves comfortable. "You know we've been talking about ways to improve our skills at being able to talk easily with Dad about subjects that normally he wouldn't want to."

"You mean sex, death, and money," Mike said before Bev could start her next sentence.

"Precisely. We all know Dad isn't alone in this. Since sex, death, and money are not our usual daily fare of conversation with different generations, we're not that great at it. With Dad's recent change in situation, we've all found that out, especially with wills. But I was lucky enough to have talked with someone recently who provided me with some insights on how to improve your communicating skills with ageing people. Hence the tape recorder."

"Is this the fellow whom you heard about, the professor

from a U.S. university who's spent a lot of time studying how people interact across generations?" Judy asked.

"Yes, you're about to hear Dr. Don Helfenbaum, who agreed to let me tape our conversation and divulge some of his wisdom. As you listen to this, you'll soon realize that there is no magic bullet for some frustrating communication problems, but there are things we can do to minimize them. So let's listen. You'll hear me as well. We start at the part where I've just finished filling him in on our situation."

Bev reached for the start button as Mike held up his right arm like an old talk-show host and announced, "Will you welcome, please, Dr. Don Helfenbaum!"

"Communication style is often part of the missing puzzle pieces that people need in order to resolve conflict. I advise many people with small businesses, including farm businesses in Pennsylvania, who continually hammer the same arguments back and forth to no avail. Particularly the issue of how to pass down the family business. Once I show them how to restructure their words and how to change their delivery, they often are quite surprised at the outcome. But like anything else, it's an acquired art that only improves with practice."

Helfenbaum cleared his voice. "First of all, talking to ageing people is quite different from talking to people our own age. It has a lot to do with a difference in what I call 'conflict styles.' Younger people, and that category includes you and me, can be confrontational, and they can get to that point quickly. Think about some of the arguments you've had with your peers and how quickly you or they can get hot under the collar. As we get older, most of us become more collaborative, though certainly not all. So we need to change our style of speaking when we talk to older adults."

Bev listened to herself responding to the professor on the tape. She cringed a bit. She hated the sound of her voice; it would sometimes crack at the ends of sentences, like Marge Simpsons'. "We've noticed my Dad has selective amnesia and gets uncomfortable and sometimes quiet when we try to approach him on the topic of money and wills and stuff. Why is that? Is it just because he's from a different generation?"

Helfenbaum spoke slowly and clearly. "There are two issues intertwined here. First, your dad's becoming quiet is likely in response to his perception that the conversation is becoming confrontational. That's the usual response from an older adult when they perceive conflict. Second, you are quite right when you say that they belong to a different generation. There is a cultural dimension at play here — many older people do not talk openly about death, money, and wills. You are up against an old tradition of reserve and circumspection, which is gradually being broken down in today's popular culture. Older people want to preserve their privacy, while new generations are celebrating their *non*privacy. Just look at the reality show phenomenon on television."

"If we want to improve our collaborative approach with Dad, what is best?" asked Bev.

"It's usually up to the children to take the first step, in your case you and your brother and sister. Don't just wait and expect your dad to take any initiative to bring this topic up. Plus it helps if you use a particular style."

"For example?" asked Bev.

"You can start a conversation by saying 'Dad, I need your help.' Your real challenge, though, lies in slowly drawing your father into the conversation. You need to use certain techniques in order to do so."

"What would I say?"

Helfenbaum took a deep breath. "Something like 'We need to solve a problem' or 'I need you to help me solve a problem.' Another strategy that works for some is to say 'I need your help with some estate-planning issues. I'm looking at doing my own will, and I thought you could share with me some of the things that you've done. Where are you comfortable starting?' Sentences like that."

"That makes sense. So, by using those sentences, I'm really asking my Dad how much he is willing to divulge?" asked Bev.

"That's right," replied Helfenbaum. "You see, it's all about the power of psychology. The key for you is to put yourself in a *powerless* position. That way it gets a parent to want to help a child by playing out the parental role."

"I see. So I need to make my Dad feel like I need his support and guidance and experience to help me solve my problem."

"Exactly," said Helfenbaum emphatically. "But remember it's an acquired skill to be able to do that. You must be very patient and calm and take it slowly. Don't forget that, if you push things along too quickly or abruptly, your father may perceive you as getting confrontational. Then the whole effort backfires. So I recommend that you begin with just one small item at a time and work from that point forward."

"Okay. Could there also be an issue of control here — I mean, could it be that my Dad wants to retain a high degree of control and that's why he won't discuss these things?" asked Bev.

"Absolutely," said Helfenbaum with authority. "There certainly could be an element of that as well. But I think what you interpret as a desire for control could actually be something else. Older people tend to be rigid in their outlook and find it very difficult to understand that, when faced with an alternative, equally valid point of view, it is possible to accept another person's view without appearing weak."

"Sounds like U.S. foreign policy," said Bev. "I'm joking," she added, having heard only a cough at the other end of the line. She continued quickly. "Are there certain phrases or words that should be avoided when dealing with ageing people?"

"Yes. It all goes back to style, as I mentioned earlier. Any manner of speaking that's confrontational, loud, or forceful should be avoided. Effective communication with ageing people is when you give them options for what to discuss and how to discuss it."

"Here's a thought," said Bev. "My Dad uses e-mail. What if I took the 'I need your help' route, as you suggest, and initiated this discussion via e-mail? That way there's no opportunity for conflict. Wouldn't it give him ample time to mull it over, without being under pressure to respond on the spot?"

"In theory, that would make sense, but I don't recommend it. E-mail can sometimes be too impersonal for an older person. There's a generation gap with respect to technology. The old-fashioned, handwritten letter is more effective — but only when that's been a standard way of communicating in the family about important issues."

"Should my brother, sister, and I meet with Dad at his home over dinner?"

"No."

"No?" asked Bev timidly.

"Not the three of you. Just one." There was a moment of silence.

"Oh — you mean because with all three of us it would appear confrontational?"

Helfenbaum chuckled. "Now you're getting the idea."

"So does it matter which one of us takes the lead? Should it be my brother?"

"Another no."

"I'm puzzled. That's contrary to what I would have thought," said Bev. "I assumed Dad might listen more to my brother about business issues since the older generation has a cultural difference about women understanding business issues and the like."

"At the risk of generalizing, fathers seem more able to accept advice about business issues, and some criticism as well, from daughters — they may react to suggestions from sons as a personal critique or even attack."

"That surprises me. We've been doing it wrong all along in our family, then!"

"Yes, this is a very interesting area. Anecdotal evidence seems to indicate that father-daughter relationships may have a better chance of success in business due to lack of rivalry. Rivalry can be quite strong in father-son relationships."

"So, if it's not my brother, then who?"

"I'll answer that question by stating the most effective

method. Remember that this doesn't mean that it works for every family. Research indicates that the best person to approach a father is either the oldest daughter or the daughter who lives the closest."

Bev sounded surprised. "That pretty much keeps it simple. It's me on both counts. Now is there an appropriate place for communication?"

"I would suggest the home of the parent because that's where he or she is the most comfortable," said Helfenbaum. "Also, I recommend you talk to him face to face, make eye contact. If it were your brother, I'd recommend a different method."

"Such as?"

"Some place where they can sit side by side. Like in a car or boat or golf cart. But assuming that you are the chosen one, I recommend you take the lead. Another thing you can do right after your face-to-face meeting with your dad is to write down the issues on a piece of paper and leave it with him. You might then say 'I'll come back next week to talk about it further.'"

"This is good — sons should be side by side, daughters face to face. Interesting. I know that time is running out. Just one more topic, if I may. The cottage — any thoughts on how to resolve cottage conflicts?"

There was a moment of silence before Helfenbaum spoke. "That's a tricky one. A cottage is emotion based, similar to the family domain. A business, on the other hand, is typically task oriented. So, if you try to treat a cottage like a business trans-action, then you may run into some patterns of emotional behaviour that are irrational. That's because of emotional undercurrents at work. I don't think I should go into a great deal of depth here, but suffice it to say that the key with the cottage is the more conversation the better. Another method you can use to persuade your dad to discuss these things is to take him to something he likes to do and discuss it within the context of doing activities. Some people take their parents to bingo and talk there. It can be anywhere that's familiar and where they are comfortable. And one more thing. Usually anything that involves dinner is a good idea. Ageing people are often planning their schedules around mealtime."

"Or their bowel movements," giggled Bev.

Helfenbaum laughed. "True. And another place for good conversation is the golf course. Does your dad like playing?"

"Playing and everything else about the sport. He's at home watching the Permian Basin Open on the Golf Channel. Enough said."

"Perfect — have a game with him and talk about all this stuff."

"Good. I have just one more question, if I may. I saved the big one for last. The presence of my Dad's youthful new partner, Mary Beth, is causing a lot of tension for obvious reasons. Her appearance on the scene also poses a real challenge to the position of our inheritance. Any advice you can give me on how to deal with that and how to talk to Dad?"

"That's a very good question and again one that can't be answered with any formula. But I can offer one piece of advice. The three of you *must* include her in your discussions. If you do not, you may lose the war before the battle has even begun."

"That will be very hard to do. Some of us feel that she's on a gold-digging expedition. It would be hard to include her in the conversation because she is the very reason we are in this turmoil."

"Agreed," admitted Helfenbaum. "But you must accept one thing. The three of you now will not have as close a relationship to your dad as Mary Beth does. That is a fact and one that you cannot change. Again, to use research to back up my suggestions, when children force a parent to side with either them or the new partner, eight out of ten times the parent will agree with the stepparent. So, if you force your father to decide on an issue that involves a difference of opinion between the three of you and Mary Beth, the odds are 80% that your dad will agree with her. He is closer to her than any of you three now because she is the one whom he's living with. So the nuts and bolts of this one are don't alienate her."

"Dr. Helfenbaum — thanks very much for your comments. You've given me some valuable strategies to start with."

"You are welcome. Please remember one thing — sometimes nothing works, but if that is the case at least you'll know it isn't because you didn't try the right techniques."

Bev pressed the "Stop" button on the tape machine.

"Seems simple, doesn't it?" said Mike. The group sat pensively as the sound of the tape rewinding itself filled the room. "Bev, this is good work you've done, and thank you for sharing it. Judy, what do you think?"

Judy was curled up on the sofa, her hand cupping her chin. "Jeez, my arm's asleep, which must mean I was listening intently. Yes, I commend you, Bev. I agree with the man on the tape — you may be the best person to talk with Dad. Are you OK with that?"

"I'm ready to give it a try, if Mike's in agreement."

Mike ran his hands through his hair, stretching out his legs from his chair at the same time. "It certainly makes sense with my living out of the city. Now that we know Dad's recovering well from his accident, it may be a good time to approach him again. Not having his power of attorney properly updated I think was a wake-up call for him."

"You're right about that," said Bev. "I think I'm now ready to talk with Dad again."

Chapter 19

THE POWERS OF COMMUNICATION

BEV AND HER FATHER sat out on the Delmore Avenue patio finishing off Alfred's time-tested speciality lunch of tomato soup and grilled cheese sandwiches. They sat listening to the summer whining heat bugs competing with the next-door neighbour's wheezing air-conditioning unit.

"One or two pennies for your thoughts," said Bev, seeing her father look pensive.

"Oh, I'm thinking about how much better I've been doing since the boat crash. I can now make lunch and move around without getting sore in the shoulder too much."

"Yes, I've noticed, that's wonderful," said Bev. "I wanted to have lunch with you today because . . . well . . . because I need your help."

"Oh?" Alfred looked concerned.

"You know, that accident. . . . I'm worried about anything happening to you again, and —"

Alfred let out a long sigh. "That accident really was a fluke — the chances of something happening again are pretty tiny."

"But what if something *did* happen again — something worse?"

Alfred looked at his daughter, rattling the remaining ice in his virgin Bloody Mary drink.

Bev continued, a bit apprehensively. "Mike, Judy, and I — we're *all* worried about you — especially if you and Mary Beth are going to travel out of the country. There are potential risks to your health. I know you're hale and hearty, but you're almost 70, and . . . when the doctor came out to talk to us at the hospital we realized none of us knew who had your power of attorney."

"I know, I know. I understand why you would be concerned," Alfred conceded.

Bev felt encouraged by her father's tepid acceptance of her point. "Actually the accident was a big wake-up call for me. It had the effect of making me aware of my own limitations."

"Mmmm, hmmm?" This was Alfred's signal that it was OK to continue and that he was listening.

"You don't have to be elderly for accidents to happen. A person my age is more likely to become incapacitated than dead. I've never really bothered to take proper care of my own affairs." Bev took a sip of her own drink and continued. "Yesterday I had my power of attorney documents and my will done. Your accident jolted me into realizing how fragile life is . . . and what would happen to my kids if anything should happen to me, God forbid. I prepared two power of attorney documents — one that deals with financial issues and one for questions concerning my health. This is one of the reasons that I wanted to see you alone today."

"All right, what have you got in mind?" Alfred thrust out his chin ever so slightly, giving him an air of authority.

"I would like to name you as primary decision maker —
that's what they call the 'attorney' in legal speak — on both my
financial and my health-care power of attorney documents.
That would mean that, if anything should happen to me, you
would have to step in. You don't have to accept — I mean, only
if you're comfortable. I could name —"

Alfred put his hand over his daughter's. "I would be honoured. As long as I'm physically and mentally with it, go ahead
and put me down. But what happens if I'm unwell and something happens to you? Jiminy, talking about this gives me the
willies. Nothing is going to happen to you!"

"I know this is a touchy subject, Dad, but it's crucial, and I
really do need to get my power of attorney finalized."

Alfred got up from his garden chair and started fiddling
with the umbrella that had come with the garden table, as if he
might find valuable knowledge there. He raised the umbrella
height one inch and then returned to his chair and sat down.
"Okay, I'm listening," he said with a smile.

Bev smiled back. "You asked me what would happen if you
were not healthy enough to act as my P.A. I've appointed Judy
and Mike as alternative decision makers, so, if you are unable or
unwilling to act, they would become the substitute 'attorneys.'"

"And, if you remarry, then what?"

"I asked my lawyer that question also. Marrying doesn't
affect my power of attorney. That document doesn't change; it
continues to remain in effect until I specifically revoke this
power of attorney and appoint my new hubby on a new one.
But since I don't have one at the moment — I mean a husband
— I can't think of anyone I trust as much as you. Add to that

the advantage that you live nearby."

"Gee, Bev. I'm honoured, and I sure hope I never have to act on it. And your will is completed?"

"Yes, and the lawyer brought up a very crucial point. He said that many individuals neglect to consider whom they would appoint as guardian for their minor children — that is, kids who are under the age of majority, which is either 18 or 19 depending on the province. Here in Ontario, age of majority is 18. Do you know what the law dictates here and in most other provinces? If you die without a spouse and a will, the courts will name a guardian for your children. The person appointed by the courts may, in fact, not be someone whom you would want looking after your kids. It was actually this issue of guardians that motivated me to get my will done. The will refers to the kids as minors."

"And children are of course anything but a minor consideration! Sounds like you're thinking this through very well. Whom have you appointed as guardian?"

"Mike and Shauna."

"Phew! No offence, but I was worried you might be asking me to accept that appointment as well. I love Megan and Harry, but at my age just a couple of hours with kids feels like a weekend at Disneyland. Have you spoken to Mike and Shauna about it?"

"Yes, I have, and they've accepted the appointment of guardian in my will. I just feel better now that I've completed these tasks."

"I'm glad you've addressed them. These are important steps that are easy to put off but foolish to ignore."

Alfred and Bev sat silently for a few moments, Alfred breaking the silence. "As for me, I'm taking better care of my health now. I'm on a health regime, allowing, of course, for my once-a-week grilled cheese and Bloody Mary ritual. I don't feel a day over 60. I'm drinking green tea regularly now — my doctor chirps about its health benefits — particularly as a cancer-preventing agent."

"That's marvellous that you feel so well. There may be another agent that you need to consider," added Bev gently.

Alfred put forth another "Hmm, mmm?"

Bev knew this was a good opportunity to continue. She was inwardly thrilled at her progress with the conversation. "You also need an agent for your own powers of attorney," she said.

Alfred nodded. "Mary Beth still feels devastated about the accident. She blames herself for the crash. It has really put a strain on our relationship. She hasn't been herself since."

"We *all* felt the strain of your accident. The short period where you were unconscious — and the doctor asking us who had power of attorney — we all just looked at each other waiting for someone to step up to the plate. We soon realized that we were all empty handed and that none of us could act on your behalf. I was worried sick. I mean, what if you hadn't come out of the coma? We were all worried sick about you, and almost as bad as that was the feeling of overwhelming helplessness — there was nothing we could do. I haven't slept very well since, and to make matters worse I have this constant nagging feeling." Bev's voice cracked a bit on the last few syllables.

"I understand your concern, Bev."

"All we are asking you to do is to appoint someone you trust and prepare one of those documents. In the future, our angst levels will be so much more manageable."

"I know. Jeremy has been badgering me to get my powers of attorney done. I just thought. . . . I was sure that, because I had drawn them up years ago when your mom was alive, that my fiancée would automatically be able to make decisions on my health. But I made a boo boo — I realize now that those old documents are useless. Even if Mary Beth were my wife, she would have been unable to make any decisions."

"So does that mean I can breathe a sigh of relief — will you get new ones drawn up?"

"Yes, I will — in fact, I'll call Jeremy tonight and see if I can get these done tomorrow."

"And then. . . ." Bev hesitated a second, still wary of her father's traditional reticence. "And then will you discuss with us whom you have named? We will need to know in case anything happens again."

Alfred let out a sigh. "I worry about starting a family fight over whom I name. If I name one child, the others may feel snubbed. If I name Mary Beth, that could cause another problem. If I name Jeremy, that might look like I don't trust you."

Bev shook her head. "Dad, all you need to do is tell us. It's your decision to name whomever you wish. We will respect that. Having proper documents and communicating your wishes to us now while you are healthy will serve as a hedge against future disputes. This is about not having surprises in the future. Mike and Judy and I now realize from experience that inaction is the worst path you can take."

"Yes, I definitely see your point. So you think it will be safe to discuss this document with all of you? No arguments? Even Judy?"

Bev smiled. "Yes, even Judy."

"Then, when I have made my decision, I'll find a time for all of us to have a discussion — Mary Beth included."

"Mary Beth included. Thank you, Dad. I feel so much better. I now realize that estate planning is not about death and dying — really it is about living with peace of mind."

"You may be right, Bev."

"My lawyer gave me some very useful information on preparing a will. I thought it would be helpful to share some of his points with you, you know, for your will. Where are you comfortable starting?"

Alfred stood up and walked over to the water sprinkler, which he relocated to the opposite corner of the garden. He returned to the table. "Not so fast, Bee. I'm getting there. One thing at a time."

"Okay, Dad. Let me know if you need any help."

Father and daughter gathered up their lunch plates and bowls, which clattered together as Bev reached up to plant a kiss on her father's cheek.

Chapter 20

THE SPIDER
BROOCH

"MARY BETH, YOU'RE QUIET today — everything okay? Are you happy?" Alfred was standing by the wardrobe, inspecting his thinning greyish brown hair and checking his tie in the mirror.

Mary Beth stood near the bedroom window. "I'm OK. I just get a bit nervous before birthday parties, especially when you're the fiancée of the birthday boy," she said, holding up a vanity mirror and tracing a dark red lip liner skilfully around her lips. "I feel like I'm under constant scrutiny by your kids, especially Judy. That I'm being criticized. And there's the age thing. What will your friends think?"

"What age thing? You make me feel younger and younger every day. C'mon, we just have to give the kids more time. This is all happening very fast for them, particularly Judy, because in some ways she is the closest to me."

"Do you think this dress is too short? Should I wear the long one?" Mary Beth examined herself in a full-length mirror. Got to make the butt look good, Mary Beth mused to herself. She surveyed her reflection with that look of pained and pensive scrutiny most women assume when objectifying themselves.

Alfred moved toward Mary Beth and placed both hands on her upper arms. "You look fabulous," he murmured, kissing her on the cheek.

"And you look flash as a rat with a gold tooth."

"Mercy! I'll accept the compliment. Your dress is beautiful. And here, try wearing this." Alfred reached into the back of the dresser drawer and produced a small velvet box. With a rustle of old tissue paper, he held up a spider brooch made from a black South Sea pearl, with two quarter-karat diamonds representing the spider's eyes and eight one-inch platinum spindles as the spider's legs. "This is a Victorian piece, in the Hilroy family for well over a century. It will look stupendous on you."

Mary Beth accepted the brooch silently. Alfred kissed her on the other cheek just as she was pulling him toward the bed, the duvet and the sheets still in a crumpled pile from earlier that afternoon.

"We're going to be late now," said Alfred.

"Who cares?"

⌗

The Terrace Hall had a high ceiling, a quadrant allotted for dancing, and two sets of French doors opening onto a terrace with wrought-iron tables and smallish white chairs. Fifty guests were attending Alfred's birthday; half the invitees were what Judy called the "blue rinse" crowd, the other half friends of Mike, Bev, and Judy.

"I'll never forget when Dad bailed me out of that situation," said Mike, reminiscing with three old neighbourhood buddies.

"I don't know how many snowballs we'd hurled at passing cars. Remember we had them lined up on the front steps and were firing away for about an hour before some college kid in a Dodge Dart took exception and chased me through nine backyards before I surrendered — you guys were faster than me and got away. Dad was waiting for me and my sputtering captor, who was going to sue the world. And Dad took care of everything in that no-nonsense way of his — the angry driver was defused and sent on his way, I got kicked to my room, and Dad then dealt with the constable. All Dad said later was 'You should be in jail,' and I spent a week waiting to be led away in handcuffs. Even though I wasn't, the waiting was enough punishment."

Mike grabbed an hors d'oeuvre from a passing tray and went over to Bev and Judy huddled at the bar. "Come on, mingling time," he instructed.

"We're just trying to coach each other on the people whose names we can't remember," said Judy. "That buck-toothed guy over there, isn't that Dad's old schoolmate Jack? We should've done the name tag thing. I like to load up on these little weenie rolls, they're great as conversation gap fillers."

At the other corner of the room, the newly betrothed Alfred and Mary Beth were aglow and basking in attention, particularly Mary Beth in her sleeveless mini-dress, black-and-red silk shawl, and designer black high heels. Her thick, wavy, blonde mane, normally tied back in a ponytail, fell loosely about her shoulders, giving her a look of cool dishevelment. Alfred, freshly shaved and wearing a blue French-cuff dress shirt and black dress pants, proudly displayed Mary Beth on his arm as he greeted old friends. She leaned in close to Alfred, taking in the scent of his Aqua Velva aftershave. He whispered softly to her, his voice in her ear sending a tickling chill up her body. "You're definitely making an impression, you look ravishing. Are you feeling all right?"

"I feel better, thanks. I'm actually a bit hot now — must be nerves."

"Why not let me take your shawl?"

Mary Beth allowed the silk shawl to slide off her shoulders. Twenty feet away, a shrimp was halfway on its journey to Bev's mouth. Then it halted, Bev's lips forming a perfect letter *o*, hors d'oeuvre forgotten. Firmly ensconced next to Mary Beth's left breast, perfectly positioned, and glittering its unique beauty against the contrast of the black dress was the highly honoured family heirloom. "Good God, is that what I think it is?" Bev inched forward for a closer look. "It's the spider brooch. Mother's spider brooch."

Judy craned her neck to see Mary Beth. "It is? It is? It is!"

Bev began to feel as if the air had left the room, with a punch in the stomach added for good measure. She could feel her heat gauge rising to the red zone. This was something Bev knew she could have been better prepared for but wasn't. The sense of rising fury was new to her. "This is the absolute fucking end."

Judy was caught by surprise at her sister's very uncharacteristic outburst.

"Looks like the big wolf has crawled into Grandma's bed," said Judy. "That brooch has been handed down all the way from Dad's grandmother, and it looks like it's been handed down once more."

Bev motioned to Judy to follow her, and they made their way to the terrace for privacy, where a few furtive partygoers stood and smoked. "I've tried. I've really tried. In fact, I've been charitable, genial, civilized, and downright magnanimous. But this is different. This is personal. Mom always said that I would own that brooch someday. So now what do I do?" Bev's hands were trembling, the uneaten shrimp mashed up in her cocktail napkin.

Mike appeared on the terrace and was brought up to date on Bev's meltdown. "I didn't know the brooch meant so much to you. If you feel that strongly about it, you could tell Dad that giving it to her is not fair," he said. "Of course, you don't have all the facts yet — you may just have more pent-up emotion than the brooch is worth."

"Perhaps so, Dr. Freud, but I need to see the brooch back in its drawer, Dad's and not Mary Beth's, even if I have to rip it off that perky little chest of hers myself," Bev said, her voice an octave higher than normal.

"I don't think her chest is so little, in fact," Mike began and then stopped as he noticed Bev's eyes starting to moisten. "We'll get this fixed. I'm probably in the best position to talk with Dad about what's going on. I'd almost forgotten about the brooch, unique and beautiful though it is."

"C'mon, Bev," said Judy, her arm around her sister in a show of sibling support. "Mike's right — we'll figure something out. I don't think the brooch is going to disappear. She's probably just borrowing it for the night anyway," Judy said, dabbing a tissue at Bev's cheeks.

"Do you really think so? Can we get a court restraining

order to keep that gold digger away from Dad?" Bev asked, blowing her nose.

Judy laughed. "There's something else to think about. I've always liked that little arachnid myself. After all, I've been known to sport the goth look on occasion."

Mike cleared his throat, lowering his voice to Orson Welles's Shakespearian tones. "Oh what a tangled web she weaves. . . . You wanted that, I do believe! But Judy brings up a good point. Assuming Dad wants his kids to inherit such things, and tonight's events suggest that's always an if, we have to be ready to handle the chance that Dad's estate will not spell out how beneficiaries are to split up physical assets. And, if Dad's estate does specify who gets what, that it doesn't create a war between us. But let's get back to the party — Dad and M.B. need us to keep things moving!"

⚭

When Bev returned from the washroom, it was time for dinner. She took her place at the buffet and picked up a plate and a napkin-wrapped bundle of silverware. She wasn't particularly hungry, but she helped herself to a meagre amount of salad and four asparagus spears. Once seated, Bev made a conscious effort to divert her attention away from Mary Beth. Fortunately she was at a different table. She would not have been able to withstand the sight of that precious piece adorning Mary Beth, the continual, overbearing assault on her eyes. To be fair, Bev realized that she was probably displacing many feelings onto Mary Beth at that time, but she was beyond being polite or circumspect, for that matter. Bev had been provoked one too many times. She busied herself with her food to cover her discomfort, though no one else around her seemed to notice. Her stomach cramped with tension. She uncrossed her legs and tried to relax, but she couldn't get comfortable. She picked at her food, making small talk with the people seated to either side of her. The waiter came by with wine, and Bev held out her glass, allowing it to be generously filled. The rest of the evening passed by in what seemed like an interminable length of time.

At one o'clock in the morning, Bev stirred in her bed, unable to remove the image of Mary Beth dazzling the guests, carrying herself with perfect composure and confidence, with the brooch on display like an exclamation point. She imagined Mary Beth rummaging around boxes and cupboards at Delmore Avenue. Ooh, what's this, dumpling? Again Bev flashed on the image of the pretty face, the wide smile, the sparkling eyes — only this time her mom's pearl necklace and earring set appeared in the picture.

Bev, along with Mike and Judy, hadn't divvied up their mother's jewellery yet because it seemed too soon, and they certainly didn't want to press Alfred and seem greedy. And now, because they had waited, Mary Beth seemed to be the lucky recipient of their mom's jewellery. Dad had no right to do that, thought Bev. Mom would not be happy, and she certainly would not want another woman wearing her stuff.

Bev tried counting in her head all the different plants in her garden in an effort to divert her mind away from the offending images. Eventually her thoughts rounded into perspective. She remembered Judy's and Mike's comments about rushing to judgement and how their dad's welfare far outweighed any piece of jewellery. After all, Bev thought, Dad still has his health and is enjoying his trip into old age as well as anyone could wish for.

Bev fell asleep at four o'clock and dreamt of wonderful days at the summer cottage, both long ago and those to come.

Chapter 21

COTTAGE
LIFE CRISIS

"STILL BROODING ABOUT THE brooch?" asked Mike the next morning, noting Bev sitting by the picture window, looking out pensively, not really taking in the sight of an acrobatic squirrel's attempts to get at the bird feeder.

Bev could feel her bowels squeeze down every time she thought of the brooch. "I feel like five kinds of crap," she said.

"Your Alice Cooper eyes don't help."

Bev ran the knuckle of her index finger under her lower lashes, where her mascara had smeared. She slouched down and leaned her head back. "I've been thinking about my own reaction to the whole scene. I'm happy that Dad has found someone. Someone to make him happy after so much sorrow. The blowup with her in the house I got over — I expected they would live there together. I didn't even mind her changes at the cottage so much, after a while anyway. But the spider brooch. That's different. That was *so* Mom. I can still see her wearing it every Christmas Eve. Dad has no right to give it away."

"I hate to say this, Bev, but he does. He could give it to Shania Twain or Michael Jackson if he wants. Of course, there's zero chance he would, but if he did I'd recommend laughing rather than crying. And, if the brooch is now Mary Beth's, magnanimity is the best course."

"Philosophical today, I see. It's more than just the brooch," said Bev. "I'm trying to put everything that's happened until now in perspective. But this whole issue is becoming serious. Dad is so cranked up with lust and newfound vigour that he's lost sight of, well, everything."

"And without a Viagra boost too, I overheard him tell Jack proudly last night at the end of the party!"

"Goody for him and her too. But how could she just grab something that's so sacred to the family? What other things is Dad going to give to her?"

"Obviously Dad's just not thinking, Bev. He, well, lots of men, they, you know . . . they just don't think in sentimental terms — excluding me, of course."

"Of course," remarked Shauna, who'd just arrived with Judy, loaded down with supplies for the upcoming postparty brunch for Alfred and Mary Beth.

Mike continued, "What seems obvious to you just probably doesn't register with Dad. Besides, you are right about one thing — Dad is infatuated, but that doesn't necessarily translate into catastrophic consequences. It just means we need to help him understand the impacts on us of some of his actions."

"I hope you're right, but somehow I get the feeling that there's more bad news to come."

"Think about it, Bev. Easy for me to say, but it's not the precious object that can get people stirred up, it's the associations that come with it. In this case, it's Mom."

"What are you saying? That what happens to the spider brooch doesn't matter?" asked Bev.

"To a degree, yes. The jewellery and other stuff are great to preserve, and to enjoy them for their beauty or value, but they're not our responsibility."

"You've got a point," said Shauna. "I had an uncle, a historian, who owned a complete set of first-edition books written by Winston Churchill, with signed correspondence from the great man himself tucked in the flyleaves. Nothing historically significant but valuable nevertheless. My cousin was very interested in the prized volumes, but the day came when they were boxed up without a word by my uncle and given away. Previous expressions of interest in the books had done no good. 'I can do with them what I will,' said my uncle. My cousin was sorely disappointed, even wondering if he was in a way being punished for some previous family transgression. He wisely dropped the matter."

"But you'd think there would be a way for such situations to end up better," said Judy. "I mean, that was a pretty teeth-grinding experience for Bev at the birthday party."

"Sure there are ways," remarked Shauna, "but the family has to be open and proactive. One good way of handling items of value that my brothers and I did, whether sentimental or practical, is for the parent (or parents) to draw up an inventory of more important things, everything from furniture to artwork. And then they let their kids put check marks beside the items they're interested in. The parents may not be inclined to do such a list at first, but perhaps some gentle hints can be dropped over time that a list is a good idea."

"And make it look like it was their creation!" laughed Judy. "Mom always said that she didn't ever want us fighting over possessions. She would have liked this idea."

"Exactly," said Mike. "That would be the way we would have to approach it with Dad — he needs to feel like he is in control — that important decisions like this originate from him. Even better is if we can get Dad to ask us to help compile the list. Artwork on one list, maybe jewellery on another, furniture on another, et cetera. A little psychology can go a long way."

"That makes sense," said Bev. "All the kids should be involved. This is critical. Parents can designate who is to receive what, but if not then the kids should mark the list with their preferences and then put it away where it can be easily found when needed."

"I'd feel like the old washerwoman in *A Christmas Carol*, where you see her going over Scrooge's belongings with her cronies after he's died," said Judy.

"That's not an optimal way to do it, though," said Mike. "The parents should be fully involved in the whole process. If it never happens, we can always do it later, not like the old hags in the movie, but as part of a planned and organized distribution."

"Assuming the whole lot hasn't been willed to Mary Beth," said Bev grimly.

"Then we live with it," said Mike. "The important thing is that, Mary Beth or no Mary Beth, we three sort out sentimental and valuable items either now or later and that we do it as fairly and as smoothly as possible. Yes, we must be disciplined enough to follow through on the task, which might become tedious at times. Like gym workouts. But everyone will thank each other later."

⚮

The brunch went quickly and informally, people perched on chairs inside, avoiding the rain pelting down outside. Alfred was no longer in his arm sling, but he was still in some minor discomfort as his shoulder healed. He couldn't move about for more than 10 minutes since the natural force of gravity inflicted more than the necessary pressure on his shoulder.

Stretched out on the sofa and finishing off the leftover birthday cake, Alfred cleared his throat, a time-honoured tradition that signalled for everyone to listen up. He sat up in a more formal, businesslike posture on the sofa. Mary Beth sat on a high-backed chair next to him. "Last weekend at the cottage," Alfred began, "a nice young man named Frank Doherty knocked at the door. He has a young family with three children, and they've been renting on the lake for the past three summers. They like their own rental cottage, but they want something more, with four bedrooms and a north- or northwest-facing lot."

Alfred's kids stopped eating all at once. All that could be heard for a moment was the old clock on the mantelpiece in the next room.

"By the time he left, we'd struck a deal for him to buy the cottage."

Bev, Mike, Shauna, and Judy sat mutely and statuelike, Bev looking more like a gargoyle as the news sunk in.

"What?" said Bev numbly. She felt powerless. She was being told something she could not comprehend.

Alfred pulled himself up to sit higher on the sofa and ploughed ahead. "The nuts and bolts of this are Mary Beth and I would like to travel a lot in the next few years, particularly while I'm still able to, ah, get around and while I have the stamina. And, you know, the wedding is planned for September, and then we plan a month in Greece. . . ."

A sickening shiver overtook Mike. "What has all that got to do with the cottage?" he said, not believing what he was hearing. He got up and placed his coffee mug on the counter, crossed his arms, and braced himself for another blow.

"Why would you want to sell the cottage?" asked Bev. "And so suddenly?"

"The cost of travelling these days — well, you know, it's very expensive. Mary Beth and I had long discussions about this, and together we came to a decision about our future plans, what our priorities are. . . ."

"This is your answer to a desire for travelling?" asked Bev. "To sell the cottage out of the blue without consulting us?"

"Consulting you three would have meant complications. Mr. Doherty gave me a week to decide, or else his offer would expire."

Mike stared into the dry kitchen sink. "But, Dad, with all due respect, this doesn't make sense. Even if you don't use the cottage for a few years, we still want to go there."

"Why sell it to an unknown person?" Bev stared at her dad, feeling faint, her brow furrowed.

"Mr. Doherty offered me a very good price."

"Can I ask how much?" asked Bev quietly, biting the insides of her cheeks, a lifelong habit that surfaced during stress.

"He offered me $50,000 more than that real estate agent told us we would get at the beginning of the summer. He offered $400,000."

"Nice," said Mike. He thought how easy it was to be philosophical about the brooch, but the impending sale of the cottage was going to test everyone's resolve. He looked over at Judy, who stared inexpressively at her dessert plate on her lap, her half-eaten cheesecake no longer holding the same appeal.

"Is your decision final, Dad?" asked Bev, unable to hide a wince and rubbing her upper left arm.

"Well, I verbally told Mr. Doherty that we had a deal. The lawyers will be drawing up the contract by the end of the week, and Mr. Doherty and I plan to meet next week when he's back from a business trip."

"Dad, obviously you must do as you see fit," said Mike. "But I just don't understand what's happening here. Why sell to some other cottager at the lake?"

Alfred had believed that his kids would be resilient enough to handle any upheaval. But now he was not so sure.

"And what's happening with the furniture — your dresser that used to belong to Grandpa and that musty, 150-year-old armoire in the living room?" continued Mike.

"Well, I thought just to keep it simple I'd sell the cottage with all the furniture — unless there's something in particular that you want, but you'll have to make up your mind fast. We can talk about that more later — we're all tired from last night and grumpy," Alfred said.

Judy had remained silent, letting her father ramble on about his plans, desires. He was unrecognizable to her; everything was unrecognizable. Her anger rose from deep inside her. Not the cottage, she thought to herself. Anything but the cottage. She put down her dessert plate on the coffee table with a loud clatter. "This is just plain shitty, Dad! Have you ever stopped for a moment to consider your kids' needs? Letting Mary Beth waltz into your life is great for you, I know, but it's damned annoying to us. She redecorates our cottage and city homes, wears Mom's jewellery, which devastates Bev, spends your money freely, and now you're cutting out a part of our life — the cottage — and I feel like it's all a slap in the face."

There was a cold silence in which everyone inspected Judy.

"Dad, you're an old fool," she said simply. And she didn't stop at that. Much to everyone's horror, she then focused on Mary Beth, her gaze narrowing. "I do wonder, Mary Beth, you having just flattened a perfectly good job you had at the bank, if you would have found our father quite as compelling if you didn't stand to enjoy a small fortune from your union with him."

Alfred's jaw dropped, and he looked at everyone with a caught-off-guard look. The kids' severe reactions seemed surprising to Alfred, but what was stranger was the implication that Mary Beth was just in it for the money. "I never —"

But before Alfred could continue, Mary Beth stood up abruptly, her napkin dropping from her lap to the floor. "Hold on to your horses. I know this relationship has been very hard on the three of you. I will freely admit that I do like the fact that I now have financial security, because I grew up living on the smell of an oily rag. And, yes, I realize now that I have initiated some rather annoying things, like redecorating your city home. And I still feel traumatized about the boating accident, for which I accept full blame."

Mary Beth then turned her head and focused her rising anger on Judy. "But, Judy, I'm not the mongrel you like to think I am. You have a few 'roos loose in the top paddock with your suggestion that I'm just here for the money. That is a load of old cobblers! What you have utterly failed to understand is the depth of my true blue love for your father — and I can give you a million reasons why. And that should be all that you need concern yourself with. I am as mad as a cut snake with your continual knockers at my expense." Mary Beth began to cry. She grabbed her purse and stormed out the front door.

Judy burst into tears and ran from the room. She stomped up the stairs, her clogs slamming against the pine boards of the staircase. She slammed the bedroom door after her.

Alfred rubbed his palms over his temples, feeling suddenly weary. He'd known there would be dissent with his decision to sell the cottage, but he hadn't expected it to be this severe.

Mike gave Bev a "Let it lie for now" look, seeing the "This brunch has ended" look on his father's face.

Alfred lifted himself from the sofa. "Well, I'd better go find Mary Beth" was all he said as he let himself out the front, slamming the door a little more forcefully than necessary.

∞∞∞

Mary Beth was sitting in the car waiting for Alfred, tears streaming down her cheeks. The drive home was subdued.

Mary Beth stared straight ahead at the road, barely blinking. "I'm sorry, but I just couldn't keep my trap shut," she said, getting a weak smile from Alfred. She continued, her voice cracking occasionally. "I was surprised by the emotions and outbursts in there, but obviously you hit a real nerve with your kids. I think you are going to have to rethink this cottage issue."

"I will. I'll talk to Jeremy. You know, I'm sorry you had to go through that. I'm sorry for Judy's insolence. I'm sorry for everything."

Mary Beth looked at Alfred with her perfectly beautiful face. "You know, bugalugs, I've been thinking lately that I need a vacation. This is all upsetting me tremendously — and this afternoon's blue with Judy has left me shaken."

"That's a great idea. Why don't we take off for a while?"

Mary Beth responded anxiously, "Actually, I was thinking alone — or maybe with a friend. I feel I'm causing you more grief than joy. Your kids are upset with my presence, and the accident. . . ." Her voice began to crack again. She looked tired, her face pinched, with dark circles under her eyes.

Alfred stopped at a red light and remained silent for a moment. He too looked exhausted. "Honey, go have a good time," he said with a brave smile. He stroked her cheek and turned back to drive at the green light. Alfred didn't agree with the idea, but he reluctantly gave Mary Beth his blessing.

Although they were excited about their upcoming marriage and about their relationship, which was flourishing, life at times for Alfred was becoming almost unbearably stressful. All in all, a fine mess, he thought.

꞊ꞌ

Judy sat upstairs in Bev's guest bedroom and stared at the wall. She took deep breaths, her eyes closed. She worked on hardening herself. Once she had her emotions in check and knew that Alfred and Mary Beth had left, she ventured back downstairs to join the other three in the den. The four sat there in silence, staring straight in front of themselves. They didn't speak for several minutes. The siblings didn't know what to say to each other. Usually it was one needing another, so there had been a way in the past to borrow from each other's strengths. Now they were unified in their melancholy.

Mike was stunned. Stunned at the news and stunned at his sister's outburst. Even though his spinal cord felt like a column of ice, he managed to drag himself out of his seat. He headed to the kitchen, donned the yellow dishwashing gloves, filled the sink with sudsy water, and went into dishwashing overdrive with Shauna by his side. "Looks like your idea of making a list of sentimental items might come in handy," he commented to her. "I suppose we should prepare such a cottage list now so that at least we can decide equitably on what items we want to bring home."

"I think we have to go up there," commented Bev as she walked into the kitchen.

Mike turned from the sink, dishcloth in hand, and looked over at Judy, who'd remained in the den chair brooding. Some of the recent changes in the Hilroys' lives over the past year were, to Mike, regrettable and sad, but he was an optimist at heart. His attitude was simple as he addressed his sister. "Judy, you're just going to have to accept all of this. We must make the best of it for Dad's sake and for the family's sake."

Her suspicion of Mary Beth was considerable. Judy thought that there was no point in lying or pretending. "No," she responded gloomily, "I can't."

Chapter 22

COTTAGE ALTERNATIVES

Not surprisingly the tension between Mary Beth and Alfred grew over the next several days, adding to his despair. Their cozy breakfasts when they planned their days were mostly silent. Their predinner glass of wine and cheer carried a resounding sadness. The following Saturday Mary Beth took a flight south for a week-long spa getaway.

Left on his own for a week, Alfred struggled to maintain a constant mood. The more he thought about the strong and hurtful words spoken at the brunch, the more upset he became. The weekend passed by painfully slowly. Bev phoned each day, but Alfred felt little like talking, and he declined Bev's invitations to dinner at her house.

On Monday and Wednesday after Mary Beth had gone, Alfred went to work and plodded through his tasks at the pharmacy, but he couldn't take his mind off the troubles of home life. He felt heartsick about the rift in the family. Waiting for Mary Beth's return, he grew more depressed about the mess he'd gotten into. He was very much in love with Mary Beth, and, while the inconveniences of his angry youngest daughter made him very unhappy, they were no reason to give Mary Beth up.

By Thursday, sadness had almost undone Alfred. Alienated from the people whom he loved deeply and disillusioned by the lack of acceptance of his kids, he went for a long walk in his neighbourhood trying to think of what to do. Here he was at nearly 70 years of age, financially secure, with three success- ful children, living in paradise with a woman whom he adored, with good health and good friends, yet he felt resounding gloom. The headwinds going forward seemed to be more than he wanted to withstand.

Alfred needed to take steps to mend the family rift. He couldn't imagine that his three children in time wouldn't learn to love this spirited and fun-loving woman. When he returned home, he sat down to compose a hand-written letter:

To my loving children,

Our last get-together was terrible for everyone. I do not fault you for your feelings or sudden outbursts of frustration. But if we don't try desperately hard, every conversation we have or you three have with Mary Beth may only result in a damaging shouting match.

When your mother was alive, it was easy to defer to her the task of resolving family conflict. But Mom's not here to pitch in with her steadfast counsel, so I must carry the task. My goal is to keep this family intact. I would never intentionally create unhappiness for you. For my part, going forward, I will discuss ahead of time with the three of you decisions concerning family assets that carry emo- tional significance for you — such as the cottage.

With Mary Beth being away for the week, I feel miserable. I do love her, and I hope that in time the three of you will get to know her good qualities, of which she has plenty. I think the best course of action is to put this all behind us and move forward. Please do not continue to assume that Mary Beth is something that she is not.

I would like all of you to come to dinner here at my house soon with Mary Beth and me. There are some things I would like to discuss with the three of you. We will schedule it when you, Mike, are in town at the end of the month for your client business meetings. Let us know your dates.

In the future, allow me to control my own life and make my own decisions, with your blessing. I know you three love me and mean well.

Love, Dad

∞∞

Alfred arrived alone at Jeremy's home, and Jeremy greeted his old friend in his usual expansive manner. "You're missed on the golf course, old boy. Bob Hinchcliffe has replaced you in the Sunday foursome — his allergies make him sniff a lot, usually when I'm over the ball. You need to get back soon. How's your injured wing?"

"Much better, thanks. You're probably stuck with Bob the rest of the season, though. Thanks for seeing me on short notice. You know when we talked the other day about my decision to sell the cottage to Frank Doherty?"

"Yes, I was wondering about that. How did the kids take the news?"

"About the same as if I'd said Mary Beth and I were each to undergo a sex-change operation, sell everything, and move to New Jersey. I wasn't ready for the sort of confrontation we received. Judy and Mary Beth got into a donnybrook." Alfred recounted the events of the brunch.

Jeremy listened attentively with deep concern over the quickly developing Hilroy conflict. "You need to stop this deterioration before it gets worse, and I may be able to help you. One thing I want you to understand today is that there are alternatives to selling the cottage outside of the family."

Alfred looked up at Jeremy. "We're selling because Mary Beth has lost interest in going up there since the accident. But I'd do anything to reverse this unhappiness that I appear to have started."

"Did you ask the kids if they wanted to buy the cottage?"

"No. But they don't have the means. They can't afford to buy."

"Isn't that jumping to conclusions? One or more of your kids could have come up with some sort of arrangement. And they might have been caught just a little off guard. Just recently you were talking about renovations up there — what happened?"

Alfred shifted uncomfortably in his chair. "I know I was. I guess it was being hospitalized that gave me time to reflect. In addition to Mary Beth not caring so much for cottage life, we want to travel and could use the extra cash. The cottage costs me close to $15,000 each year in property taxes, utilities, and repairs, not to mention boat storage and fuel."

"What if your kids were to assume some of those costs? Would that change your mind?"

"Not really — that could cause more problems. I don't want to see a situation where one or two had the means but the other didn't. That would be a surefire way to stir up resentment in the family. Selling outside the family seemed to be the easiest solution. And Mike lives out of the province and can't spend a lot of time up there."

"True, but, if he's still spending his summer holidays up there every year, that might suggest he hasn't lost interest in it. And Bev, being with the Board of Education, she can spend most of July and August there, no?"

Alfred remained silent.

"Have there been any fights over handling of ongoing expenses?"

"So what are you saying?" asked Alfred.

"Look, I don't want to get too pushy, but I'll risk it. Cottages can cause a lot of heartaches and headaches in families. I want you to consider all the options before selling to this Doherty fellow. Here's a thought for you to consider. What if you rent the cottage during the month of June? That should allow you to receive a good chunk of rental income. You can apply that rental income to the operating costs of the cottage. Any expenses over and above what you collect in income you split equally with the kids — that is, one-quarter each."

Alfred remained silent, but Jeremy knew he was listening. There was no glazed-over look of someone who's thinking of other matters.

"Before you answer that, remind me — what were you planning to do with the cottage before your idea to sell?"

"I don't know — as you know, when Joyce was alive, our wills stated that our kids would get the cottage after our deaths. But since Mary Beth came on the scene, I hadn't really decided on what to do. Then, over the course of the past couple of weeks, we thought selling might be the simplest solution."

"That will is no longer valid, by the way — but later on that. Alfred, would you still consider leaving the cottage to the children? What are your thoughts about putting the cottage in the names of Mike, Bev, and Judy?"

"Well, the first problem is the high cost of running the place each year. I don't want to keep paying the bills given the fact that Mary Beth and I probably won't use it much in the future. But that's not all. The bigger issue is the large capital gain on the cottage. I thought that by selling at least the proceeds would cover the taxes owing."

"What's the adjusted cost base of the cottage exactly?" asked Jeremy.

"I inherited it from my mother about 20 years ago. The cost at that time was about $125,000."

"And you say that the market value today is about $350,000, if I remember correctly," said Jeremy, flipping over a notepad and scribbling down the numbers. "Alf, the reason you want to sell — is it financial or emotional?"

"Financial, I guess." He couldn't think of any emotional reasons at the moment.

"Have you ever thought about gifting the cottage?"

"Gifting, um, you mean just giving it up as a present to the kids?"

Jeremy nodded once.

"That would still kick-start a taxable gain — that's a boat-load of tax to pay. And now that I work only part time, my income is much lower."

"Just a sec. Renovations — you've done some in the past decade — don't forget the brand-new dock you put in a couple of years ago."

"That dock sure was expensive — I must say the cost of it rambled through my mind as I lay there semi-conscious last month."

"Well, you can add the cost of renovations to your cost base of the cottage — doing so reduces your gain when you sell. What did you pay for that dock?"

"Egads, about $50,000."

"I hope you kept good records of your renovation costs. Okay, so your cost base is really $175,000 — the amount you inherited from your mother plus the cost of the new dock."

Alfred nodded. "Okay, so $350,000 less $175,000 — that gives me a taxable gain, then, in the amount of $175,000," said Alfred, proud that he was able to come up with the numbers so quickly.

Jeremy waved his pencil like a windshield wiper. "Not so fast. It might not be as bad as you think. First of all, the tax-able gain is not $175,000. That's the *full* capital gain. It's not the amount that you need to include in your income tax return. You need to report only 50% of capital gains in this country. So your *taxable* capital gain is therefore $87,500."

"It's still too much tax. Eighty-seven grand buys a lot of golf balls, and I need a lot of them."

"One thing at a time," said Jeremy steadily. "If I found a method of reducing your taxes to a minimal amount, would you at least consider gifting the cottage to your kids?"

"I need to see some numbers — show me, maestro."

"Forget about numbers for a sec. I'm just talking hypothetically now. I'd like to know if you're open to the idea of keeping the cottage in the Hilroy family."

"Let's just say I'm listening," said Alfred.

"Good. There are several alternative methods for keeping a cottage in the family. Specifically, the more common methods include giving the cottage to your kids, selling the cottage to one or more children, joint ownership with your kids, willing the cottage to one or more children, or putting the cottage in a trust. These are five ways that title can be transferred." Jeremy had counted off each of the options on his right hand, starting with his right pinkie and ending with his thumb.

"Lots to consider," said Alfred. "Is there any way that title can be transferred without incurring any tax?"

"Absolutely not — that is the biggest technical problem with cottage ownership," answered Jeremy. "There are thousands of families in the same position as you. It's funny — people really like to boast about how much their cottage has appreciated in value over the past decade or two. Everywhere — look at cottage prices in the interior of British Columbia, or the Muskoka region, or the Lake District of New York — cottage prices have soared just about everywhere in North America. But, when you really think about it, the increased cost of cottage life is rotten for estate planning. It would actually be better if the cost of a cottage never changed one dollar from one year to the next. Cottages are not considered by most families to be financial assets; they are perceived as emotional ones — a gathering place for families. How do you hand a cottage down to the next generation when it entails a whopping tax bill?"

"Exactly — how do you?" asked Alfred.

"In each of those five ways I mentioned, there are capital gains involved. The amount of the gain is simply determined by taking the fair market value of the cottage at the time title is transferred and subtracting the adjusted cost base — which, as we determined in your case, comes to $87,500."

"So, if the cottage is left in my will, there is a capital gain on my death, right?"

"That's correct. That tax bill owing on that capital gain must come from some liquid assets in your estate, such as bonds, or from your investment account. If needed, some assets would be liquidated to pay the tax before title to the cottage is transferred according to the wishes in the will."

"Liquidated, eh? How very resourceful," joked Alfred, borrowing from *The Wizard of Oz*. "By liquidating, I presume you mean selling off the car, furniture, et cetera. Just curious — what if there is no money to pay tax from the estate? What if I've spent everything on travelling and eating out with Mary Beth and using up crates of golf balls?"

"Then the tax authorities would look to the beneficiaries, who might then be forced to sell the property or somehow come up with the taxes owing. But, in your case, there would be a means to pay tax from the estate. But there are disadvantages to leaving the cottage through the will."

"Do tell," said Alfred.

"First, the cottage will continue to grow in value from now until your death. Hopefully that will be a long time — 20 more years perhaps? That could also amount to an enormous growth in fair market value if the prices of cottages continue to escalate as they have in the past several years. Ouch! By getting the cottage out of your name today, future growth becomes someone else's responsibility."

"So it's kinda like an estate freeze that I hear people talk about."

"Exactly — it is an estate freeze on the cottage. Second, by leaving the cottage in the will, probate and executor fees may be payable on that cottage. Also, if it isn't left to *all* the children and other assets are given to remaining children, it can sometimes be very difficult for the parent to achieve certain estate objectives, such as equalization."

"Why is that?"

"Because each asset has its own cost base and market value, and market values change over time. Also remember that, with a principal residence, the capital gain is usually fully exempt. So you may designate property to each of three beneficiaries based on today's fair market value, but at death each asset will likely have a very different after-tax value. So, if your intent is to leave the same amount to each child, it is easier in my view to put them all as beneficiaries on assets you want to have remain in the family and then have them split the residue of your estate at one-third each. That way you know everyone will receive an equal amount."

"That makes sense to me. What do you recommend, then? What about the trust thing you mentioned?"

"That's one of the other alternatives. To maintain a high degree of control over the cottage, you could transfer owner- ship of the cottage to a trust for the benefit of your three kids. There's a capital gain in this instance also. But I know your family well, and I don't think this is the appropriate solution for you. Typically trusts are used for minors, or financially irre- sponsible children, or children in unsettled marriages. That's not your situation, right?"

Alfred paused a minute before answering. "Maybe it was a concern a few years ago, when Judy was still acting like a hip- pie come lately and Bev was going through a bad marriage. But they're over that, and, besides, they're in their 30s and 40s now. Maybe a trust set up 10 or 15 years ago but not now. I guess my decision to sell the cottage was based on the notion that I was avoiding a huge tax bill and relieving my children — and myself too — of the stress of coming up with all that money. Let's discuss the gifting alternative you mentioned before."

"All right," said Jeremy. "Frankly, this is the alternative I recommend for you. Give the cottage today to the three kids equally. As I said before, any *future* growth in the value of the property would be taxed in the hands of the new owners — the children. But here's my idea. It won't exactly be a gift. Alfred, I recommend that you sell the cottage to your children."

Alfred had a puzzled expression. "But I thought that we just established that the kids can't afford to pay for it now?"

"So you believe. Even if they are able to buy it, what you do here, Alfred, is" — Jeremy leaned forward in his leather office chair, which squeaked slightly — "take back a demand loan from your kids."

"A demand loan?"

"Yes, old boy. Since you are selling the cottage, the transfer would trigger capital gains, but with a demand loan you aren't receiving the proceeds right away, correct?"

"Okay, so what good does that do?" asked Alfred.

"Simple. There's a special rule in the Income Tax Act, and there's a formula too, but you don't need to know that much detail. Suffice it to say that, when you sell a capital asset with a gain, and you don't receive all the proceeds immediately, you can spread some of that capital gain over a maximum of five years."

Alfred's eyebrows went up, and they were more noticeable than usual because, with all the recent stress and shoulder pain, he hadn't bothered to trim them. "So, by granting a demand loan, I'm not receiving any cash from the kids, correct?"

"Correct — at least not right away," said Jeremy. "And, if you're not collecting any cash on the sale, then the entire capital gain, not just a portion, can be spread equally over the ensuing five years."

"When do I collect on the demand loan?" asked Alfred, still looking doubtful.

Jeremy just held up his hands, palms facing the ceiling, and shrugged his shoulders.

"What do you mean you don't know?"

"You leave it as a demand loan until your kids can afford to repay."

"So what happens if they can never afford to repay?"

"Then you have the flexibility to forgive that demand loan in your will."

"Flexibility won't be one of my strengths when I'm freshly dead. Although I know what you mean. Do I charge interest on that loan?" asked Alfred.

"That's up to you. If you do charge interest, however, you must claim on your tax return any interest received from your kids on the loan. The problem is that if the kids pay you annual interest, they cannot deduct that amount for tax purposes."

"Why can't they deduct it?"

"Interest can only be deducted generally on amounts paid with respect to a loan that was incurred for generating regular income. For example, interest paid on a loan for investment purposes — that's okay because in most years you are reporting some income from those investments. But because a cottage doesn't generate income, your kids would not be able to deduct any interest paid to you."

"Interesting."

"Now I know that you need not worry about loss of ability to use the cottage. You are a tightly knit family. However, by using a demand loan, you do have the option of retaining control over the cottage since you can demand payment at any time."

"Sounds good. So what are the figures, then?" asked Alfred.

"Let's say you do that today. The fair market value is $350,000 less the adjusted cost base of $175,000. As we said earlier, the capital gain becomes $175,000, and the taxable capital gain is $87,500. So we then spread that taxable gain over five years, and you end up with a taxable capital gain each year to report in your tax return of about $17,500. Your marginal tax rate is about 40%, so the tax you actually have to pay on that comes to roughly $7,000 each year."

Jeremy remained silent for a moment, letting the numbers sink in.

Then he said, "But the best news, in your case, old buddy, is you won't owe anything in the first year and very little in the second year."

Alfred scrunched up his formidable eyebrows. "Qu'est que c'est? Je ne comprend pas."

"Remember the stock we sold last year at a loss?"

"Oh yeah, how could I forget? How much was that loss exactly?"

"The full capital loss was seventy grand and the allowable capital loss, at 50%, was thirty-five grand."

"But you already did something with that, didn't you?"

"Not completely. The rules with capital losses are that, if you have an allowable capital loss in a year, you must net that loss against any taxable capital gains in the same year. If you still have a loss remaining, like you did, it is called a net capital loss. This loss cannot be used against other income. You have the option of taking that net capital loss back to any of the three preceding years and using some or all of it in any of those years against capital gains that you had already reported. In your case, I was able to use $5,000 and claim it against a taxable capital gain you reported three years ago."

Alfred was very interested in these numbers. "And then what about the remaining $30,000 — do we lose it?"

"Well, first I'll explain the general rule. Any remaining net capital loss that you cannot or you choose not to use up in the three preceding tax years can be carried forward indefinitely to be used only against future capital gains. So, in your case, you are still sitting with a $30,000 net capital loss to be used up in any future year or number of years."

"So you're saying that this amount almost offsets the first two years of tax on the cottage."

"Exactly. The year of sale your taxable capital gain of $17,500 is completely offset, and, in the first year after the sale, you still have $12,500 remaining of the net capital loss. So, in that year, you would report a net $5,000 taxable capital gain, with tax owing of about $2,000. So it therefore wouldn't be until the second year after the sale that cottage tax bill for that taxation year would appear at the $7,000 mark."

"I wonder, though, how it would feel to be a guest in my own cottage if I no longer own it."

"Nah, hogwash. Listen, Alfie, Kay and I did this with our kids, and absolutely nothing has changed. Even though title to our farm passed to the two kids three years ago, that is just a formality. We still hold say in what gets done up there, and we go up there every weekend just as we always did. And in your case — there's a lot of respect from your kids — you don't, in my view, need to worry about feeling like a guest."

"Thanks, Jer. Well, that gives me something to chew on."

"One more thing. When dealing with your cottage, whatever you decide, this subject demands an around-the-table discussion. It is one of the more difficult areas of estate planning. You must flush out long-term intentions of your children for cottage use. And . . . no more sudden, out-of-the-blue, shock announcements."

Chapter 23

GETTING IT DONE

"HILROY, HILROY, HILROY, let's see, here it is," said Jeremy, producing a file folder and plunking it down on his desk. "Have a seat, Alf. I'm glad we're finally getting around to this piece of business. You'll breathe easier afterward."

"I know, I know," said Alfred. "I should have done this sooner — but the horses are still in the barn, with no harm done yet."

"Right. First, let's do your financial power of attorney. We should review what that means."

"That's a good idea — I didn't pay much attention earlier."

"A financial power of attorney is a document that grants another person or persons the right to manage your affairs on your behalf while you are alive. Basically there are two kinds of financial powers of attorney or P.A.s for short: a *continuing* P.A., which is very general, authorizing the named persons to do almost anything you can do; the other kind is a *restricted* power of attorney." Jeremy emphasized "restricted," almost rolling the *r*.

"Explain what you mean by 'restricted,'" said Alfred, sitting forward in his chair.

"Certainly. The name might vary from province to province; for example, it might be referred to as a *limited* power of attorney in some provinces. But basically, with a restricted power of attorney, you can name someone to act on your behalf solely with respect to a *specified* matter. For example, you could have a restricted power of attorney document just for the closing of a house if you are away on vacation. Or if you are away for an extended period of time — say more than six months — you can restrict someone to act only for that specified time period."

"So, in my case, I'll need a restricted power of attorney that allows someone to act on my behalf only when I become incapacitated?"

"That is incorrect, sir," said Jeremy, imitating a Regis Philbin-like game-show host.

"Here we go again," said Alfred, pinching the bridge of his nose with his thumb and forefinger.

Jeremy produced his familiar guffaw. "The term 'restricted' or 'limited' only applies to a specific event or time frame — these types of limited attorney powers are generally not valid in the case of your mental incapacity. Unless your power of attorney document contains the correct language, it will be automatically revoked by mental incapacity."

"That seems silly — isn't that why we have them drawn up in the first place?"

"It is, but let's say you get bonked on the head again, this time by a wayward golf ball on our 13th tee, and bundled off unconscious in the greenskeeper's cart. If you want your power of attorney to continue to be valid after you've been knocked out cold, it must contain the correct wording so that the document *continues to be valid* beyond your mental incompetence. So I recommend that you have the first type of document I mentioned drawn up — a 'continuing financial power of attorney.' It allows you to choose a person to deal with your property if you lose your mental competency and cannot do it yourself. The word *continuing* simply means continuing beyond incapacitation."

"Okay. I already have a power of attorney at Empire Bank. I've appointed Mary Beth on that one. Isn't that good enough?"

"No. You see, the power of attorney document that you signed at the bank is likely limited to dealing with matters at that particular bank. It will be of no use in dealing with other property. For example, if you were still in a coma in the hospital now, that power of attorney would be useless in terms of having some of your stocks sold, which you hold at a discount broker, not your bank."

"All right, so I need another one. Whom should I appoint as the attorney?"

"I can't answer that for you. The person you choose must be someone whom you trust, who understands your personal values, and who will follow your instructions."

Alfred pursed his lips but said nothing.

Jeremy continued, "And, if you haven't left detailed instructions, he or she will need to make decisions based on what's in your best interests and must stand up for your wishes."

"Can that person make decisions concerning my will too?"

"No. Not at all. The person you name on this document can make almost any financial decision except preparing or changing your will." Jeremy paused momentarily. "And decisions concerning medical treatment are addressed in a separate document."

"What sort of duties am I giving this person the right to do?" asked Alfred.

"Locating assets and debts, collecting income, paying bills, managing investments, filing tax returns —"

"Taking care of the hockey playoff pool," added Alfred.

"Sure, any money stuff like that. And the person you name is expected to maintain good records and consult with you, if possible."

Alfred shuddered slightly. "Yikes. Naming the wrong person to act as attorney could lead to some major abuses of power."

"Indeed. I know of another advisor's client whose mother died after a long bout with cancer. The client's brother had power of attorney at the bank for the mother. The client believed that some money had gone missing from the bank account. She wanted to know what she should do. She was told that mismanagement with a power of attorney can happen. And it does happen — it is open to abuse. Unfortunately I have seen abuses of powers of attorney by business associates as well as family members. What if that person you choose decides to access your funds, buy himself a new Cartier watch, and go on an extended trip to the Fijian Islands? So I always tell my clients that the powers they are giving someone should not be assigned lightly."

"Well, that would be Mary Beth or any of my three kids. But because Mary Beth is the closest to me now and understands my wishes — after all, she will be my wife — I suppose I should name her. Or what if I name more than one person?"

"Yes, that's often a good idea too. You might also consider appointing more than one person — let's say you appoint your two daughters and Mary Beth. You can put 'joint and several' so that all three of them can act in your best interests either together (joint) or alone (several). But it's important that they communicate and get along with each other. Putting those three as attorneys on your document is not the best way to bring together people who, shall I say, are not the best of buds, at least not yet."

"Right. I suppose that could be a recipe for disaster with those three, couldn't it?"

"Quite possibly, old boy. There is also one other option I haven't mentioned. You can also consider a professional who handles complex estates such as yours. Your affairs are a bit complex. There is the matter of your kids and Mary Beth getting along. Such a professional will be experienced in all your business needs — and impartial. You just need to shop around — I can help you with that."

"Let's get started, then," said Alfred. "I'm now a man of action!"

"Wait a minute. You need to give thought to *another* power of attorney document along with the continuing financial power of attorney. Here in Ontario, we call it a 'power of attorney for personal care.' Some provinces refer to it as a 'healthcare directive,' B.C. refers to it as a 'representation agreement,'

Quebec a 'health-care proxy.' In practical terms, they're all the same document providing guidance with respect to health-care wishes."

"You mean a document stating whom I'd like to give me sitz baths and find and install my dentures when I'm no longer able?"

"A little more important than that. But it's a very significant document nonetheless. There are many places — hospitals, nursing homes, for example — that require this type of document. And, of course, with an attorney for personal care, there can't be a professional trustee — the attorney you appoint really must be a trusted family member, one who will make decisions based on your wishes. And bear in mind that the attorney for personal care doesn't have any authority to make these decisions for you unless you really are incapable of making a medical decision yourself. Do you want to live hooked up to a machine when there's no hope of survival?"

Alfred laughed. "Only if the machine can be programmed to rub my feet every hour."

Jeremy continued. "It's a good idea in this document that we specify what you mean by 'quality of life.' I'm reminded of the 84-year-old retired nurse who, while still in good health, had the words *Do Not Resuscitate* tattooed on her chest."

Alfred grinned. "Maybe I should have 'Resuscitate' tattooed on me, with the 'Do Not' to be added later. I'm having too much fun right now. But I know what you mean; it's for really grave situations late in life. Does the doctor have to follow the instructions in the document?"

"Yes and no. Basically the Canadian Medical Association

supports powers of attorney for personal care. In some cases, some doctors may fear being charged under the Criminal Code — but only in instances where someone has put down his or her wishes that involve clearly unsanctioned behaviour, such as assisting with suicide. When you direct that you do not wish to be kept alive by heroic measures, that will be respected."

"I can just see them now squabbling over my bedside. One opting for cryogenics, one for mummification, one for regular burial."

"You're such a cutup, old man. Can I get you to think about both types of documents now and whom you would like to name?"

"Let me sleep on it one night, and I'll let you know tomorrow, s'all right?"

"Fine. As for your financial power of attorney at Empire Trust you'll need to have some forms completed at Empire. I have a contact there and would be happy to set up an appointment. But really, before we make that appointment, you need to decide if you would also like Empire Trust to be the executor or co-executor of your will."

Jeremy took out Alfred's old will from the folder, prepared not quite a year before Joyce's death. He turned the document around and placed it on the desk in front of Alfred.

Alfred examined the last will and testament and thought of Joyce, how she'd cajoled him to get their wills done. Maybe she had a premonition, he thought, smiling to himself. He could barely remember having signed it, but there it was, on his friend's desk, his signature with a flaring *y* at the end, preceded by Jeremy's more subdued, legalistic-looking autograph. Alfred tried to push thoughts of Joyce to the back of his mind. "Oh. Another exercise in morbidity?" he asked casually, glancing up at Jeremy.

"What would Joyce's advice be to you?"

"But that's just my point. It seems as though making a will is a bad omen. I mean, it was just 10 months after we redid our wills that Joyce died suddenly, unexpectedly. I really don't want to deal with my own mortality, when it comes down to it."

Jeremy cocked his head to one side. "Is that what is bothering you? Superstitious twaddle? It's precisely because it isn't just the little old lady down the street who dies that we all need wills. Remember, if you and Joyce hadn't done these when you did, her death could have had devastating consequences, compounding your grief with a whole pile of other headaches and problems for you and your family."

"I know, I know, it's just. . . ."

"Signing a will won't hasten your death. But it will prevent you from leaving Mary Beth, Judy, Bev, and Mike to mourn more than just your passing."

"But I'm not even married yet. Don't we need to wait until Mary Beth and I are betrothed?"

"No. You see, as long as your will states that it was written *in contemplation of marriage to Mary Beth*, then we don't need to write a new will after your marriage."

"Egads. I'm starving. Let's continue over a sandwich at La Gamboni, what do you say?"

"Fine. But no more postponement — we're getting your will done, and that's final."

Alfred snapped off a salute at Jeremy. "Yes, sir!"

◌◦◌

"Alfred, here are two statistical facts for you to chew on," said Jeremy, smiling at Jenny the waitress as she plunked down two glasses of water beside the already ordered wine.

"What? Where?" asked Alfred, feigning confusion.

"Second marriages," pronounced Jeremy, placing the top layer of bread back on his sandwich. "I have a lot of clients on their second or even third journeys through marital bliss. Listen to this. In Canada, almost half of all marriages now end in divorce. In the U.S., one in every five marriages involves not one but two divorced spouses!"

"Thank goodness," exclaimed Alfred, "Mary Beth and I aren't candidates for those statistics."

"Oh?" asked Jeremy.

"Because I'm not divorced — I'm a widower. As for Mary Beth, she's from Australia."

Jeremy sighed. "I'm just making the point that you must think about the end of a marriage almost as much as the beginning, however unromantic or unsavoury that may be. Have you given thought to a marriage contract?"

"No. Er, yes. And we aren't doing one."

"Very well. In that case, as we do your will, we must address the subject of property division and distribution."

"Okay. I suppose it is a good idea that I do my will now," conceded Alfred. "After all, with all the agony and stress in my life over the dissension in my family, I might just seize up and die any day."

Jeremy chuckled. "You're too fit for that, old boy. But your first decision: whom do you wish to appoint as executor?" asked Jeremy, running his forefinger over the rim of his wine glass.

Alfred sighed. "It was easy the first time around."

"Yes, much easier then. You and Joyce simply appointed each other as executors, which is very common in simple first-marriage situations. Now things are a bit more complicated. You really need to understand how important the role of executor is."

"It's just the person who distributes my assets according to the instructions in my will, no?"

"Yes, but it's more than that. Here's a pamphlet on executor duties." Jeremy extracted a booklet and handed it to Alfred. "It's not exciting reading, but it's certainly not as complicated or dense as the *Rules of Golf*. You'll be surprised at the amount of work that the job involves. As with a power of attorney, an executor appointment shouldn't be taken lightly. The optimal person for this job is someone whom you trust completely and who has the financial and business sense to manage and distribute your assets. Someone who has never filled out a tax return might not be the best answer."

"Mike probably has the best business sense for that responsibility," said Alfred, looking around for Jenny, who was known to disappear longer than he liked.

"True. Problem is Mike lives in British Columbia. A sole executor from out of province will have to post a bond since the jurisdiction over executors is provincial."

"How about you? Why don't *you* be my executor?"

"Aha!" said Jeremy, making a quick gesture and knocking over the pepper shaker. "Good question. I'm not the best choice either because, don't forget, I'm not exactly a svelte spring chicken. I'm 65 years old and could die before you."

"So what would happen then?"

"Then, believe it or not, the executor of my will could end up handling your estate too! Not necessarily a good situation."

"Yecch. So that leaves Mary Beth, Judy, or Bev as my choices. None of them has great experience in business matters, but they're smart enough to get by."

"And there are other considerations," said Jeremy, using his thumb and three of his fingers to emphasize each point. "Are they willing to accept the job? Do they have time to do the job? Do they all get along? Are they able to handle the significantly large responsibilities? Anyone who has ever acted as an executor will confirm that it's a job and sometimes not a well-paid one at that."

"How onerous is it?" asked Alfred.

"Quite. Some of the more common duties are arranging the funeral; acting as trustee and managing the assets for the benefit of the beneficiaries; closing the deceased's accounts; cancelling the driver's licence, telephone, cable, credit cards, et cetera; reviewing all bills and bank statements and getting a value of the investments and RRSPs or RRIFs; contacting insurance companies; obtaining deeds for real estate; settling all bills of the estate; filing the tax returns; establishing any testamentary trusts that have been set up according to the will; telling the golf club they have one less member to whine about fees, but could they please prorate and refund his unused annual membership dues? —"

"Okay, I get your point."

Jeremy barrelled ahead. "Oh, there's more. An executor has to be prepared to do a lot of administration and deal with lawyers, Canada Customs and Revenue Agency, accountants, creditors, beneficiaries, appraisers, you name it. Also, before all the assets are distributed to beneficiaries, an executor has to obtain a clearance certificate from the CCRA, or else he or she can be personally liable for the tax bill."

Jeremy reached for his glass, thirsty after his talk. He remained quiet to allow Alfred to chew on his thoughts.

Alfred looked deep in thought. "Maybe, then, Mary Beth is the best answer."

"Maybe, maybe not. If there is any chance that she might make a claim against your estate under family law, there would be a potential conflict of interest between her role as executrix and her spousal entitlement."

"Why would she?"

"If, under family law, her entitlement to your estate amounts to a greater sum than what is left under your will, then she could make a claim under the Family Law Act. A lawyer might present her with the options at the time, and it's up to her to choose. This is just hypothetical — I'm not suggesting that she would necessarily do this. We have to look at all angles. But we don't know — we never know — what will happen down the road. And, despite what Mary Beth agrees to now, she could change — especially after you're gone."

Alfred decided not to argue the point. As much as he hated to admit it, on a deeper level he didn't entirely disagree with what he was hearing. "It doesn't look like there is anybody to appoint, unless I appoint Bev only or Bev with Judy."

"You could appoint all three of your kids — that keeps it equal. Even though Mike is out of province, Judy and Bev could do most of the work."

Alfred frowned. "But then Mary Beth might not be happy. Maybe I should consider a professional executor."

Jeremy nodded. "That works too. And appointing a family member to work with the professional executor is a great idea for you to consider because the family member understands the family situation and the professional can handle the administrative and legal requirements of the job."

"What do I have to pay for an executor?"

"Good question. You don't pay anything now. Compensation occurs after you die. First, remember that any executor is legally entitled to receive compensation out of an estate. But family members, especially if they are beneficiaries, don't usually charge trustee fees."

"That makes sense, or else it would be like taking from the right pocket and stuffing the left pocket. What about the cost of a professional executor, then?"

"In most provinces, an executor's entitlement to compensation is established by legislation. The professional executor is entitled to take a percentage of the assets administered under your estate. But generally this fee guideline accepted by the courts today is up to five percent. Some trust companies have their own tiered fee schedules. Your estate is substantial and it is likely the trust company will negotiate a lower fee."

"Five percent in my situation is a ton of money. I hope I get a lot of service for that. Speaking of service, where's Jenny?" Alfred looked around plaintively for their waitress.

"Generally the trust company will do a personal inventory, provide ongoing consultation, and administer the estate after you go. Also, because Empire Bank currently manages most of your accounts, Empire Trust may charge you less than the legal maximum."

"What happens if the person who is assigned to my estate leaves his or her job?"

"Oh, the trust company will automatically assign someone else to handle the job. These are all good questions, my boy, and it's best if we get these answered at Empire. I will set up the meeting, but for now let's get the rest of your will done."

"Then let's do that. I would like to name Empire Trust as a co-executor with Bev," said Alfred with an air of formality.

"Remember, before we formalize this document, you should talk to Bev first to see if she is willing to accept the responsibilities. And don't forget to discuss all these decisions with Mary Beth too!"

"I will. In fact, I plan on having all my kids over soon to discuss everything. I'll let Mary Beth know all the details before that."

Jeremy and Alfred discussed remaining details of Alfred's will over dessert and coffee, which finally arrived, prompting Alfred to mutter that his "tip meter" had just been adjusted downward. Jeremy outlined further options for Alfred to consider, including life insurance policies and ways of reducing income taxes and probate fees. Although Alfred didn't reveal this to Jeremy, lately he had thought quite a bit about his will. He was prepared for this "will-making session" because, while in the hospital, he had mulled over various arrangements and combinations of legacies and bequests. For this reason, Alfred reached a final will draft quite quickly. After a brief fight over the tab (won by Alfred), including the proper tip to award the always morose Jenny, the two good friends made plans for their next get-together.

Just before he set out down the street to walk to the public transit, Alfred turned to look at Jeremy. "It's amazing, but it's like how you feel after cleaning out the garage or after finishing a workout you didn't want anything to do with. You feel a lot better!"

Chapter 24

A PEACE OFFERING

BEV OPENED THE DOOR of La Palazzo Trattoria and walked in off the rain-slicked street. The restaurant was jammed; Bev cast her eye over the crowd, wondering if Judy and Mary Beth were already seated. When Mary Beth suggested that the three women get together for lunch, Bev was sure that Judy would decline. Much to her surprise, Judy had agreed, after considerable thought, to come along. But Bev didn't want to leave her sister and Mary Beth alone together if she could help it. She approached the maître d', who was standing behind a podium at the front of the room.

"Hello, yes, table for three at 12. Hilroy is the name."

The maître d' showed her to a booth and took her coat and umbrella. Bev opened the newspaper she'd brought with her. She skimmed the same article several times, looking up frequently to glance at the door. The clock showed 12:07. Bev began to feel anxiety whispering through her bones. Would Judy show up? The thought of Judy standing her up stuck in Bev's throat like a tiny morsel of food — not enough to make her choke but enough to be annoying.

Mary Beth arrived next. Her latest outfit consisted of a long-sleeved, ribbed black turtleneck, hip-hugger jeans with a wide black belt, and black chunky-heeled boots. After a few pleasantries, Mary Beth took the seat opposite Bev.

Bev breathed a sigh of relief as she caught sight of Judy pushing her way through the door. Judy walked determinedly across the room and without hesitation took up her position next to Bev.

Bev and Mary Beth chatted absently; Mary Beth, as usual, did most of the talking — about the weather, her trip, Carling. Judy remained silent for the most part, smiling occasionally, her smile never quite reaching her eyes. So far so good, thought Bev. Judy is trying.

Mary Beth suggested a glass of Chardonnay for everyone. "If I drink this stuff at night," she said, "I find it promotes the most vivid dreams. Why, last week, I had this amazing sequence where I'm a high-wire acrobat inching my way across the Horseshoe Falls."

Bev saw Judy start to open her mouth and expected her to ask Mary Beth if she was just the top part of a human pyramid balancing on the wire, supported by a cluster of Hilroy family members. But Bev deftly turned the conversation to other matters until the Chardonnay arrived.

After they ordered their lunch, Mary Beth took a big gulp of her wine and said, "Thank you for agreeing to meet with me."

"Thank you for inviting us," said Bev.

Mary Beth downed the rest of her wine; Bev noticed her hand tremble slightly when she put her glass back on the table. "Your father is very pleased that the two of you and Mike are coming to dinner this Thursday. He has a lot he wants to go over with you. I've been worried because he's been showing signs of strain the past several weeks. He hates family discord. But he seemed very pleased about the three of us meeting here today. He's not expecting us to come away as best friends, but he would very much like us to try to get along. The wedding is in a couple of weeks, and I'd like to take a stab at making amends. I love your father very much."

Judy remained silent, playing with her fork and making plough lines along the edges of her napkin. Bev motioned for the waiter and ordered another round of wine for the table.

"I'll speak for the three of us — Mike in absentia," said Bev. "I'm sorry about our outbursts at the brunch. Our anger is not directly at you per se, it's just that we have had to endure a lot of changes in the past couple of months."

Mary Beth nodded and fiddled with the bracelet on her left arm.

"That's not entirely true," Judy said. "How can our anger *not* be directed at you? Think about it. You march into our lives barely half a year after our mother's death, our home starts to look quite foreign to us, you wear our late mother's jewellery, and then we're told the cottage we love so much is being sold, probably because you snapped your fingers one day and suggested —"

Mary Beth interrupted, "I can understand how all this must look to you. But I have to set the record straight on a couple of things. First of all, it was never my decision to sell the cottage — your dad came up with the idea after the accident. Of course, I'm sure my stupid boat-driving antics played a big part in that decision."

Judy suppressed a laugh. "It's more than just that. You've done a pretty good high-wire act of financing purchases on Dad's line of credit — a new fancy car and vacations at luxury spas. Nothing but the best for —" Judy stopped mid-sentence and lapsed into silence.

"We're having a lot of fun at the moment," Mary Beth said, "no question about it. I've dated lots of guys in my day, but your dad is streets above the others. He's having fun too, you know. He enjoys spending some money for now, something that he says he is ordinarily not accustomed to. That won't continue forever."

Judy summoned a smile. "He never spent a dime before in his life on frivolous purchases. That's why this all seems so unusual."

Mary Beth shrugged. "He was very lonely when I met him. Aren't you pleased that your dad is so happy?"

Bev answered gently. "Of course — that is what we want most of all. To be perfectly honest with you, we hope that your infatuation with him isn't just temporary. We worry about Dad getting hurt and hope that you're committed and sincere."

"Can I add to that?" Judy said. "Mary Beth, if you are around until the end, that would make us all very happy. The cottage, the house — all that is peanuts compared to the underlying question: will you always be there for Dad?"

"Your dad's passion for life is unparalleled. I don't notice the age difference — he's so interesting, he has a very gregarious nature and a keen mind."

"Oh, you'll feel like that for a while," Judy said. "But have you really considered the age difference? Dad's nearly 70. Soon he'll be demanding dinners at six, while you'll be wanting to head out for a lively meal at eight. He'll need heavy doses of fish oil, flax oil, you-name-it oil, and certain foods will upset his digestion. Most nights he'll be in bed before 10, an orange-flavoured Maalox in his mouth. The state of his bowels will obsess him, and every forgotten name at a cocktail party that he'll make you leave early will be, in his mind, the first stages of Alzheimer's. At some point, he may be reduced to nothing more than a helpless infant. Will you still be there for him then?"

"Why would I not?" Mary Beth asked. "What makes you assume that I haven't thought all of that through? Since you know everything, what happens if it's me who gets sick first?"

"I just worry about Dad," Judy said quietly. "You're a beautiful woman, and I have no doubt that you're half in love with him now. But it will take a lot in the years to come. I just hope that this marriage isn't a mistake. Why don't you be prudent and just live together for a while?"

Mary Beth flinched. "I've been told by friends the younger-woman-older-man syndrome gives off a gold-digger-with-visible-claws appearance. We just need time to prove that this isn't just a passing phase for me. Look, I know you probably think of me as a 'bee' with an 'itch,' but all I can tell you is that I really love your dad and plan to take care of him always — right to the end." Mary Beth took a piece of bread from the basket and spread it with butter. "In the meantime," she continued, "I just ask that you accept our relationship, which is flourishing. I'll make you a deal: if you stop assuming the worst of me, I'll stop assuming the worst of you."

Their food arrived, and the conversation lapsed while the three women concentrated on eating. After they finished their lunch, Mary Beth pulled a box from her purse and placed it on the table beside Bev. She also summoned the waiter for the bill.

"For me? What's this?"

"A belated birthday prezzie from your dad. Go on," coaxed Mary Beth with a quick nod of her head.

Bev pulled the cardboard lid off the box. Inside, to her surprise, was the spider brooch. She looked at Mary Beth, her eyes twinkling with delight.

Mary Beth laughed at Bev's startled look. "Judy mentioned how upset you were when you saw me wearing it at your father's birthday party. Your dad just let me borrow it for the occasion. It's an absolutely spectacular piece, but I never meant to upset —"

"Thank you," Bev said. "Thank you. I'm happy to have this back in the family. Not to say that you're not going to be family. I just mean. . . ."

"No worries. I know exactly what you mean. Right, I'd best be off now," said Mary Beth.

Judy's response was limited to a neutral-sounding "Mmm, hmm."

To Mary Beth, this indicated acceptance; to Bev, it was a signal that Judy would have an opinion on Mary Beth's gesture but not now.

The three stood up to leave after Mary Beth paid the bill. Bev gave her a quick embrace. Judy did not embrace her future stepmother but did summon the good manners to thank Mary Beth for the lunch.

"What do you think?" asked Bev out in the street after they had waved good-bye to their lunch companion.

"Marvy. I'm glad the brooch is back. But there's just one thing. You don't think that brooch is now yours, do you?" Judy's eyes flashed aggressively.

Oops, thought Bev. "You saw it was a gift from Dad, didn't you?"

"For sure, but that's my point. We all know the brooch is one of Mom and Dad's items of sentimental value, or ISVS as businessman Mike likes to call them, so I would feel a lot better if Dad hadn't made a birthday gift of it. It should be part of the inventory that we draw up with Dad, and then, if the brooch goes to you as part of an equal distribution, that's fine with me. Do you see where I'm going?"

"Yes, but I thought you weren't interested in the brooch."

"True — but only as an ISV. But it's also, forgive me, an IFV, an item of financial value. If the brooch is valued at $10,000, then do you think it's wise for Dad to just be giving it away to one of his kids? I think you and Mike would agree that, if Dad did a lot of that with other items, it might get us at each other's throat more so than if he donated the brooch to some museum."

"Judy, my hat's off to you. The brooch as well. I'll talk to Dad. Maybe it's a better idea to get the brooch evaluated and then put on the list along with any other items that interest us, and I include Mary Beth in the 'us.'"

Chapter 25

LAST WILL AND TESTAMENT ALFREDO

The front door of 75 Delmore Avenue was open wide enough to see in. Mike approached first, Bev and Judy instinctively staying back a few feet on the front steps. "Nothing lewd going on in here, I trust?" he said, poking his head around the door.

Jeremy's trademark guffaw echoed in the hallway. "Haw! I wish there were."

"Didn't know you'd be here," said Mike, enthusiastically pumping Jeremy's hand several times.

Bev and Judy followed, each giving Jeremy a warm hug.

"Ah, yes, lad and lasses. I'm here to smooth the flow of information and to answer any of those tough estate-planning questions your dad can't answer — and to enjoy a good meal too, naturally."

"Jeremy allows me to pay off my golf debts with dinners, and he doesn't hesitate to take advantage of Mary Beth's cooking," smiled Alfred.

They moved to the back of the house, Bev and Judy not failing to notice additional changes since their last visit. Mary Beth had continued to assert her own taste. New Oriental rugs had been laid together like a puzzle, and new upholstery had been applied to the den sofa and chairs and decorated with plush down pillows. Coffee table art books dominated the den's table space. More were on the built-in bookcase and were bracketed by new bookends made of green soapstone and shaped like elephants. Judy picked one off the shelf. "I guess these could do double duty as weights for Mary Beth," she said to no one in particular. Two vases of dried flowers completed an overall comfortable effect. The doors to the patio stood open, a light August breeze filtering through the room.

Mary Beth appeared from the kitchen. Judy replaced the bookend with a clunk, pretending to be reading the book titles.

"Hello, Mike, you handsome bloke! And Bev, Judy, it's nice to see you all again."

Mike had the warmest greeting for Mary Beth, a double-cheek kiss, Bev applied a one-cheek peck, and Judy waved a hello from her corner at the bookcase.

"It's barbecue chicken and ribs night," said Alfred, filling in the gap.

"Yes, and barbee sauce made Aussie style," beamed Mary Beth. "Help yourself to drinkies, and we'll be eating within the hour."

"Ow-wa," mimicked Judy after Mary Beth left the room, echoing her future stepmother's Australian accent.

At dinner, they ate and drank at a brisk clip. Judy maintained her decorum and behaved respectfully toward Mary Beth. Bev thought that perhaps their lunch together had improved their relationship somewhat.

Judy helped Mike with the dishes while the others were still on the patio. Mike reached for another bottle of wine to open but was stopped by Judy. "Better keep a cork in it for this meeting, the wine I mean," she said. "For our own good, we shouldn't be slurping more wine than necessary. I don't know about you, but extra vino might make me more lippy than usual."

"Good point," said Mike. "We need clear heads for the next while."

Business began right after dessert. Jeremy retrieved his briefcase and set up shop in the den, where everyone had gathered.

Alfred cleared his throat. "All right, we have coffee and a great ice wine for us, and I thought we could have that in the den while I go over my, um, my will and other documents."

He must be referring to a marriage contract, thought Judy.

Mike chose the wing chair opposite where his father and Mary Beth would sit. He reflected on the ensuing discussion. On the one hand, he was pleased that his father had at last taken the time to draw up proper documents; on the other hand, he was uncertain about wanting to hear the contents. In fact, all three Hilroy children were feeling a similar disturbing mixture of emotions: relief and curiosity, apprehension and anxiety.

Mary Beth was the last to enter the den and sat down beside Alfred on the couch.

He began hesitantly. "Time is moving on. That's why it's now important to discuss the inevitable — my personal estate documents. Being hospitalized for a few days gave me time to reflect." He became philosophical for a moment. "You never know when it's going to be over. Listening to my hospital roommate Jimmy Heim made me realize that much can go wrong in a family. The last thing I want ever to see is a Hilroy family dispute. Jeremy has also convinced me — although it required a whopping deal of patience on his part — that discussing my estate plan is not a surrender to mortality but rather a commitment to a better quality of life. This meeting tonight, therefore, is my catharsis."

Bev proposed a toast in appreciation, with everyone raising a glass except Mike and Judy, who hoisted their coffee cups.

"Jeremy has convinced me that I don't want to die intestate," added Alfred.

"Nobody wants to die on the interstate. Why, I-70 can be . . ." started Mike. He felt glad he'd stopped drinking before dinner.

"I've also discussed the details of my will already with Mary Beth. And, I might add," Alfred said with a hand reached over to Mary Beth's, "Mary Beth has done her own will and powers of attorney with her lawyer. She has also obtained independent legal advice."

Mary Beth nodded. "I'm just here to listen tonight."

"Right, then, here we go," began Jeremy. He took some papers from his briefcase and handed copies to everyone.

"Jeremy has handed each of you two documents," said Alfred. "These are my two power of attorney papers. Everyone here knows why we need these. First take a look at the document titled 'Continuing Power of Attorney.' This is my financial power of attorney."

Alfred gave everyone a minute to look over the papers.

"The person who is appointed to act on my behalf is called the 'attorney.' On this document, I have named two attorneys to act jointly: Mary Beth and Empire Trust Company."

Alfred explained that he wished for his wife to be the co-attorney along with a corporate attorney. He indicated that, with a second marriage situation, his estate settling may not be straightforward.

Jeremy then supported Alfred's decision by explaining the advantages of using a trust company as co-attorney with a family member. He finalized his thoughts. "Essentially, you see, by choosing a trust company, you have the advantage of impartiality *plus* the added benefit of someone with the technical expertise."

Alfred added, "Basically, kids, I feel that with the involvement of a trust company there is no need to add any of you as further attorneys on this document. Too many attorneys could just result in confusion. Questions?"

Mike glanced sideways at Judy, expecting an objection. "I think that makes sense," Judy responded calmly. "I think what's important here is that you have included the trust company as co-attorney. That will maintain objectivity and fairness in all decisions. What happens if there is dissent between the trust company and Mary Beth on a particular issue?" Judy asked.

Jeremy responded. "Good question. Some powers of attorney are 'joint and several,' which means that each of the attorneys can either act jointly (together) or severally, which means independently. But trust companies usually insist that, when they are named with another individual, both must act jointly. So Mary Beth and the Empire Trust Company must act jointly in all matters. If they don't agree on a major issue, generally speaking a trust company might step down or go to the court for advice and direction."

"Hmmm," Judy replied, sitting back in her chair like an MP in the midst of Question Period.

"*I* have a question," said Bev. "Let's say that Dad is incapacitated for a long time — for example, a year or two. Who has the say in what happens to this house?"

Jeremy adjusted his reading glasses. "Let's take a look at Section Four, the matrimonial home. Everybody there? Mary Beth is living in the house so obviously that would be the last asset to be touched; however, the power of attorney document does give the attorneys the authority to sell the house if absolutely necessary. That typically would only happen in extenuating circumstances. For example, if your dad is not expected to regain his mental capacity and money is needed to pay for his ongoing care."

"Then what happens with the money from the sale of the house?" asked Mike.

"It would be used judiciously for the benefit of your father and his property. Remember he's still living at that point — and missing more putts than ever. Money isn't paid out to a beneficiary until death. This power of attorney only allows someone to act in the best interest of the donor, in this case your father. And one more thing; see this clause?" Jeremy held up the document and pointed with a pen. "The attorneys here also have the authority to make gifts to family and or charities should the need arise."

Once assured that everyone understood, Jeremy moved ahead. "Now let's take a gander at the 'Power of Attorney for

Personal Care.' This document gives legal authority to another person to make decisions about personal care if your father becomes incapacitated." Jeremy moved his hands like a practised teacher. "Things like hygiene, health care, nutrition, clothing. As well, medical practitioners will look to the person listed on this document for consent for medical decisions if the patient cannot give consent directly. There is no question in my mind that each of you here understands perfectly the importance of such a document."

Hilroy heads bobbed up and down in confirmation of understanding.

Jeremy looked at Alfred, a cue for him to continue. "The person named in this document is Mary Beth. She is soon to be my wife, and of course, as a spouse, she is the best choice for personal matters. Also, Mary Beth has named me as her attorney in her documents."

Mike was the first to speak up. "Mmm, I see." He pulled at his earlobe. "Another question. Who makes a decision about whether Dad needs to be admitted to a care facility?"

"That's a good one," responded Jeremy. "If your father is incapable of making a decision, consent to place him in a care facility may be given or refused on his behalf by Mary Beth because she is the person appointed on the 'Power of Attorney for Personal Care.'"

For a moment, the only sound was the churn and whine of a neighbour's postdinner lawn mower. Mike didn't agree that Mary Beth should have autonomy to make such a crucial decision. He felt his jaw tighten but knew that he must hold judgement at this point in the proceedings.

Judy, less circumspect than her brother, narrowed her gaze at Jeremy and spoke slowly, which made her voice sound lower than normal. "Shouldn't there be more than one person involved with that kind of power?"

"Why?" asked Jeremy.

"To minimize the chances of a bad decision." Judy looked at Mary Beth. "I'm not suggesting that you would make such a decision hastily, but it would seem prudent to me to have more than one person involved in life-altering decisions."

Alfred answered quickly and firmly, shaking his head. "I have appointed Bev as a substitute decision maker if Mary Beth is for any reason unable to act. But if Mary Beth is capable, I am satisfied that she would act wholeheartedly in my best interest. She is aware of my wishes; we have spoken many times about them. I've always been independent. I have no wish to be parked in a long-term-care facility — I would rather languish at home. And, if Mary Beth needs help managing my serious debilitation, she would be able to access some cash to pay for required nursing care." Mary Beth rubbed Alfred's back. "But I would want that here in my own home," he finished, hoping that Judy would let it go at that.

"Judy, it's often a spouse named on these documents," added Jeremy, noticing the slight edge in her voice. "I'll use Mary Beth in an example. She must consult from time to time with supporting family and friends. She must act honestly and in good faith. If, for some reason, Mary Beth does not act with fiduciary duty and she is found to be negligent by a court, she could be removed from the power of attorney under court order. Those are all very good questions, but we must move on.

You should also be aware that your dad will have a third power of attorney."

"A third?" queried Mike. "I thought you only needed two."

"Most people only need two. But your dad should have another one for his condominium in Florida. You see, his continuing power of attorney is technically acceptable in Florida, but the problem is that it still may not by usable if the person being asked to accept the power of attorney, for example a selling agent for his condo, isn't familiar with the layout or the wording of that document. That person could refuse it — it has happened before. So my suggestion to your dad is to have a Florida power of attorney drawn up by a lawyer in Florida."

"How does Dad do that?" asked Bev.

"When he sashays off to Florida in the winter, he can have it done there. It shouldn't be too expensive; it'll run between $150 and $300 U.S. So far so good. Any questions?"

"Last one, I promise," pleaded Judy. "Can Dad change his mind about any of these documents?"

"Uh-huh, absolutely. On these documents, the first section revokes any previous powers of attorney. Then you just replace the old one with copies of the new one. Simple. Now let's move on to the will, shall we? Actually, before we do, I suggest we all take a quick coffee-nature-wine-whatever-you-need break."

∞∞

"And now the will," said Jeremy, rummaging through his briefcase. He looked like a magician about to produce a rabbit or a dove. "Before I hand each of you a copy, let me say this will was prepared with several objectives in mind. First, we looked at where trusts might be appropriate, and, second —"

"Second," interjected Alfred, "my will's been prepared in a manner that I feel is fair and equitable. I spent considerable time deliberating on how to allocate assets to benefit each of the three of you and also Mary Beth, who will, after all, be my wife very soon."

Mary Beth smiled, a correct, perfunctory, First Lady-type smile.

"And, third," continued Jeremy, "I kept in mind the need to always look for areas where there was an opportunity to reduce income taxes and probate fees."

"That's good," observed Judy. "Wherever we can find a way to dodge the taxman."

Jeremy shook his head. "Not dodge or cheat, Judy, but rather use government-sanctioned tax-planning strategies to ensure that Alfred and the four of you do not pay out any more tax than is legally required."

"Hear, hear," offered Bev.

Jeremy redirected his gaze to the contents of the briefcase. "I have copies for each of you." He handed out copies of a document titled "DRAFT" on the top. Mike felt he could use a cold draft at that moment. "Now, we are going to go through this methodically, and I would ask that we stay together and go through each section piece by piece. Please don't read ahead."

"This feels like school examination time," said Bev.

"Yes, it does require some mental gymnastics," said Jeremy. "Page 1 — the first section revokes all former wills. The next section appoints the executor. Alfred, you can discuss this section."

Alfred took his cue and proceeded. "I have chosen two executors — Bev and Empire Trust. Empire Trust I have chosen for the same reasons I mentioned earlier — they have the technical expertise and objectivity I think are prudent in my situation. I had to choose one person to handle softer issues like sorting through all my personal items and stuff, so I selected Bev to handle that end of things. I spoke at length about this with Mary Beth." Alfred placed his hand on her knee. "The executor of a will is also the trustee of any trusts that are formed after my death. Empire Trust suggested that, because Mary Beth will have a spousal trust, there may be a conflict of interest if she is also acting as executor."

Jeremy removed his reading glasses. "Also, because Empire Trust manages most of Alfred's nonregistered accounts and all of his RRSPs, we have negotiated a slightly lower executor fee than the standard. If there are no questions about executor roles, we can move on to the next section of the will." Jeremy looked around, eyebrows raised.

Mike, Bev, and Judy nodded in agreement — they didn't seem to be unhappy with what they'd heard so far. No fidgeting, no yawning, no running to the washroom in the middle of someone's remarks.

Jeremy kept his eyes on the will document as he spoke. "Remembering others in your will is typically accommodated in two parts of the will. The first part sets out specific gifts of property and cash, and this is where some trusts are set up. The second part deals with the residue, which is the remainder of the estate after specific gifts have been allotted in the first section. We will begin with specific gifts. This is where Alfie should have left me his hi-tech driver and that old hickory-shafted putter."

"No, I think you're getting the Simon and Garfunkel and Smothers Brothers records instead," replied Mike.

"I think Dad's given you enough in betting losses, hasn't he?" said Bev with a laugh.

Judy ignored the light humour, preferring instead to make notes along the margin of the will copy.

Alfred continued. "I didn't feel that there were many items of significance that needed to go directly in the will — including my golf clubs — so I've listed only three. The items addressed here are: to Judy, the signed Robert Bateman print; to Mike, the baby grand piano; and, to Bev, Grandma Hilroy's china and silverware."

Judy looked up from her note making. "Shouldn't *we* be included in how important items are allocated?"

"Uh, Dad, Judy has a good point," said Mike hurriedly before his father could respond. "We thought that, with your concurrence, we could prepare a list of items that we feel are important to the three of us. You could look that over to see if you agree with the list, and then the three of us could allocate them between ourselves. You would, of course, be free to remove any item from the list you'd like to go to someone else. Then they could be itemized in this section of your will. What do you think?"

Alfred pondered the thought. "Well, I'm reluctant to do that because it might lead to squabbles on your part. However, your mother always thought it was important to ensure that you three never squabble over possessions after we're both gone."

Bev nodded her head emphatically. "Mom was right. It will greatly minimize the chance of a dispute. We have an idea on how to do this."

The three children explained their ideas to their father about preparing two lists: items of financial value (IFVs) and items of sentimental value (ISVs).

"Please let us try," Bev said with a calm firmness.

Alfred looked at Jeremy. "It might be possible. But I may want to make changes over the next few years. For example, I may want an item to remain with Mary Beth."

Jeremy shifted his weight in his chair. "It doesn't hurt to go through this process, though. I was going to mention this to you as an option. I have a lot of clients that do this sort of thing. I think Bev is right about a list helping to prevent future disputes. You know, a 'memorandum of personal effects' can be prepared to specifically list those items. Then, when any changes are made to the items on that list, only the memorandum needs to be changed, not the original will document itself. You may not know this but if that memorandum is mentioned in the will, the estate's court will want to see that memorandum along with the will after death. Therefore we will leave reference to that out of the will."

"Sounds good, let's do it, then," conceded Alfred. "As long as I'm involved. Before you begin, though, I would have to tell you which items are to be omitted from that list. I would obviously like to leave some things to Mary Beth."

"Oh?" Judy remarked.

Mike and Bev both wished they were at the dinner table so they could each give her a kick from underneath.

Jeremy quickly answered. "We don't need to go there just now. Let's finish the will first. Alf, do continue."

"The next part involves a bequest I will make to the Canadian Cancer Society by donating my Empire Bank stock which sits in my safety deposit box. Its value today is about $25,000. Not only are there generous tax credits for charitable gifts, but also, if that stock is donated in kind and if the tax rules have not changed in the interim, my estate would only need to include in income 25% of the accrued capital gain on that stock."

Alfred paused to take a sip of his wine. "Next, the following paragraph is where I have authorized my executors to sell whatever assets are still around at the time of my death — specifically the remaining equity in the pharmacy and this house here on Delmore Avenue. Let's leave out the Florida condominium for now. That asset is not in this document because it will be addressed in a separate will that I will prepare when I'm in Florida, along with the power of attorney. In that way, it will meet the requirements of Florida legislation."

Alfred did not look up. "Next, my nonregistered investments. It's my wish to leave Mary Beth enough money so that she is financially taken care of. The value of my investment accounts at both Empire Wealthline and the discount broker is about $250,000 *before tax*. My will specifically directs that title to these accounts, which are now in my name solely, be transferred directly to a spousal trust in Mary Beth's name."

Mike and Bev kept their silence, their eyes fixed on the will document. Judy, in a flat voice, asked what it all meant.

Jeremy took Alfred's cue to provide an explanation. "Let me answer that. A spousal trust protects the capital for the final or residual beneficiaries, that being the three of you. The trust deed stipulates that Mary Beth is not allowed to encroach on the capital in the spousal trust. In the meantime, Mary Beth will have access to all of the income generated from that capital. And Empire Trust will be the trustee managing the spousal trust investments."

"I'm curious — the $250,000 stays intact and doesn't get depleted?" asked Mike.

"That's right," answered Jeremy.

Judy had now turned over the will document and was writing notes on the back.

Bev looked puzzled. "But . . . I don't get it. How will the capital eventually fall to us? I mean, we're essentially the same age as Mary Beth."

"Another good question. The balance of the spousal trust will be split equally among the three of you, or, if one of you does not survive Mary Beth, that third will be paid in equal amounts to your offspring."

"And if I'm gone and haven't sprouted any offspring?" Judy asked, wishing there was a cigarette available even though she quit smoking two years earlier.

"Then that one-third lapses back into the trust, and the capital is split between two remaining siblings, and so forth."

Judy wasn't pleased with this section. She told herself to keep her eyes fixed on the document, her head still, and her mouth shut.

"So . . . that trust could potentially exist for a very long time — conceivably it could exist for, say, 40 years," said Mike, rubbing his chin like a farmer evaluating his livestock.

"That's correct," responded Jeremy.

"But I thought all trusts have to declare a capital gain every 21 years so that assets don't build up indefinitely without the ever-vigilant CCRA wanting its cut."

"I'm impressed you know that tidbit," said Jeremy. "You are correct with that statement except that there is one exception to the 21-year taxation of accrued gains in a trust — a spousal trust. Capital gains tax, if any, is owed when the spouse dies. Then the after-tax amount rolls out from the spousal trust to the final beneficiaries."

Judy's quick mind and wit were at hand. "Mike, it's great you know your taxation of trusts, but there won't be large accrued gains in the spousal trust, so it's a moot point." She overenunciated the t's on the last two words.

"Why?" asked Bev and Mike in unison.

"Because all income generated in the spousal trust will be paid out regularly to Mary Beth. It's her spending money. That capital won't grow much."

"Oh, right."

"I'm going to list a few very good reasons, tax and otherwise, for using a spousal trust," added Jeremy. "From purely a tax perspective, the simplest way to defer taxes on death is to name a spouse or spousal trust as a beneficiary of any asset. So, in this particular case, tax will be deferred until Mary Beth passes on and you three become entitled to the trust's assets." He took a few breaths and continued. "Because of the special rule that allows tax on capital gains in a spousal trust to be deferred until the spouse dies, the best assets to choose to transfer to a spouse are those that have and will be expected to have the largest accrued capital gains. In your father's case, that relates to his investment account at Empire Wealthline and his discount brokerage account. The fair market value of both accounts is now about $250,000, comprised mostly of mutual funds but also a few stocks. He bought those stocks and mutual funds many years ago, so the original cost, or the adjusted cost base in tax terms, is only about $100,000. So, if he leaves these assets to anyone other than Mary Beth, right off the top his estate would have a sizeable tax bill to pay on the growth in those two accounts."

"What would that be, roughly?" asked Mike.

"Getting technical, are we?" Jeremy said, poking fun. "The full capital gain would be the fair market value of $250,000 less the approximate $100,000 cost, which comes to $150,000. The capital gains rules today are that 50% of the gain is reported on the tax return. So therefore $75,000 would be the taxable capital gain, and, assuming the top tax rate at the time of your father's death is still about 46%, the tax comes to about $34,500. Plus keep in mind that, over the remaining years of your father's life, these investments will hopefully continue to grow, so the tax amount at death, assuming that your dad doesn't liquidate any of these investments in the interim, could be much greater."

"Jeremy," said Judy, feeling pleased with her own patience. "You mentioned other advantages of using a spousal trust. What are they?"

Jeremy spoke with cautious precision. "I'll name some for you. Amounts that pass into a spousal trust are subject to probate but only once. You see, when the assets from the spousal trust eventually pass to you three, probate fees are avoided. Also, each year the spousal trust is in existence, it will be taxed as a separate entity, thus keeping taxes down. In other words, Mary Beth benefits from a doubling up on the lower graduated rates of tax. Finally, another advantage to using a spousal trust is that your father wants to make sure that the ultimate beneficiaries are you three children or your offspring."

Mary Beth spoke up, having sat quietly all along beside Alfred. "Of course, I'm not used to the investing side of things. So, having Empire Trust act as trustee, the assets will be professionally managed and invested wisely."

"That's good," said Bev. "Um, Dad, what would happen if you died suddenly before you had sold the remaining equity in the pharmacy or this house here on Delmore?"

"Another good question," answered Jeremy. "The executors in the will, in this case Empire Trust and you, will have authority to sell any asset at your dad's death."

"Actually that is the next area we will address," suggested Alfred, anxious to continue. "Essentially we have covered the first section of the will-specific gifts of property. Let's have a break."

⚬⚬

The group reassembled, with Mike and Alfred slightly behind the others because they were checking up on U.S. Open tennis scores on the Internet and arguing over the relative merits of the Williams sisters.

"Now we begin the second part of the will, which deals with

the residue. The residue amounts to everything left over after specific gifts. I have split the residue of the estate equally among the three of you children."

"I'm confused," interrupted Mike. "What's in the residue? You mentioned that the executor is to sell Delmore, so does the residue include the cash from that sale? The cottage?"

"Slow down a bit, son. We'll discuss the cottage later. The residue in my will contains everything that is left in my will after the charity payment and the spousal trust for Mary Beth."

"That being?" coaxed Mike.

"That includes the proceeds from the sale of this house, the value of the remaining equity in the pharmacy, the value of the shares I own of Mike's company in B.C., about $50,000 in Canada Savings Bonds in my safety deposit box at Empire Bank, and a GIC of about $100,000 at Empire Bank. The GIC and Canada Savings Bonds were purchased with the proceeds from the partial sale of the pharmacy. The rest of the funds were used for general spending money — and the new dock."

"Just a minor clarification," said Jeremy. "First, the residue contains the *full* proceeds from the sale of this house, which are tax free because your father deems this place to be his principal residence. Second, the residue will contain the *after-tax* proceeds from the sale of the pharmacy and the shares in Mike's business. Remember any capital gain that exists with those two investments is taxed if those assets are being either sold or transferred to you children. As for the GIC and Canada Savings Bonds, interest is reported, and the tax is paid thereon each year. Therefore, the total of $150,000 for these two assets represents the after-tax amount."

"Dad, about the pharmacy — I'm confused. I thought you were selling the rest of the pharmacy soon — like in the next two to three years," said Bev.

"Correct — I probably will. The after-tax proceeds from the sale of the pharmacy will be placed in an account at Empire Bank, and I would likely invest the money in mutual funds and GICs. So those monies will still form part of the residue of my will. But, if I start pushing up daisies next week, the executor will have to negotiate the sale of the remaining equity."

"Okay, if I understand everything," said Judy, an encouraging tone in her voice, "that means that the three of us split that residue equally?"

"For the most part," said Alfred. He looked at Bev. "Bev, you have a loan with me in the amount of $25,000, which I plan to forgive in my will. So, in effect, it becomes an advance on your inheritance. Your third of the residue will be less that $25,000."

Bev smiled wanly. "Fair enough," she said.

"Also, I have decided to establish trusts in my will for each of you three and your families. The residue will pass to each of you in a testamentary trust rather than into your names directly because —"

"A what?" asked Judy, her head jerking sideways.

"Just listen," said Bev hastily to her sharp-tempered sister.

Judy felt her cheeks blaze and gripped the armrests covered with Mary Beth's favourite fabric.

Jeremy jumped in. "It's actually a great idea," he said enthusiastically. "With this trust, each of you is both the beneficiary and the trustee. The trust deed gives you the absolute discretion as to how you invest the assets and full access to the capital at any time."

"So why the need for a trust, then?" asked Mike.

"Purely to save money," answered Jeremy. "To save some pennies. You see, by using a trust, you're saving on income tax in two ways. Testamentary trusts are taxed like individuals — that is, on a progressive scale. As a result, we can 'income split' with trusts. Let's use an example that I've already prepared."

Jeremy extracted a sheet of paper from his briefcase and quickly scanned the numbers.

"Mike, let's say you inherit $250,000 outright, you invest it in a pile of good stocks and bonds, and the dividend and interest income from that lump sum generates $20,000 each year for you. Let's ignore the dividend tax credit for purposes of this example. Because you already earn a good living, you will be taxed at your marginal rate, which is almost 44% in British Columbia. Therefore, on that extra $20,000 of income, you would pay tax of about $8,740 each year. But let's look at the other scenario. Let's say that, instead of receiving your inheritance of $250,000 in your hands directly, it is left to you inside a testamentary trust. That capital is still invested in the same stocks and bonds in the trust name, so you are still earning income of $20,000 each year. The big difference is that now the yearly income is taxed inside that trust. The total tax would now be only about 25% or roughly $5,000. So you'd be saving more than $3,700 each year just by having a trust."

Jeremy stopped and let the concept ferment with everyone.

"Cool," said Mike. "I like that. That would essentially pay for a grand vacation for my family every year! Jeremy, you said there were two ways of saving tax with a trust. What's the other?"

"Glad you asked, old boy. Remember that each and every one of us in Canada receives roughly the first $8,000 of income tax free. The beneficiaries of these three trusts are yourselves *and* each of your immediate family members — spouse and kids. So, assuming that your kids have no other income, you can pay about $8,000 of interest income from the trust right into the hands of each of your two children. The trust does not pay tax on that amount paid out, and your kids essentially don't pay tax either because the amount falls within their tax-free personal limit."

Mike looked at the ceiling, drumming five fingers on his chin and calculating. "Shauna isn't working. Can I do the same with her?"

"Absolutely you can."

Mike grinned. "So, in your example, by paying out all of the income of $20,000 each year to Shauna and the two kids, there is no tax to be paid and my savings are now more than $8,500 each year."

"Correct, as long as the three of them have no other income and you pay them no more than the tax-free amount each. So you see the difference? Approximately $8,740 of tax paid on income of $20,000 earned in your name if you are left an amount out-right, and possibly no tax on that inheritance if left in a trust for you and your family and you pay all of that income out to Shauna and the kids each year. Furthermore, if there are capital gains generated on the investment in the trust, each beneficiary can actually receive approximately $16,000 of capital gains tax-free because only 50% of capital gains need be included in income."

"Yes! I really like this part a lot," beamed Mike.

"You would, Mikey," retorted Judy. "I don't have a family, so the benefits aren't the same for me."

Jeremy was anticipating Judy's concern. "Perhaps not as significant at this point. But that trust will still save you in income tax each year versus receiving your inheritance directly in your name. Plus remember your dad isn't going anywhere just yet. And, when he does, it will be a long time from now, and at that time you probably will have a family."

"Perhaps," Judy said without much conviction. "Or just a significant other," she added dryly. Judy didn't agree with Jeremy's prediction, but how could she argue with the future?

"I think this is a great strategy," added Bev quickly, trying to defuse Judy's apparent growing tension. To Bev, Judy looked like an untended boiler in its early stages of overheating. "But . . . I don't understand. If Empire Trust is trustee of these trusts, doesn't that mean there will be restrictions on us accessing capital from the trust if we need the cash?"

Jeremy shook his head. "None whatsoever. The trust deed is written in such a broad way that gives the trustee all the discretion you need to allow you to access the capital in your own trust. There is just a formality in that you need to apply in writing to Empire Trust to access your capital, and therefore there may be a time delay of a week or two. And, if you choose not to take out any income from the trust in a given year, then that's fine too. But the added benefit of having Empire Trust act as trustee is that you have the benefit of Empire's investment management team so that the assets in those trusts are professionally managed."

"That's comforting," Bev said.

Alfred added his own points. "This way you can give your kids some cash from the trust without having them access any capital. I don't know what your kids' financial priorities will be at age 18 or 19, but when you were that age, Mike, your objective in life was to buy a cool car. Remember that brown Firebird with the stripe down the sides?"

"That was my chick magnet."

"It collected a few hens too, I recall," said Judy with a little-sister look.

"Dad," said Bev, "what's the amount in the residue we are looking at?"

"Hmm," Alfred said, studying the ceiling with casual attention, "I knew you'd be wondering that. I don't know what the value of the residue will be when I conk out, but today I gather this house would fetch in the $350,000 range, which, as you know, is tax free. The value of the GIC and Canada Savings Bonds I mentioned is $150,000. The value of the remaining half of my business after tax today is about $250,000. And, Mike, what's the value of the shares I own in your business now?"

"You have about 5,000 shares worth $10 each, so about $50,000. And that's expected to grow too!"

"Good. So, when you total all of that up, it comes to about $800,000 in today's value. That amount will be split equally three ways, and each third will transfer into a trust for each of you on my death. But when I go, which hopefully isn't for a long time from now, that amount could be greater than that."

"Or a lot lower if you spend it all first," pointed out Judy with her usual less than admirable use of tact.

Alfred ignored the raw irritation in Judy's voice. "I'm trying," he responded jokingly but sounded to Judy like a cornered politician at a press conference.

Bev glared at Judy. "It's wonderful you're sharing your plans with us, Dad, in such a clear way."

"So that's the will — or at least everything except the standard legal-speak paragraphs and such," said Jeremy with satisfaction. He looked at his watch. "And it took only an hour and a half. Not bad."

"Dad," said Mike, "you said we could talk about the cottage. What are you doing with the funds from the sale of the cottage?"

Alfred smiled. "I was leaving this to the last. I have good news for you. I'm not selling it." He laughed at the varied expressions he saw around the room: Bev wide eyed, Mike sort of stunned, and Judy with a disbelieving look. "It isn't in the will because I have decided to 'gift' the cottage now to the three of you."

Alfred explained his reasons for the gift, and Jeremy pointed out the tax issues and resulting capital gains reserve provisions that allowed the spreading of his gain over five years.

"So you see," Alfred said, "by spreading my capital gain over five years, and by using my capital loss carry forwards, I can pay the tax on the cottage out of my current earnings from the pharmacy. I plan on working for several more years."

Mike shot up from his chair, letting the will document fall to the floor. Bev and Judy weren't far behind. Mike stood in place, running his fingers through his hair in a kind of happy stupor. "Yesss!" he exclaimed excitedly.

Bev's eyes were bright with delight. "This is the best news of the night."

"It sure is," added Judy, feeling buoyed up after the earlier disappointments.

The Hilroy children immediately dove into an excited discussion on cottage sharing. Alfred sat back in his chair, letting the others release their excitement.

Ten minutes later, Alfred held up his hand to stop the discussion. He spoke slowly, with cautious precision. "I want to manage the cottage succession like a business," Alfred stated authoritatively. "To this end, I would like us to draft a formal agreement, not now but soon, that covers every aspect of our long-term intentions with cottage ownership — stuff like usage, expenses, allowance of guests, that sort of thing."

Judy spoke anxiously. "And that agreement should also stipulate how one of us can break the agreement and how we would be compensated for our share of the cottage should we decide not to go anymore. You never know — one of us could move away."

"Precisely," said Alfred. He then discussed his desire to rent out the cottage from June 1 to July 15 each year to help defray some of the costs. He spoke of designing a system of keeping track of fixed costs versus variable costs. He agreed to pay for the fixed costs, such as property taxes, each year from the rental income he collected. Variable costs, such as hydro and propane, would be split each year between Alfred and the children in relation to their respective times at the cottage each summer. The Hilroys unanimously agreed to take a more businesslike approach to their cottage.

Once the cottage euphoria had dissipated, Judy looked back at the will document and scratched her head. She looked up and narrowed her gaze. "I'm still confused. There seems to be some missing information," she said hesitantly, flipping the pages of the will back and forth. "You had an insurance policy when Mom was around, and I don't see it here."

"I was going to mention that too. I can't find a reference to your RRSP either," added Mike. He put his pencil down and threw an arm over the back of the couch, watching his father placidly, his right leg moving up and down rapidly, a habit from childhood.

Alfred smiled without surprise at the questions. "The insurance policy and the RRSPs have direct beneficiary designations and are therefore not mentioned in my will. Only assets that pass through my estate on death are addressed in the will." He shifted stiffly on the couch, prompting Mary Beth to prop a blue pillow behind his back.

"So who is the beneficiary?" asked Bev.

"Both the insurance policy and the RRSP have Mary Beth designated as the beneficiary." Alfred took a deep breath while he let that information sink in. "Because they are not in the will, those assets have creditor protection, and probate fees won't need to be paid."

Bev bridled at that revelation. Judy reverted to looking like an untended boiler. Mike just stared blankly at his father.

"Uh, what is the value of those two assets?" asked Judy, rubbing her reddened forehead.

"The value of the insurance policy is $100,000. This house, as you know, will be sold at my death, and the proceeds will go to you three. So I would like Mary Beth to use the insurance money to purchase a small condo or townhouse for herself."

Alfred hesitated and then continued slowly. "The RRSP, soon to be a RRIF, currently has a market value of $310,000."

Judy's tone was mild, but her words had a cutting ring to them. "But some of that money was Mom's RRSP which rolled over to you, did it not, on her death?"

Bev winced. The memory of her mother seemed heavy in the presence of the young woman sitting beside her father.

Judy looked at Mary Beth as if she'd just noticed her presence. They held each other's gaze for a moment. Mary Beth's lashes dropped first, and she reached down to give the dozing Carling a pat. Judy did not care to look at Mary Beth again for the rest of the evening.

Alfred cleared his throat. "Yes," he said unforcefully.

Judy looked at Mike, then at Bev, then at Mike again. "Any thoughts?"

Bev glanced at her father. "If I may make a suggestion," she asked politely, "couldn't Mom's RRSP portion be willed to the three of us?"

Alfred answered with calm, genuine authority. "My children, please listen to me." His words were like the careful steps of a man walking a tightrope over the falls, slow and deliberate yet precise. He stared at the fireplace. "RRSPs are another ripe area for tax gathering by the CCRA. If I leave you three any of my RRSP, that amount is deemed collapsed, and the tax hit is similar to one of the shark's bites in the movie *Jaws*." Alfred turned his head slowly and looked at his three children, his eyes weary. "I wanted to take advantage of the spousal rollover provisions. Plus I want very much to provide enough money for Mary Beth to live on comfortably."

Judy laughed dismissively at the handling of her enquiry. "Well, she could get a job."

Alfred put his hand up to his forehead.

"Are you feeling okay, bugalugs?" asked Mary Beth.

"Yes, it's nothing really. Just a mild headache."

"Let me go and retrieve an aspirin for you." Mary Beth headed out of the room.

Alfred smiled at her prompt concern.

"There is just one more thing I haven't mentioned," he continued. "The Florida condo is to be sold at my death, and the funds are to be split equally between the three of you. It's not a lot of money — at the moment, the condo is worth about $90,000 us."

"Does that money go into a trust as well?" asked Mike.

"No, the money from the condo will be paid directly to each of you. Income tax is paid here in Canada on the accrued gain and there may be some U.S. estate tax to pay as well. As I mentioned earlier, the condo will be addressed in a separate will to be handled by an executor in Florida."

"Why might there be U.S. estate tax?" asked Mike.

Alfred looked to Jeremy for the answer. "U.S. federal estate tax is based on the fair market value of the U.S. asset on the date of death. As you know, in Canada we do not have estate tax; rather, we have capital gains tax that is owed on deemed dispositions at death. However, there is a Canada-U.S. tax treaty, which allows you to claim foreign tax credits on the U.S. estate tax paid against capital gains tax owed here in Canada, if any. So what this means is that, on your father's death, there may be U.S. estate tax assessed against the fair market value of the condo at that time, but the foreign tax credit should essentially mean that you are not doubly taxed. So, Mike, in answer to your question, there probably won't be an excess of U.S. estate tax to pay over the income tax owed here. Now, having said that, there are situations where some people owe an excess of U.S. estate tax above what they can offset against Canadian tax payable. We won't really know the full details with the Florida property until later on."

Mary Beth reentered the room with a glass of water and two aspirins.

Alfred took the pills. "I must be getting tired," he said. "So, before we wrap up, just one more thing. As Jimmy Heim suggested, there is no one way to celebrate a life — it can be done simply or elaborately. But funerals are expensive, so I have taken the decision out of your hands and prearranged my funeral with The Other Side Funeral Home just a couple of blocks away."

"How does it get paid for?" asked Judy.

Alfred smiled. "I've prepaid the funeral and cemetery costs. I signed a contract last week with the funeral home — the same day that Mary Beth and I selected wedding invitations! Now that's planning!"

"So everything is taken care of?" asked Bev.

"Yes, my contract guarantees that the prearranged services will be fully paid for. The prepaid funds are put in trust, and the interest earned on that asset remains tax free provided the amount is used entirely on funeral and cemetery costs. I do wish to have a funeral service in a church, so the funds will allow a good-sized funeral. I have also picked my casket, and I chose burial, not cremation. A 'burier,' not a 'burner,' as the old joke goes."

"Do the funds pay for the North African belly dancers that we plan to have at your funeral?" asked Judy.

Alfred laughed along with everyone else. "Sure — anything you wish."

"That's great, Dad. Of course, this is never an easy topic, so maybe it's time to change the subject," said Bev.

Jeremy wrapped up the meeting, making sure everyone understood the information divulged over the evening and making sure to collect the draft copies of the will from everyone.

"You can be proud of your dad," Jeremy said to Bev as she saw him off to his car in the humid August night.

Bev smiled in agreement, then headed back into the house to hug her father.

Chapter 26

THE RIGHT STUFF

MIKE AND JUDY STUDIED the oil portrait of their mother mounted prominently on the wall of Bev's dining room.

"You call that an item of sentimental value, or ISV, as Mike puts it?" asked Judy. "I remember Mom hating it."

"Yes," said Mike. "You can see in her a look of trepidation. She sat for the artist during the Cuban Missile Crisis, and I remember Dad telling us she would come home after a sitting asking if any strategic nuclear missiles would fly that day and whether she should bundle the babies off to the cellar. Dad would watch the nightly news and yell 'Armageddon outta here!'"

"That's why it's sentimental for me and Mike, in an odd sort of way," said Bev. "Let's put it on the list anyway so if either of you wants it we'll sort it out later with the other items. I've had it only since Mom died; it was mouldering away in the basement anyway."

Judy ran her fingers along the frame of the painting. "Mom always said that, after she and Dad were gone, she didn't want us ever feuding over possessions. That's why she would have liked the list idea."

"That's not all," said Mike. "She once said that, if she went first, not to get upset if Dad 'took up' (as she put it) with a younger woman."

"She must have had a premonition," commented Judy. "If Mom could somehow see what's happening now, she is probably taking this whole Mary Beth situation better than me."

The three Hilroy children sat down at the table to look at a computer spreadsheet put together by Mike. Along with their father, they had considered other methods of handling the task of splitting up family items, everything from drawing lots to picking items one by one in order of age, but Alfred had thought they should try the more systematic yet flexible list method. The list was organized by category:

Pictures
China and Silverware
Jewellery
Furniture
Other (e.g., scrapbooks)

Across the top of each category were headings:

Item (ISV, IFV, or both)
Current Location
Family Background
  (e.g., Alf's or Joyce's parents, gift or purchase)
Comments
  (other interesting background info like Joyce's portrait)
Evaluated or To Be Evaluated (if applicable for IFVs)

The final two columns were spaces reserved for the initials of one or more of the three Hilroy children, to be used if the item appealed to them. The last column was for Alfred's initials, to be used for items he'd already designated to others or reserved the right to do so in the future.

"Once we complete this list, we'll send it to Dad for any changes, additions, or deletions, and he can change or update his memorandum," said Bev. "It's a fair bit of work, but it will save a lot of hassle down the road, don't you think? And we don't have to make it as organized as this. As long as we have a list of some sort."

"I can't argue," said Judy. "I don't have the 'lust for lists' that Mom did, but I can see the benefits. If I understand this concept right, we should list as much as possible, no matter where it's located? We're not going to get down to listing wastebaskets or doorstops, are we? What about the pull-out bed Mom let me take a few years ago?"

Mike grinned slyly. "No, the little everyday things aren't necessary. Not unless they have special significance for someone. When I was in Dad's basement last week, a box (yes, a box) of condoms surfaced from under a pile of newspapers from the 1950s. Now this is a case where for Dad these days they're an everyday item and should not go on the list. For me, they're just purely sentimental, even the more modern ones."

His sisters looked at him.

"I kid, I kid!" he said, arms out and shoulders raised. "As for the pull-out bed, Judy, again that's something we can agree not to worry about. This is stuff all of us already have, like the big bookshelf I took to B.C."

"That's fine," said Judy. "What about the more important stuff, such as the, um, spider brooch, which you recall Mary Beth recently handed to Bev rather ceremoniously, I thought. I think it should be on the list as both a financial and a sentimental item. It should be evaluated, and, yes, I would put my initials where the brooch is listed, and I know you will too, Bev. What if Dad then puts down his own initials, meaning it's bound for Mary Beth's bosom?"

"One thing at a time, Jude," said Mike. "If you and Bev both would like the spider brooch, then at the end of the exercise we would go over the list to see how it all looks in total among the three of us. We might make changes, especially if I've asked for $50,000 worth of IFVs and you've got only $10,000. I think we agree we want to split IFVs reasonably equally. You and Bev would have to agree between yourselves about ownership of the spider brooch within that framework. At that point, we may have to further devise a method for ordering our picks within a particular category. Or you could also agree to share something like the spider brooch."

"And Mary Beth?" Judy asked, her eyes narrowing.

"Dad could still designate M.B., thus overriding your agreement with Bev. But you'd have to live with that."

"Besides," said Bev, "I think Mary Beth was pretty sincere about not wanting the brooch."

"And Dad did mention that he only meant to lend the brooch to her," added Judy.

"Again, Judy," said Mike, "you've got to accept the fact that Mary Beth may end up with some of the items."

"OK, but how about all the items now in Dad's house? We

can make up a list now, but how do we know it's complete? Dad told us he listed the baby grand piano, the signed Bateman, and Grandma Hilroy's china and silverware, but he didn't talk about any others. Yet I know there's that armoire that's kind of nifty or that Victorian sofa with bee's fabric."

Bev looked at her younger sister. "Don't you think we sound just a bit, you know, grabby?"

Mike didn't let Judy answer. "Come on, guys, let's stick to the list. No one gets anything, really, until Dad gives his blessing. As long as Dad endorses what we're doing, *I* don't feel grabby. Instead, I feel that we're united as a family and that we're insuring ourselves against future misunderstandings."

"I agree," said Bev. "Having a list endorsed by Dad, which we can refer to down the line, will lessen the chance of any muss or fuss over who wants what."

"Let's keep going," said Mike. "Do you remember that old cribbage board that stood on four iron legs? It's still in the basement, in great shape, with the 1978 Hilroy Cribbage League standings taped to the bottom. That's an interesting one."

"Jiminy, I forgot about that. That was the only time Dad was allowed to smoke a cigar while playing cribbage. He would usually win, while Mom would try to lose to us on purpose," Bev said with a wistful look. "Now that's something that I'd put my initials beside. Or maybe it's better off at the cottage."

"OK, we'll sort out that one once we get the list completed. Speaking of the cottage, what about the items up there?" asked Mike. "Since the property's not going to be sold, hallelujah, perhaps for now we can exclude the cottage from this exercise."

Bev and Judy signalled their agreement.

"I have a suggestion, though," said Bev. "We should still do the ISV list eventually. Even though we have a lot of our own stuff up there, there are still items like the old scrapbooks. In a few years, the ownership situation may change, and we should do the exercise then."

"Put on the list that fridge door handle," said Judy mischievously. She put one elbow on the table and idly scrolled up and down the computer page with her free hand. "Just one other thing. We know the Delmore furniture list won't be too big, because a good chunk of it is now close to land-fill quality. However, there are still some good pieces, like the armoire or the dining room sideboard. You'll agree I'm a bit light myself as far as furniture goes." Judy got up from her chair. "I heard a story in which one child of an aged parent backed up a van virtually in the middle of the night, and off went some of the nice furniture, not for his or her own use, *but for his or her own kids.*"

Bev went a little red. "You're not suggesting —"

"Of course not, silly," said Judy. "I just think it's an interesting phenomenon how one sibling might allocate some items for his or her own kids without consulting the other, innocent or otherwise."

"Well, it's good we're bringing this up now, huh?" said Mike. "Judy is just reinforcing the need for us three to keep the dialogue going, and this list is a good tool for supporting that."

"I still sometimes feel we're all being incredibly rapacious by doing this," said Bev quietly.

"I might agree with you, Bev," said Mike, "but don't forget we would never have thought of this process without Dad's suggestion. None of us is being greedy by being proactive. Picture us a few years down the road and *not* having had Dad and ourselves agree on all the items. Everything might turn out fine by not doing a list. Then again it might not."

"You're right," said Judy. "Better to do this now, then get our suggestions to Dad for his memorandum of personal effects, then forget about it."

With a crack of his knuckles and a long stretch, Mike suggested they get started.

Ninety minutes later, the semblance of a usable list was in place, with the next step being a second meeting with Alfred at his home to complete the inventory of more practical items, such as china. Many of the items had little monetary value, but they all evoked strong memories. Bev came close to getting frustrated when she lost the 1960s Alvin comic books they loved as kids. And they all wanted the wall-mounted deer head, Alfred's only hunting or fishing prize. But the sisters agreed that, since Mike had been with their dad when he'd made his kill, he should be the recipient of that item. And, of course, all three wanted the cribbage board, so in the end they agreed it would go up to the cottage. During this process, they were determined that all viewpoints would be considered. There were compromises and sacrifices, not to mention tears as they listed their mother's belongings.

"True to Mom's wish, there have been no fights yet — well, no serious ones anyway," said Judy, rubbing her eyes from the overflow of memories associated with some of the items. "Bev, you'll see I've put my initials beside yours for the spider brooch. Other than Mike refereeing an arm-wrestling match between us for the brooch, how is this supposed to work?"

"Remember we must complete the list and then have Dad go over it," said Mike. "He may decide to name his own preference for who gets the brooch, or anything else for that matter, but I think he knows we can work out our own arrangements once the list is complete. That may mean factoring in the brooch's monetary value with everything else you've initialled and comparing that with Bev's choices and mine. Where we have overlaps, like with the brooch, then it'll come down to common-sense give and take. If not, then I'll have to set up the arm-wrestling table. But you'll be a bit older and with fewer muscles, because remember this won't happen until after Dad dies."

"I think we've come a long way over the past couple of months. And, with one more meeting, we'll have finished this part," said Bev.

"Because Mom died early, we'll never get to toast Mom and Dad on a 50th wedding anniversary like some families do," said Judy sadly.

"That's right — we'll never get to tell them how, as a testimonial to both of them, we three have been given the best inheritance ever — 'the right stuff,'" said Mike.

"How very true," said Bev. "But we can always toast Dad. And, really, it's our sensible and organized division of Mom and Dad's physical belongings today that provides a testament of having inherited 'the right stuff.' That in itself is a very lasting tribute to Mom and Dad."

Chapter 27

ONE YEAR LATER

The phone in the study rang, and Alfred reached across the desk to pick it up. It was Mike.

"Happy anniversary, Dad!"

"Thanks, son." It was hard for Alfred to believe that a whole year had elapsed since he and Mary Beth were married.

The outdoor wedding took place at Selwyn Gardens on a beautiful Saturday in September. After considerable discussion, Mary Beth had capitulated and agreed to get married in Canada. Her family flew in from Melbourne, and her parents stayed as house guests at 75 Delmore Avenue. The wedding was a fairly modest affair; there were about 60 people in attendance, including all three of Alfred's children and his four grandchildren. Judy was there in a blue dress and a string of pearls that Joyce had given her on her 21st birthday. Alfred's youngest daughter was a bit standoffish at first, but she opened up at the reception and even danced the Funky Chicken with her siblings and Mary Beth.

In the year following the wedding, Judy was a frequent dinner guest at 75 Delmore, and in recent months it seemed to

Alfred as though she and Mary Beth were really beginning to warm to one another. They talked about food and gardening, and Judy even floated the idea of their taking a yoga class together.

"How are you feeling?" Mike asked.

"Like I could go a few rounds with Lennox Lewis," Alfred said. "Okay, maybe not that good, but much better, thanks."

In June, Alfred collapsed one night at the dinner table. Mary Beth immediately phoned for an ambulance. Once he was ensconced in the emergency room at St. Alphonse hospital, Mary Beth called Bev and Judy, both of whom rushed over to wait with their stepmother. After several hours, which seemed to the three women like several years, an emergency room doctor came out and explained that Alfred had suffered a very mild stroke.

"Of course, we'll have to do a series of tests and have a number of X-rays taken," the doctor said. He glanced at the three women. "Who has power of attorney over Mr. Hilroy?"

"I do," Mary Beth said. "I'm his wife."

Judy flinched almost imperceptibly. Bev reached out and placed a hand on her sister's arm.

"Your husband should pull through just fine, Mrs. Hilroy," the doctor said. "The stroke was really very mild. It doesn't look like it was serious enough to do any lasting damage."

"Oh, thank God," Mary Beth said. Fresh tears sprang into her eyes, which were already red and puffy from crying. "I was so scared."

"But," the doctor cautioned, "there is always the outside chance of complications."

Judy sucked in her breath. It had been only a year and a half since her mother had died from complications arising out of a routine appendectomy. If that had been possible, how much more likely was it that her father could succumb after having a stroke? The thought of losing both her parents in such a short space of time was almost more than she could bear to contemplate.

The look in Bev's eyes, like those of a wounded animal, indicated that she was thinking the same thing.

"Mr. Hilroy is unconscious at the moment and is being fed through an IV drip. We have every reason to expect that he will regain consciousness within 24 to 48 hours, but if he doesn't we may need you to make some decisions about his care. Do you understand, Mrs. Hilroy?"

Mary Beth made an effort to stand as straight as she could. "Yes, doctor," she said. "I understand."

After he departed, the three women stood together holding on to each other. They sat there together for the rest of the night, each taking a turn staying awake or going to get coffee.

Alfred regained consciousness 36 hours later. His speech was slurred, but he appeared to be attentive and even laughed when Bev cracked a joke. Mike had spoken to Bev the day before, and she'd managed to convince him that it wasn't necessary to fly in from B.C. just yet. Two days later, Bev phoned him on her cell phone from her father's room, and Alfred spoke haltingly to his son, assuring him that everything was fine and that there was no need for Mike to get on a plane.

Alfred remained in the hospital for a month following his stroke. The day he returned home, Mary Beth organized a party for him at 75 Delmore Avenue. All of his children attended — Mike and Shauna had flown in with their children the day before — and the house was festooned with brightly coloured floral arrangements and balloons. Harry and Megan had painted a large sign that read "Welcome Home, Grandpa"; the large pieces of multicoloured Bristol board hung outside the front veranda of the house.

Thinking back on the experience, Alfred realized how lucky he was to have a family that cared so much for him.

"I've started a regular walking regimen," he said into the phone to Mike. "Nothing spectacular, but I'm up to about half an hour each day. I feel very healthy."

"That's great news, Dad. Big plans for tonight?"

"Mary Beth and I are going to dinner at La Gamboni. It's been a while since I've been out of the house, so an evening out should be just the thing."

"Super. Listen, Dad, I've got to go. Shauna's out with her girlfriends, and it sounds like the kids are getting into a bit of a tiff downstairs."

"Okay, son. Thanks for calling."

"No problem, Dad. Give my love to Mary Beth, and I'll talk to you again soon."

"Bye, son."

"I love you, Dad."

Alfred hung up the phone and sat back in his desk chair. He was thankful that he'd allowed Jeremy to talk him into updating his will and powers of attorney. Fortunately he hadn't needed them in June, but he realized that he was 70 years old and that the day would come when he would. It was comforting to know that his affairs were in order and that his wife and children would be well provided for after he was gone.

Alfred glanced at his watch: 6:30 p.m. The dinner reservations were for 7:30; I should probably think about getting dressed, he mused. He looked wistfully at the picture of Joyce and his three children on his desk. There was now another picture beside it. Inside a simple silver frame, the image of himself with his new wife stared back at him. The picture had been taken on their wedding day. Surrounding the happy couple were Bev, Mike, and Judy. Alfred picked up the picture, taking off his glasses to get a closer look. In it, all five people were smiling broadly.

ALFRED'S GLOSSARY OF ESTATE PLANNING TERMS

Adjusted cost base: The cost of a capital property for tax purposes. Cost is the original purchase price plus certain additional costs of improvement. (Pages 220–221)

Alter Ego Trust: A personal trust created by a taxpayer 65 years of age or older whereby that taxpayer is entitled to receive all of the income of that trust until his or her death. An alter ego trust may provide for the trust capital to be passed to other beneficiaries on the death of the settlor. The tax treatment of an alter ego trust is similar to that of a spousal trust. If two persons wish to set up this type of trust it is refereed to as a 'joint spousal or common-law partner trust.' (Pages 13–18)

Annuity: A contract that provides for a series of payments to be made or received at regular intervals. (Page 89)

Attorney: The person(s) named in your financial or medical powers of attorney who has the power to act on your behalf. In this instance, the 'attorney' does not refer to a lawyer. (Pages 105–106, 189, 233–235)

Beneficiary: A person who receives a benefit under a will, an RRSP, insurance policy, or a person for whose benefit a trust is created. (Pages 54, 59, 86–91, 99, 260)

Bequest: A gift of property made in a will, for example a specified amount of cash or a specific item of personal property. (Page 268)

Capital Gain: A profit reported on an asset that is disposed or 'deemed' disposed of. (Pages 223–229, 270–271)

Continuing Power of Attorney: A Power of Attorney that contains a continuing clause so that it continues beyond incapacitation. (Pages 231–233)

Deemed Disposition: A procedure whereby Canada Customs and Revenue Agency deems that you have disposed all of your assets even where no actual sale took place. This happens on certain title transfers, death, and emigration from Canada. (Page 18)

Estate Freeze: A legal procedure which limits the growth in the freezor's estate by diverting the growth in the estate to a subsequent generation. (Page 224)

Estate Trustee: The legal term in Ontario for executor (see below for definition). (Page 14)

Executor: Person or trust company named in the will to follow out the instructions in the will the testator (person who made the will) dies. (Pages 14, 86, 91, 240–244, 264–265)

Fair market value: The price that a seller would get for an asset if he/she were to sell it to an arms-length buyer (not related) on the open market. (Pages 224, 227)

Fiduciary: an individual or institution under a legal obligation to act for the benefit of another party. (Page 262)

Guardian: The person(s) named in a will to act as the legally responsible guardian for the minor children in the event that both parents are deceased. (Page 190)

Inter Vivos trust: This type of trust is one that is set up during the lifetime of the settlor. This type of trust is taxed at top marginal rates. May also be referred to as a 'living trust.' (Page 13)

Joint Tenancy: An asset that is owned jointly with one or more individuals. Could be 'joint tenants in common' whereby an asset is divided at death according to the respective owner-ship of each party or 'joint tenants with rights or survivor-ship,' where in most cases, full title to the asset is transferred to the surviving joint owner(s). (Pages 98–105)

Life Insurance: An important aspect of estate planning. Life insurance provides protection against economic loss caused by the death of the person insured. (Pages 11, 115, 244)

Power of Attorney: A written document by which you appoint someone you trust (called the attorney) to manage your affairs on your behalf. A power of attorney is com-pletely different from a will — the authority given to the attorney in this document is valid only while the grantor is alive — a power of attorney ceases to be valid in death of the grantor. There are different types of powers of attorney; some deal with limited circumstances, some general finan-cial issues, and others with health care issues only. (Pages 105, 188–192, 231–237, 260–263)

Power of Attorney for Personal Care: A document which gives your stated representative the authority to make deci-sions concerning your personal care should you become incapacitated. This document also may include 'living will' instructions which allow the individual to convey their wishes with respect to procedures used to prolong life in the event of terminal illness

Some other terms applied to this document include: a 'healthcare directive' in several provinces, a 'representation agreement' in B.C., and 'health care proxy' in Quebec. (Pages 235–237, 260–262)

Probate: A process whereby an application is made to the court to obtain a 'Certificate of Appointment of Estate Trustee with a Will.' This certificate confirms the validity of last will and testament of the deceased and confirms the authority of the executor to administer the deceased's estate. (Pages 14–19)

Probate fee: A fee charged on the value of the assets that flow through someone's will that has been probated (see definition above) by the courts. (Pages 13–18, 98–101)

Registered Retirement Income Fund (RRIF): A plan registered with Canada Customs and Revenue Agency for the purpose of receiving regular income. A RRIF is an arrangement with a financial institution under which regular payments are made by that institution to the annuitant under the plan. Payments made must be not less than a certain minimum amount. (Pages 88, 99)

Registered Retirement Savings Plan (rrsp): A plan registered with Canada Customs and Revenue Agency for the purpose of saving for retirement. Assets in the plan grow on a tax-deferred basis. Contributions to an RRSP are deductible for tax purposes subject to certain maximums based on 'earned income.' (Pages 54, 85–94)

Residue: The portion of an estate remaining after specific bequests (for example, to charities and individuals), taxes, and bills have been paid. (Pages 265, 273–274)

Spousal Trust: A trust, under which the spouse is entitled to all of the income from that trust during his or her lifetime. No one other than the spouse is entitled to encroach on the capital. A 'qualified spousal trust' does not create a capital gain when assets are transferred over. A capital gain is assessed on the death of the spouse, when the trust assets are passed to the intended beneficiaries. (Pages 70–71, 270–273)

Testamentary Trust: A trust which is created under the terms of a will, i.e., a trust created as a result of the death of an individual. (Pages 274–275)

Trustee: Person or institution appointed in a trust deed who is required to follow that trust agreement and manage assets for the benefit of the beneficiaries. Also refers to the person or institution named in a will (usually the executor) who acts as trustee of any trusts that have been established after the death of the testator. (Pages 14, 71, 90)

Will: Estate planning document that spells out the instructions of the deceased for distributing assets to chosen beneficiaries. The will also names guardians for minor children. The will is a written document that conforms to strict provincial guidelines. (Pages 29–35, 98–99)